Pelican Books
In Defence of Opera

Born in 1933, Professor Swanston read English at Durham University, and did graduate work in Theology there and in Canterbury. Having taught for some time at various universities in North and South America, he returned to the University of Kent in 1972 to be tutor in Eliot College, and was elected in 1977 to the Chair of Theology. He has published a clutch of theological works, most recently *Ideas of Order*, an account of nineteenth-century English divines, and *A Language for Madness*, a study of the Christian creeds. Professor Swanston writes that he 'collects East-Anglian watercolours and fossils from anywhere, without knowing much about either, and without thinking time spent with either anywhere near so generous in excitements as those evenings in the opera house to which he devotes whatever he can manage in energy and cash.'

IN DEFENCE OF *Opera*

HAMISH F. G. SWANSTON

PENGUIN BOOKS

Penguin Books Ltd, Harmondsworth,
Middlesex, England
Penguin Books, 625 Madison Avenue,
New York, New York 10022, U.S.A.
Penguin Books Australia Ltd, Ringwood,
Victoria, Australia
Penguin Books Canada Ltd, 2801 John Street,
Markham, Ontario, Canada L3R 1B4
Penguin Books (N.Z.) Ltd, 182–190 Wairau Road,
Auckland 10, New Zealand

First published 1978
Published simultaneously by Allen Lane 1978

Made and printed in Great Britain by
Richard Clay (The Chaucer Press) Ltd, Bungay, Suffolk
Set in Bembo 10pt.

Contents

PREFACE 7

ONE WHAT DOES IT MEAN? 17

A single success: Beethoven 19
Varieties of success: Mozart 27
A revolutionary art? 42
A revolution of the mind: Wagner 50
More single successes: Tchaikovsky 58
Debussy 62

TWO IS IT FOR REAL? 66

The real and the conventional 70
Aria and ensemble 73
Verdi's melodramatic realism 78
A slice of life 81
A new realism 89
The new hero 90

THREE DO THE WORDS MATTER? 103

Romani, Bellini and the beautiful word 109
Scribe, Verdi and the theatrical word 114
Wagner, Wagner and the universal art-work 125
Wagner as paradigm 132
Strauss, Hofmannsthal and the elegance of form 136

FOUR HOW DID IT BEGIN? 152

The Florentine Camerata 156
La Favola d'Orfeo 159
Dido and Poppea 165

	The French tradition	168
	Mechanical heavens	172
	The first reform	174
	The second reform	179
	Alceste and Iphigénie	184
	The myths again?	191
	A series of attempts: Benjamin Britten	200
FIVE	HOW IS IT DONE?	209
	Money matters	209
	The producer	215
	From convention to convention	217
	Versions of Wagner	222
	A revival of French opera	231
	The singer	237
	The conductor	251
SIX	WHO GOES THERE?	266
	Speaking and singing	267
	A common sense	272
	In what language?	279
	In two languages?	287
	Individual and community	292
	At curtain fall	301
	READING LIST	305
	ACKNOWLEDGEMENTS	
	INDEX	309

Preface

Possessed of what he considered a tidy sum through his bet on a Grand National winner, and fortified by a most substantial supper, my grandfather looked about Liverpool for ways in which he and his eldest son, then aged seventeen, might fitly continue their celebration. The music hall and the circus evidently failed him and so, determining that they should have some new story to tell my grandmother and the other children, he bought two tickets for *Aida*. My grandfather seems to have slept through most of the performance, waking up only at the 'triumphal march', but for my father the evening opened upon a wonder. He had had a most exciting day. The startling sequence of the race, the win, the meal, had readied him for some great experience, and here it was. He was entirely transported to the splendours of Verdi's imagined world. He concentrated wholly upon the struggle of the wilful princess Amneris and her rival, the tender Aida, for possession of the gallant Radames.

The night's excitement came to its climax for him when Radames and Aida, having chosen to die together, were slowly buried beneath a mound of sand. Doubtless they simply stood behind a glass sheet and the sand piled up between them and the audience, but the effect was tremendous. It was this moment which convinced my father that going to the opera was the only way for a man to celebrate the great occasions of his life, and, indeed, that going to the opera would be thenceforward a great occasion in his life.

Though he came in the next fifty years to enjoy all kinds of opera, *Aida* remained, for him, *the* opera. He would undertake immensely complicated arrangements to get us to a performance. And doubtless he was always hoping to recapture the excitement of the Grand National day, and for us to have our share of that experience. No night came near, of course, to the remembered wonder, though some were splendid enough. I can hear him now saying after a Covent Garden performance in which Edith Coates had astounded me and everyone else in the audience by her magnificent Amneris, 'Very fine. But not quite good enough.' 'What was lacking?' I asked, though by the age of twelve I knew what the answer must be. 'Real sand,' he said with decision.

My father's experience at Liverpool seems to me a paradigm of what can happen to the audience at the performance of a great opera. His awareness of a wonder expressed itself in a memory of a stunning theatrical effect. At a different performance the singer or the conductor might have taken in his mind the place of the designer as the mediator of the composer's work. But he then, like every other member of an audience at every performance, came to recognize that the wonder was generated in the music and that all others concerned in the making of the performance had their function in what was definitely 'Verdi's *Aida*'. His evening at the opera revealed both what a great composer can achieve in this art and the degree to which he depends for the realization of his idea upon the sensitivity and artistry of those who undertake the staging of the opera. The memory of real sand is not an improper starting point for a discussion of the experience of opera. It seems possible from a consideration of *Aida* and ways in which it has been more recently produced, to suggest some elements to be taken into account when talking of the performance of operas generally.

Aida has some notoriety as the modern opera which lapsed into the old nonsenses of lavish and expensive court diversions, and it is this opera which has seemed to some the perfect example of opera as an exotic and irrational entertainment. And certainly Verdi's music has prompted usually serious-minded opera-goers to demand scenic wonders. Verdi himself described 'the Egyptian business' as 'a work of vast proportions', and the first staging was fit for such grand music. Verdi had to accept the postponement of the first performance because the elaborate scenery was caught in the siege of Paris, and himself took advantage of the delay to have 'six straight trumpets of the old Egyptian kind' made for the Cairo production, and to request the mayor of Milan to rebuild the stalls in La Scala for the first European performances so that the double-basses in the orchestra pit might be re-arranged to make a fuller sound. Verdi was happy to employ every artifice in presenting his work. That he understood the way of the theatre and had given his producer every chance to make a success of *Aida* was acknowledged years later by Richard Strauss in a note to his famous librettist, Hugo von Hofmannsthal, in 1907, suggesting that their new opera should be set among spectacular gardens in order to please the many opera-goers who stayed away from 'Wagner's pieces' and flocked to *Aida* 'simply because of this lovely new Egyptian set'. They flock still to the amphitheatricals at Caracalla in Rome and the Arena of Verona, to elephants at Cincinnati, and the marvels of the bi-centennial celebrations of the Metropolitan Opera in New York. *Aida* is certainly, as the Liverpool management so thoroughly convinced my father, a grand opera.

It is a grand opera, however, in more than one way. The excitement of a performance derives from the producer, conductor and singers having realized the diverse elements of Verdi's imagination. It is possible to go to performances of the opera time and again because, like the work of any great master of an art, Verdi's composition is rich enough to allow diverse interpretations. Verdi evidently had a care for much more than the construction of scenic spectacle, and it is not by elaborate sets alone that a producer should think to put across the content of the opera. If he puts too great a reliance on the camel and the sand, the music will alert the audience to his ignorance of elements which mattered much to Verdi. 'I have revised, polished, corrected, and perhaps ruined it,' Verdi wrote in September 1871. He had not been able to leave the opera alone while he waited for the sets to be released from the Paris siege. Verdi hoped that in *Aida* he might at last manage a convincing paradigm of human affairs. He knew he had something to say, and he was determined to get it right.

Verdi harried his librettist, Ghislanzoni, from scene to scene, demanding ever more careful attention to the distinct characterization of the princess, the slave girl and the general. Only if they were precisely differentiated in words as in music could their common involvement in one disaster be appreciated. The dramatic effectiveness of *Aida* does not depend on an audience's anxious hope that Aida and Radames will escape the anger of Amneris – it is clear from the beginning that the drastic violence of Amneris and the patient tenderness of Aida are headed towards the same catastrophe – but on the audience not knowing whether Radames will choose to destroy himself by accepting the persuasions of Amneris, or be destroyed by acknowledging his love for Aida. The drama is in the uncertainties of Radames's choice. Its resolution is signified by the lovers' duet in the tomb, for which Verdi wrote both words and music. Verdi hopes to bring those members of the audience who might, like my father, be expected to appreciate only the simplicities of his narrative, to an awareness of the psychological drama within that narrative. It is an indication of his success in organizing the music according to this intention that, while the grand Khedive, who had commissioned the opera, might, after the dress rehearsal, remember only the march tune, it was the final duet which an untutored boy recognized as summing up the significance of the evening, and which gave a most sophisticated modern producer the necessary suggestion for his staging.

Those who attended the Berlin Deutscher Oper in 1961 for Wieland Wagner's production found themselves confronted by an aspect of *Aida* which previous interpretations had left unstated. The production was startlingly effective not because the audience was required to abandon a previous understanding of the opera but because, that understanding being assumed by the producer, another was proffered which had to be held in conjunction with it. The story had thus to be appreciated according to two interpretations at once. Going to the opera had become exciting in a new way — and yet a way which could not have been appreciated if the audience had not experienced the old way of real sand.

While he gave proper attention to the public events of the story, Wieland Wagner determined that the audience should recognize those events as having significance only because they offered scope for the interaction of love and honour in the hero's mind. The splendours of imperial Egypt were pushed aside and the opera set in some primitive pre-dynastic time so that the elemental force of contrary passion might be immediately appreciated. In Verdi's words and music for the final scene Wieland Wagner heard a way of staging the whole opera. At their deaths the lovers sing joyfully:

> Heaven opens and our wandering souls
> Fly fast towards the light of eternal day

To Wieland Wagner Verdi's music had made it clear that only in this final choice of love and death had Radames achieved the integrity and freedom which he had sought throughout the action of the opera. And Wieland Wagner made this equally clear to his audience. While the triumphal march had taken place on an almost darkened stage, figuring the darkened puzzlement of Radames's mind, the entombment duet was sung in a blaze of light. Radames had chosen to see. As he sat in the theatre and faced Wieland Wagner's production, a man had now to become aware not only of his accustomed reaction to the force of the story, but of the immediate origin of his reaction in the hidden springs of his own psychology. He would begin to see how the story of Radames was about himself. The final scene was for me as absolutely stunning as that of the Liverpool production had been for my father fifty years before.

That Wagner's grandson should have presented Radames as another Tristan, caught between the claims of love and honour, is not greatly surprising. But there is an element of rashness in interpreting one great composer according to the pattern of another. And Verdi's particular grumbles about those critics who found 'Wagnerisms' in his music must make one hesitate before accepting Wieland Wagner's production as fulfilling all the possibilities of *Aida*. Verdi worked in his own way. The characters in his later operas may often be best understood as the mature expression of his early perceptions about human behaviour. The musical presentation of Radames, for example, develops much that was hinted at in phrases composed for the anxious hero of *I Lombardi* in 1843. Verdi himself provides the proper frame of references for those who would understand his art. Neither by the drift of real sand nor by the rush of psychological light is Verdi's gift to his audience exhausted. He is a composer whose relevance to our lives is not to be defined by any one production. And audiences know this well. They attend each new production hoping not for an interpretation which will persuade them to forget all others but for one which will assist them to recognize something more of the richness of the composer's design.

Wieland Wagner's production gave less prominence to the modernity of certain aspects of the opera than the music suggests. That triumphal march which sets so many listeners' feet a-tapping – and which the Khedive wished to make into an anthem for his state occasions — cannot be as easily suited to the fertility cult of a savage tribe as to the review of a modern nation's regimented troops. It is a forceful tune, fit for an imperialist army and its victory. It is not to be ignored or played down. But how are the blaring trumpets to be reconciled with the psychological drama that Wieland Wagner properly emphasized? Not, assuredly, by accepting the Khedive as the most perceptive of Verdi's critics and simply accepting the march as a celebration of conquering force. Everything we know of Verdi's lifelong devotion to the cause of Italian liberty, everything we hear in the rest of his music, prevents that quirk judgement. And, in 1971, Filippo Sanjust, putting together his production of *Aida* for the Hamburg Staatsoper, came to the attractive conclusion that the trumpets were just a little too blaring and that Verdi was making through their loudness a comment on the emptiness of imperial triumph. Sanjust heard in this music Verdi's comment upon every regime of oppressive rulers and persecuting clerics. He presented the march not as a tuneful celebration at which the Pharaoh might congratulate himself on his military might and the High Priest rejoice at the coming sacrifice, but as a revelation of how hollow these men and their ambitions were. At the sound of the trumpet returning wounded and threadbare prisoners limped across the stage. Gradually the patriotic crowd fell silent and only the heartless priests were left to sing the demand for further slaughter of the prisoners. Sanjust, recognizing the continuity of Verdi's humane concerns, heard in *Aida* that compassion for the weak which had inspired Verdi's writing for the prisoners in *Nabucco* and for the disheartened crusaders of *I Lombardi*, and that detestation for the bully which he had expressed in the *auto-da-fé* of *Don Carlos*. That the producer had heard something which was truly in Verdi's music was perfectly shown in the new dramatic propriety of Radames's change of heart as he joined the crowd in asking reprieve for his own captives. Everything in the scene came together, the music, the text, and the meaning, in a way that fully justified the novelty of the producer's reading. And the remembrance of this presentation of the scene helped the audience, later in the evening, to recognize the barbarous consistency of the priests' refusal to spare Radames himself.

The success of this production, as well as those at Liverpool and Berlin, suggests that quite a number of opera-goers are ready to regard a performance as an occasion at which they may enlarge their understanding both of the art and of life. The diversity of productions is a response to the expectation of audiences that a producer will elucidate further the meaning of the composer. And the diversity of works which are maintained in the repertory of the opera houses is, equally, an indication of audiences' appreciation that just as one production does not exhaust the meaning of an opera, so one opera or the operas of one composer cannot exhaust the possibilities of the form. The eagerness of opera audiences to achieve a greater understanding of life has been responsible for some remarkable stretchings in the usage of 'opera'.

It becomes evident to anyone who attends performances of more than half a dozen works that the term 'opera' is used of a wide range of entertainments. Much certainly is common but much else is particular to the dramatic works of Verdi, Wagner and Gounod, the three composers whom the Khedive thought worthy to be considered in a short-list for his *Aida* project. And when those composers who lack the contemporaneity of the Khedive's chosen few are taken into account – Gluck, Mozart and Beethoven, say, from those who went before, Puccini, Strauss and Richard Rodney Bennett from those who came after – it must appear that there is an immense range of entertainment for the opera-goer's maturing enjoyment.

Not every opera-goer, of a surety, will enjoy or take profit from every opera. None of us possesses quite catholic enough a taste. Composers have to learn early in their careers that they cannot hope to please everyone. There is a story of a member of the first-night audience at La Scala complaining that only the lavish sets had made *Aida* bearable, and of Verdi refunding the price of his theatre seat and railway journey.

As it is with composers so it must be with critics. Those who think to say something useful when opera is discussed should not aim to please every listener. Those who put together a hurried newspaper piece and those who compose a monograph at greater leisure will not, by their pronouncements, still the liveliness of crush-bar and gallery debate. Nor, if they have a proper sense of their own limitations will they attempt, with Olympian prudence, to keep their own enthusiasms within the mean. The writers who have been most helpful in forwarding my appreciation of what is going on at a performance have been often those with notable prejudices and, though I have attempted here to avoid any remarkable idiosyncracy in my choice of composers and operas to exemplify my notions of the art, the legitimate interests of quite a number of opera-goers had to be neglected if I was to put together an account that had any coherence. Each opera-goer makes his own story of opera. If some other opera-goer had been given my commission he might have allotted more space to French composers and less to British, more to singers and less to librettists, more to economics and less to the differences between productions, but I, who have had no opportunity to see more than a couple of Meyerbeer's operas, and who, on the famous night of

Miss Beverley Sills's triumph in *L'Assedio di Corintho* at La Scala, spent much of the time grumbling at the uneven music of the piece, and who have each time an excited hope of a fiery dragon in *Die Zauberflöte* (*The Magic Flute*) or *Siegfried*, have thought it best to write of what I have heard and liked.

One

What does it mean?

Tchaikovsky once remarked to his patroness, Madame von Meck, that 'to refrain from writing operas is the act of a hero, and we have only one such hero in our time – Brahms; such heroism is not for me'. Nor for a great many other composers. There is, for example, not one major French composer who has not attempted an opera. Of those who make the attempt, many are unsuccessful, and among those who would have done better to have exercised a heroic restraint are some of the most distinguished composers.

In September 1821 Schubert began work on his only grand opera, *Alfonso und Estrella*, but when he had finished it was apparent that he had made a perfect example of the type of nonsense folk commonly associate with opera. His villain sings happily before performing abduction, rape, and murder, and his victims delay the horror further by singing of their fear of abduction, rape, and murder. It was never performed in Schubert's lifetime. Liszt produced a mauled version of it in Weimar in 1854, but this succeeded not at all.

Schumann, in his correspondence with Reinick while they were working on their adaptation of the tale of Genoveva, exhibits greater awareness of the possibilities of opera. But then Schumann had the example of Wagner to keep him closer to the mark. Schumann had from youth been ambitious to have a part in the establishment of a truly German school of opera, and in Dresden he had been a frequent attender at the opera house under Wagner's direction. He had searched for a subject in the tales of Faust, Till Eulenspiegel, Abelard, Mary Stuart, and even wondered if he might not emulate Wagner in treating of the Nibelungs. In 1847 he discovered the legend of the lady Genoveva falsely accused of adultery but finally vindicated by her husband. He set to work. His first draft was done in a style derived from Weber's *Der*

Freischütz and Wagner's *Tannhäuser*. He thought it marvellous. When he showed his work to the Master he was not prepared for criticism: 'He simply wanted me,' wrote Wagner, 'to be swayed by himself, but deeply resented any interference with the product of his own ideals, so that henceforth I let matters alone.' Schumann could not exercise heroic restraint, he took his opera away and tinkered with its structure. When Reinick saw what had been done he withdrew from the collaboration. Schumann tinkered a little more. He then defiantly presented his opera to the Leipzig audience. Though *Genoveva* had three much-clapped performances in 1850 no more came of it than of *Alfonso und Estrella*, and it dropped out of sight.

Others have risen to command attention for a night or two. Like Tchaikovsky, at least in this, Hugo Wolf felt unable to be a hero: 'How I envy all those men who have no need to write operas,' he sighed. He obeyed the command of necessity. He turned over stories of Alfred der Grosse, and rummaged in the legends of Alboin, the Lombard king. Some fragments of his early operatic music survive, enough at any rate, one would have thought, to warn him off composing a piece for the theatre. But he did not give up. In January 1895 he wrote excitedly, 'The long-desired opera text is found,' and he set off to make Pedro de Alarcón's *Three-cornered Hat* into *Der Corregidor*. The presence of Wolf's friends secured for him, as Schumann's friends had managed for Schumann, a first-night success, and Wolf cried delightedly that some parts of his opera 'couldn't be better imagined, let alone composed'. But he had not managed anything much. *Der Corregidor* remains in his imagination. It is not composed for the theatre.

Other composers should have taken warning from such examples. Most did not. There are dozens of bad operas deservedly unrevived. Some composers have been saved by their circumstances from making such a mess of things. Mahler was unaware of his own good fortune. What he termed his 'damned employment as an opera conductor' prevented his trying his hand at an opera. He had to content himself with being allowed to complete

Weber's *Die drei Pintas* from the dead man's notes. And in writing Weberian music he showed himself both apt as an imitator and insensitive to the demands of opera. It is good that he got on with his symphonies.

Some composers, on yielding to the temptation, have been able to fulfil their ambitions once and once only. Debussy sent the score of *Pelléas et Mélisande* to the Secretary-General of the Opéra Comique with a message that he had 'for a long time sought to write music for the theatre'. And he had this once produced a marvellous musical drama. But this single success was all that he could manage. Leoncavallo's *I Pagliacci* is another example of a composer bringing something off superbly well, just once. But the most famous is, of course, Beethoven's *Fidelio*.

A SINGLE SUCCESS: BEETHOVEN

Beethoven's endeavour in the shaping and reshaping of *Fidelio* ended in such a magnificent achievement that it is possible to understand from this one opera what other, less successful, composers have been ambitious to accomplish. And, of course, Beethoven himself was so delighted at what he had managed that he wanted to repeat his success with another opera, but he could not find a proper text. In his puzzlement he even thought of writing in the fashion of another composer. Not a characteristic idea – even though the composer was Mozart. Mozart's exposition of the value of human love and faithfulness had long before claimed Beethoven's admiration for *The Magic Flute*, and in his search for a libretto to set him going again, Beethoven accepted Schikaneder's suggestion of a sequel to the opera he had written with Mozart. But the librettist seemed to think that Mozart's opera had owed its success to the various magic tricks he had suggested for the plot. He wrote similar magic sequences for Beethoven. Beethoven knew that this was not his style at all. He sent the libretto back. Schikaneder sold it to another composer. And Beethoven resumed his search for something he could make into an opera. In about 1824 Beethoven thought for a little while of making a romantic opera from Grillparzer's *Melusina*, but, though he once assured the delighted author 'your opera is ready', it seems that he never put any of this project down on paper. Nothing else occurred to him. *Fidelio* remains his only completed opera.

It remains so not, evidently, because Beethoven's musical invention failed him, but because neither Schikaneder nor Grillparzer, nor any other, except perhaps Goethe, could give him a subject through which he might disclose something of his inner assessment of what it means to be human. For a composer to complete an opera successfully he must work in the assurance that he is saying something which is necessarily of importance to his fellows. The discipline of story-telling in opera form forces a composer who takes his business at all seriously to attend most carefully to his presentation of human experience. The effort involved is considerable. A composer must therefore be convinced that the story he is telling is going to be worth his effort. He must be convinced that others are going to listen with appropriate seriousness to what he is saying. At least this was how it was with Beethoven, and with all those who have distinguished themselves in the form.

Beethoven's success in telling just such an intelligible and persuasive story about matters which everyone in his audience will accept as important makes *Fidelio*, though it be his single achievement in this form, a fit instance of the kind of thing an audience hopes to hear and see in the opera house. Beethoven had within himself something worth saying, in the tale of *Fidelio* he recognized a way of saying it, and the opera is its perfect expression.

The libretto of *Fidelio* was evidently one to stir a composer into music. Beethoven was not the first to recognize its possibilities for opera. It had seemed to several others that here was a text fit for music. Bouilly's words had been set by Pierre Gaveaux in 1798, by Simon Mayr in 1805, and by Paër in 1804. Beethoven had much admired Bouilly's libretto for Cherubini's *Les Deux Journées* in 1800, in which a good aristocrat and his faithful wife are saved by a good bourgeois to the cheers of the populace who declare at the end 'To serve humanity is the best thing in life.' In the Bouilly libretto which began as *Leonore, ou l'amour conjugal* and ended as *Fidelio*, Beethoven recognized another such stirring story of the goodness of man and the providence of God. Based on Bouilly's own experience, this story of a girl searching for her husband in the Spanish political prisons and by her fidelity and bravery finally discovering him in his enemy's lowest dungeon, roused in Beethoven a grand desire to express in opera his devotion to the principle of human freedom.

Of his success in fulfilling that desire there can be no doubt. In his single opera Beethoven is recognizably a composer who appreciates the possibilities of music drama. He has evidently understood that through an opera, as through no other musical form, a composer may exhibit his understanding of life. And he manages to do just that. Beethoven shows his audience, through the action of his opera, just how noble human beings, themselves included, can be.

Anxious to make a popular work of art, Beethoven had several shots at improving both libretto and music after the disappointment of a first-night failure. He might have left at least the penultimate version alone, but certainly the present opera is a fine one. Beethoven has been careful to establish a sound musical structure. He holds in balance the disjointed first act with a perfectly ordered second. In the first half of his opera he thrusts before the audience a heap of disparate images. The sound shifts from spoken word, to recitative, to a great quartet in canon form, to a catchy, clinking song in praise of money, and a superbly poised aria. The plot shifts from domestic laundry to prison chains, from a wife disguised as a man, to a girl in love with this supposed man and a boy in love with the real girl, from a cheerful warder to a demon-king governor. And then, suddenly, everything is brought together as the sound rises, and the theatre is filled with the stupendous chorus of the prisoners in the prison yard: 'O Freedom, will you return?', they sing. That demand for freedom is answered in the second part of the opera. One of the great moments in opera is the sounding of the trumpet in Act II of *Fidelio*. This trumpet announces the coming of the king's minister just when Pizarro, the wicked governor, is about to murder the manacled Florestan. This might be vulgar melodrama, but in Beethoven's music the audience may hear a deliberate pre-echo of the Last Trump. Every character on stage signals just how this scene should be appreciated. At the sound Pizarro exclaims in eschatological terms at the closeness of hell and death, the warder Rocco is stirred from weary worldliness to recognize the day of wrath, and Florestan and Leonora joyfully acknowledge the intervention of heaven. The scene is wholly one of divine judgement, and the effect is shared by the audience.

Beethoven's effective structuring of this moment in the action may suggest ways in which he is engineering that the whole opera shall be accepted by the audience as an intelligible interpretation of those complexities of human experience about which he thinks himself bound to say something. What he says at this moment is paradigmatic of what he is saying throughout the opera.

Beethoven is not writing a dogmatic treatise. He is not attempting to get the scenario of the Last Day perfectly straight. He is not in competition with the theologian. He is not even making an effort to do the moralist's job. He is writing an opera. Whatever he hopes will come across to the audience must come across through the music – through the interplay of the voices and the orchestra. Through his music's power he hopes to bring his hearers to appreciate and feel things which no theologian, no moralist, and no one working in any other art, could convey to them. He hopes to convey something at least as complex as anything any other intelligent man might offer them. His musical design is complex. And the moment of the trumpet is evidently as complex as any in his opera. It presents rather more than everyone could be expected to take in at once. Beethoven helps his audience to appreciate what is going on by a purely musical device, and one which shows that he did not think of himself as a theologian. The trumpet sounds again. A theologian would certainly have held that one Last Trump was enough.

That repeat in the music is the device by which Beethoven summons again the original moment. At the first moment the trumpet sounds divine justice for all. Each character pauses. Pizarro with his dagger raised in the act of murder, Leonora with pistol in her hand ready to shoot him, Rocco wavering between them. We all need time to take this in. It is as if a film had been stopped at a significant frame. The trumpet sounds again. We look again. Pizarro, still holding the dagger, curses his lack of time. Leonora has flung away the pistol, the divine intervention has shown her that she has no business engaging with death, she acknowledges that God has saved her husband. Rocco has determined to serve the tyrant no longer. The moment of the trumpet sound has two aspects. By the musical convention of repetition an audience may appreciate both. The recognition of the divine and the realization of the significance of the divine for each of the characters, though necessarily sequential, is made simultaneous through the music.

Beethoven obviously believes in the overseeing wisdom of God. His belief is made obvious through his music. From the trumpet scene we are moved at once – unless the stage-hands and the wretched 'traditionalists' demand the 'Leonora Overture, No. 3' at this point – to the chorus of ordinary folk who sing of the Day of Light and to the Minister, who, 'at the bidding of the best of kings', releases those who have sat in darkness. This is the people's day of freedom. Beethoven understands the revolution as the human community's share in the Day of the Lord. His politics of freedom is composed in the confident belief in a Providence.

Dr Philip Barford in the *Beethoven Companion* declares that 'Beethoven believed in Freedom and in God, and like many others in his day and ours saw no reason to waste time saying what he meant by these terms.' What he meant can be understood at the end of *Fidelio*.

Gradually through the action of the opera all human values have been called in question. Rocco has learnt to throw away the bag of gold. His daughter Marcellina has been undeceived about the handsomeness of outward appearances. Pizarro's trust in the strength of force and political power has simply landed him in prison. Leonora's reliance on human endeavour has been shattered by the trumpet's sounding. The Minister's authority has been put aside as the townsfolk condemn Pizarro and Leonora releases Florestan. Each has become not a simple agent but a communicator of the divine freedom to others. When Florestan rises from the dark beneath the ground they all share in the glory. At the end everyone on the stage has found some other to share happiness.

Those who listen to what Beethoven is saying in this opera are brought to his contemplation of the final wonder through a series of doors. From the street into the opera house, from the auditorium on to the stage, from the spoken dialogue into the song, from the prison into the sunshine. And all the time, as they go through these doors, their hopes are enlarged. They may have come first in expectation of what Evelyn termed 'a most magnificent and expensive diversion', but they have been brought through the comedy of mistaken identity and the triumph of courage to witness the reconciliation of love. At *Fidelio* we may come at last to a sense of belonging to each other member of the audience, and perhaps, as we go out from the opera into the foyer and thence into the street, we may enjoy some sense of being with every other. Beethoven has seized the opportunity that opera has provided and he has shown what the world might be.

The audience learns through the musical structure what Beethoven thinks of them, and they may well begin to think of themselves in his operatic way. The opera is an expression of the composer's will to change men – as the warder Rocco is changed – from creatures who are satisfied with the ordinary values of worldly commerce into people capable of recognizing the divine action in their midst, and their own capacity, as human beings, for the divine. Through his music Beethoven confronts his audience with the conviction that a divine agent is to be acknowledged in the structuring of social order. He was right to see in opera a means peculiarly appropriate to the communication of ideas of social change. Even ideas of revolution.

Composers had recognized this some time before Beethoven made it plain to everyone else. Lully had backed away from such dangerous possibilities; the French court theatre was not the place for revolutions to be played out. He told Quinault that the titular hero of *Phaëton*, since he was a rebel, could not be shown with that vigour which the librettist had intended lest the King detect an anti-monarchist tone. So at the end of the opera Jupiter is displayed as the outraged governor of a well-ordered world. There was a more lively political comment in the final scene of Voltaire's *Samson*, which he put together in 1750, when the blind judge of Israel cried to the people, 'Awake, break your chains! Liberty calls you; you were born to be free!', but the philosopher could not find a composer daring enough to set his words. Beaumarchais's *Tarare* in 1787 led up to the great moment when the hero defies the tyrant king with the fine shout: 'You have all power against one man; against all men you can do nothing.' This brave sentiment found a composer in Salieri, Mozart's popular rival. But Beethoven, quite rightly, remarked an even more revolutionary impulse in *The Magic Flute*, which celebrated the triumph of man against all the deceits and terrors that monarchs and priests could devise. Beethoven properly understood the tradition. If a composer would change the world it is through the writing of opera that he may make the attempt.

That opera is commonly a revolutionary's art is perhaps not so interesting as that the form demonstrably allows the most serious use. From everything in the music it is clear that Beethoven hopes to persuade his audience that there are in their lives opportunities for love and courage still. Beethoven is properly employing the form of opera to open his mind to the audience upon matters of huge importance. It is a measure of the capacity of the form that opera can bear the fullness of meaning which so noble a composer as Beethoven hoped to communicate. *Fidelio* exemplifies opera as an instrument by which a sympathetic and intelligent man may convey his sense of large debates to those who are carrying on the discussion. Schubert, Schumann and Wolf, though they never managed a communicative opera, at least realized that this was precisely the kind of thing which they wanted to compose. Debussy and Beethoven managed it once. Mozart found more than one way to express his humane understanding of experience in opera. This need not, of course, be indicative of the greater importance of Mozart's ideas, but it does suggest that Mozart found opera a more diverse instrument than Beethoven did. Mozart might have made something of those librettos that Beethoven discarded. He could see the good in a greater variety of sources, and his work demonstrates the versatility of the form.

That versatility is further discernible in the works of the great nineteenth-century composers, notably in the works of Richard Wagner and Giuseppe Verdi, and in the experiments of those writing in the later nineteenth and the early twentieth centuries. It seems sensible to move forward in this consideration of opera by making reference in this opening chapter to the ways in which various composers have thought to employ the form.

The history of opera in the last hundred and fifty years or so has been of an art form moved forward by the exertion of will by a few composers of distinction. The present diversity of operas to be heard in a season at a great opera house reflects the vitality of mind of a few great musicians. As with any critical assessment, it is easier to recognize the influence of composers of some years back than of those who are still at work. To begin by saying something about the intention and accomplishment of Mozart, Wagner and Verdi must be the safest way of approaching the critical appraisal of Bizet, Richard Strauss and d'Albert, and of Sir Michael Tippett, Benjamin Britten and Hans Werner Henze. It is to be hoped that the following discussion of the composers who have worked for the opera house since Mozart will prompt questions not only about the reference of what these composers say in their operas to the world we inhabit, and the part undertaken by the librettist in the expression of the composer's meaning, but also about how earlier opera composers first discovered those possibilities of the form which the men who came later found ready for their use. It is these three matters which are discussed in the chapters which follow this present appraisal of some great composers and the meanings discernible in their operas.

VARIETIES OF SUCCESS: MOZART

While Schubert demonstrates in *Genoveva* how difficult it may be even for a really accomplished and intelligent composer to put his thoughts into such a shape that they will make a convincing opera, and while Beethoven demonstrates in *Fidelio* how one overmastering thought may drive its way through an opera so that no one in the audience is left in doubt about the composer's intention, Mozart in *Lucio Silla*, *Idomeneo*, *Le Nozze di Figaro* (*The Marriage of Figaro*), *Don Giovanni*, *Così fan Tutte*, *La Clemenza di Tito*, and *The Magic Flute*, demonstrates the serious versatility of the form. In each of these operas Mozart manages to say something complex about the human race and its doings, to say it in ways appropriate to the different actions of his librettos, in ways which illumine different aspects of experience, and in ways which should make each individual in the audience pause a while to consider just what things mean for him.

Mozart is obviously a composer who realizes that the varieties of his experience are most properly expressed in operatic form. He certainly knew himself that it must be through opera that he would find self satisfaction. 'I have an indescribable desire to write operas,' he wrote in October, 1777, and by February in the next year he was announcing that 'writing operas is an obsession with me'. Mozart, unlike Schubert and Beethoven, was able to gratify his desire. He found libretto upon libretto to stir his musical imagination, and he fitted each story with music which made the opera perfectly his own.

At the least subtle level of Mozart's intention there is a commitment to bring his audience to question the social conventions within which they are conducting their lives. Mozart is always prepared to give his compassion a revolutionary scope. When da Ponte gave the Emperor Joseph II of Austria his assurance that he would not be party to anything that smacked of social unrest, he was not being entirely frank. Da Ponte must have known that, as soon as Mozart set to work on the smooth piece of love and manners he had extracted from Beaumarchais's play, the new *Figaro* would have not only some of its original power to disturb, but something more radical yet. Mozart is not to be caught in a crowd shouting political slogans. His instinct is to question everything, not the political establishment alone. In place of the upturning of aristocratic assumptions in the name of democratic ideals that the French originally suggested, Mozart offers a criticism of the servant as well as the master and his criticism is only incidentally concerned with their social attitudes.

Beethoven had hoped that through his presentation of the ordeal and vindication of Leonora he could make his audience aware of the great principle of freedom upon which a just polity must be based. In *Fidelio* opera has a social relevance. Mozart, equally aware of the possibility of opera conveying a truth of moment, and equally anxious to express his estimate of human commerce, chose generally to put his meaning in individual terms. In *Figaro* opera has a personal relevance. Through the changing relations of his characters Mozart stimulates his audience into examining how they treat those close to them. In particular he provokes consideration of a man's attitude towards his wife.

Figaro and the Count are not equal in intelligence and generosity to Susanna and the Countess. The women are always more aware of what is going on than their complacent and preening menfolk. And the women in their easy, confident friendship are certainly less caught up in class prejudice than the men, however much Figaro may think himself on equal terms of rivalry with the Count, or the Count pursue his coquetries with the village girls. The dim-wittedness of the men is brought out first. Figaro, happily measuring the room for his new marriage bed, is quite unaware, until Susanna makes him realize it, that the Count plans to come in through the connecting door once he has ensured that Figaro is away. And when he does get the idea in his head it at once occurs to him to boast of his skill in handling affairs: 'Little Count, you may go dancing, but I'll call the tune.' Mozart's music makes it impossible not to think Figaro rather a fool. And later in the scene when the Count, thinking himself alone with Susanna, does make his aristocratic advances to her, she manages to leave him totally at a loss by revealing that all his loving talk to her has been overheard by the page-boy she concealed under the armchair covers. The page-boy too is discomforted. From this carefully presented situation the rest of the opera follows.

In the central action of the opera the Count, quite outrageously jealous of his faithful and generous wife, is shown being defeated by the clever invention of Susanna. Figaro, when the Count attempts to get rid of him by declaring his contract with the aged Marcellina quite legal, shows the hollowness of all his quick revolutionary slogans by declaring that the birthmark on his arm proves him to be a gentleman and therefore above such a marriage.

In the final section of the action Susanna and the Countess, by disguising themselves in each other's clothes, bring about the total discomfiture of the Count which Figaro had boasted he would achieve. And they give Figaro a moment's shock too. The plot and counterplot of the last act lead up to the moment at which Mozart's whole design for the opera is fulfilled. An assignation with the Count being arranged, the disguised Countess receives the attentions he meant for Susanna, while Figaro enacts a love scene with Susanna disguised as the Countess. On seeing this the Count, summoning all within earshot, prepares for the public humiliation of his wife. The disguised Susanna asks for mercy. The Count will none of her. He is all outrage. Then, adding her plea for forgiveness, the Countess steps forward, throwing off her disguise. The music, giving a dimension not present in Beaumarchais's play or da Ponte's quick brushing-aside of comic complexity, suddenly reveals a new power at work in the action. Everything is changed. 'If he who makes strange and startling modulations unnecessarily is certainly a bungler,' wrote Wagner, 'so he who does not realize the compulsion to modulate forcibly in the proper place is nothing but a politician.' Mozart is never a mere politician. Every step in the plot has been working towards this modulation. At this moment the women's constant love is vindicated, the games of the men are ended, and a power of forgiveness is opened upon all the world. And in response to this the Count provides the answer to his wife's question at the centre of the opera: 'Where has love gone?' The reunion of the Count and Countess is exemplary. Through his music, as Hegel thankfully acknowledged, Mozart 'expands and floods our imagination and warms our hearts'. We become more understanding and more generous. At the finale we agree with those who sing that such tangles as they have witnessed can only be resolved by love. It is to this that Mozart has been leading them.

If he had written no other opera, Mozart would have been reckoned with Beethoven as a composer who knew precisely the single effect he wanted to achieve, and found the perfect operatic means to achieve it. *Figaro* is, in many listeners' estimation, the most complete of operas. Mozart's musicianship stretches the pleasant little play until it accommodates his great concerns. In the lively progress of his music from ensemble to ensemble, held apart by the perfect self-declarations of the characters, Mozart expresses a world of harmony. The perfect order of the music figures an order for us. The opera is called not simply *Figaro* but *The Marriage of Figaro*. Mozart is celebrating the harmony that may come to a man and a woman when they unite in forgiveness and love.

This is a great theme and one which is patient of no little abuse from those of a more cynical mind. It all seems so unlike the actualities of our own experience and what we know of other people's experience. Mozart was never cynical in his music. He was always a realist. He impresses many, as he impressed Karl Barth, as a man who is 'pure in heart, far transcending both optimists and pessimists'. Barth heard in Mozart's music 'clear and convincing proof that it is a slander on creation to charge it with a share in chaos'. But we may also hear in his music a warning that within an ordered creation we are capable of making a chaos for ourselves. The ordered love realized by the Countess in *Figaro* will only be given to men and women who have readied themselves for it. If they indulge in selfish passion the world will become a chaos for them and they will perish in torment. This is a theme which interested Mozart from the very beginning. It was, for example, a major part of what he wanted to say in *Idomeneo*.

In that early opera Mozart presented an almost melodramatic version of those psychological subtleties which occupied him in his later works. The action of *Idomeneo* depends from a contrast between the drastic demands of King Idomeneo and the Mycenean princess Elettra, and the patient endurance of Idamante, the king's son, and Ilia, the captive Trojan princess. Idomeneo clings to kingship even at the cost of his son's life, he attempts to marry the girl who loves his son, and at the penultimate moment is prepared to kill them both on a sacrificial altar, all the time assuring himself that he is caught in a situation where he is the chief victim. His selfishness comes near to destroying not only the social order of the family, but the cosmic order of the elements. He brings a plague upon his people and rouses a sea-serpent in their harbour. Elettra presents a more personal image of disintegration. In her we see how personal order can collapse into chaos. She is driven through the action by gusts of her own unruly passion. Her schemes to seize Idamante for herself, though at one savage twist of the action they seem to promise sexual satisfaction, lead her into self-tormenting delusion. Her passion overpowers her. A raging madness destroys her. Her final aria is essential frenzy. She shrieks as imagined snakes writhe about her. Mozart signals in his music that the mind must lose its hold on order if love be so abused. He signals too, in the joyful music of Ilia and Idamante, a restoration of harmony for all those around them. And it is a universal harmony in which the god Poseidon acknowledges the claims upon his justice of their patient love, and

Amore, Hymen and Juno, the divinities of marriage, arrive to bless them.

Idomeneo is an impressive piece of work, and is now taking a place in the repertory of great opera houses which it has not had since its first performances. I have lately attended performances in Cologne, Munich and at the English National Opera. A new production is promised at Covent Garden. In this opera Mozart revealed himself as a composer already subtle enough for us. But he was capable of a yet more impressive treatment of the same themes. Most opera-goers will be more familiar with *Don Giovanni*, that one of Mozart's operas which is wholly concerned with the archetypal snatcher at sexual pleasure and with his effect in the society of others. Da Ponte, when he was putting together the libretto, is said to have enlisted the help of his crony, Casanova. Mozart's appreciation of reality needed no such expert prompting. The music of *Don Giovanni* is witness to his understanding.

For some distinguished critics *Don Giovanni*, rather than *Figaro*, is the opera in which Mozart performed his greatest wonder. It was with *Don Giovanni* that Goethe and Shaw were most pleased, and Claudel, who always claimed to be bored by opera, remarked that once, at the Metropolitan Opera, after a short refreshing nap, he found to his great amazement that he was following the action of *Don Giovanni* with some interest. Kierkegaard described *Don Giovanni* as the one work of which it is possible to say that the idea is absolutely musical, so that the music does not appear as an accompaniment but reveals the idea as it progresses. It was, he said, 'the perfect unity of the idea and its corresponding form'.

Da Ponte adapted a famous tale which had been made into an opera several times before. And the political significance of the story had not been ignored even by those who were more immediately attracted by the philandering episodes in the plot. In Bertati's original libretto, used by Giuseppe Gazzaniga in 1787, Don Giovanni is not a romantic figure, nor a licentious demon, but simply the ordinary aristocrat who takes and never pays, and who is rightly condemned at the end because of his offences against social justice. He is, for example, from the first scene carelessly rude and rough in his treatment of the village sweetheart of the peasant girl he is pursuing. Da Ponte diplomatically toned down the revolutionary content of the Bertati libretto, but he could not wholly eliminate the original's social criticism, nor did Mozart require him to do so.

In da Ponte's version Giovanni is certainly not presented uncritically. In *Don Giovanni* as in *Figaro* however, Mozart makes it clear that while aristocratic arrogance may be frustrated by peasant cunning, true order is only to be restored by love. Mozart believes in the power of human compassion. Every other engine for the running of society is shown in this opera to be wholly ineffective. The Commendatore's appeal to the social conventions of honour is murderously thrust aside by a masked intruder; the bargains struck between men who distrust one another are voided by Leporello's final refusal to serve his employer; the shouts of liberty and fraternity of the popular revolutionary are mockingly echoed in the songs of the seigneur Giovanni; the nunnery is shown as simply a bolt-hole for the uncertain affections of Donna Anna; Donna Elvira's belief in her own unique attractions is cruelly undermined when Leporello catalogues Giovanni's conquests; and, at the end, the glibness and arbitrariness of Giovanni's hellish punishment calls into question the very idea of a divine justice. The whole design is unsettling. Nothing seems to fit. The plot has no logic to it. The audience must ask themselves at the end of Act I why, when Giovanni has been revealed as a rapist and murderer and has been cornered by the representatives of virtue and law, the opera is not wound up with a final ensemble of general satisfaction. They must also, unless the producer is very slick indeed, ask themselves how Giovanni manages to make good his escape. After the interval the audience must wonder whether, if he can get out of such a scrape, Giovanni will ever be caught. It must be debatable whether there can be any logical direction for the further action of the opera, and Mozart at once assures them that there is not.

He offers simply a series of superb songs, each connected by the merest thread of plot to those before and after. There is no overriding order here. The music slices up the action. Each incident is presented in isolation. It seems quite fortuitous, for example, that Giovanni goes through the graveyard just when the statue happens to be in a nodding mood. When Mozart writes for the threatening statue he anticipates Schönberg's use of a tonal row but the plot itself unnerves the listener. At the end there seems no reason at all for Giovanni to be visited by so frightful a menace at a moment when he isn't chasing another girl.

The musical breaks make it plain that the audience should not entertain hopes of elucidating the shape of the action in terms of Providence. There is no governing order in the nice confusion of the tunes. The extract from *Figaro* played by the chamber orchestra on stage during Giovanni's last supper perhaps suggests that the resolution of his difficulties could be managed by someone of the calibre of the Countess. The music for the entrance of the tempestuous Donna Elvira tells the audience that there is no such person in Giovanni's life. With no providential resolution possible in such a chopped-up plot, and no human agent of effective forgiveness among the characters, Giovanni is lost irretrievably. His end might indeed have come at the close of Act I. His end might come at any time. When he wants to finish the opera Mozart simply announces that end. This opera does not reach a finale, it simply stops. Mozart is not much interested in the conventional way of talking about the just punishment of the wicked by gods or God, and Giovanni's final defiance of the retributive statue is admirably done. When the other characters line up to say dull things about 'the decree of destiny' Mozart makes them go through the old-fashioned paces of a fugue. When the librettist is announcing the completion of the action, Mozart has provided music of a kind which suggests that the story is no more complete than it was at the interval pause.

The old religious fugal form, associated with Bach, here mocks itself. Mozart is not placing much reliance on the divine. What little good there is to be found in the world of *Don Giovanni* is expressed in the tender music of the peasant girl, Zerlina. Her last comforting scene with Matteo is an assertion of human communion, but Zerlina is not a strong enough character in the opera to bear responsibility for the resolution of the action. The music of *Don Giovanni* is designed by Mozart to focus attention upon the hero. All other characters live in a world of Don Giovanni's imagination. They are meaningful only so far as he appreciates them. As Kierkegaard remarked, 'the existence of all the others is a derived existence'. Therefore only those thoughts and emotions which Don Giovanni could conceive of himself are effective in the action of the opera. Zerlina's kindness and love cannot be brought into play with any strength. *Don Giovanni* exhibits the consuming power of unordered sexual passion on a larger scale than the isolated frenzy of Elettra in *Idomeneo*. Her vision of writhing snakes pales before the imagined hell of Don Giovanni. The hero's inability to order his life with love brings him to a point at which he is prey to forces of damnation which he himself has conjured. He makes hell for himself.

In *Figaro* and *Don Giovanni* Mozart has stated clearly in his music his belief in the possibility of ordered love between human beings, and in the impossibility of any grab at such love being successful. These sentiments, however beautiful and compelling, may not seem sufficiently subtle to constitute an anatomy of love. They certainly did not seem so to Mozart.

In *Così fan Tutte* he remained true to his appreciation, expressed in the plot structure of *Don Giovanni*, of the discrete character of human experience. Life consists in a temporal sequence of broken events which can only make a single sense under the eye of that love celebrated in *Figaro*. But in this opera Mozart allowed himself to explore the stranger movements of love. He wondered what truth there was expressed in the old comedies of mistaken identities, disguise and spouse-swapping; and how whatever truth there was could be related to his conviction of an original disjointure in experience. In this opera, while the text is generally no more subtle than that of any other sex comedy, the music reveals the discrete character of emotion, the possibility of truly loving one human being one moment, and another the next. The music, like the libretto, makes it quite evident that Dorabella is a fickle girl who shifts her love easily from boy to boy. But the music alone makes it equally evident that her sister Fiordiligi is at first truly and deeply in love with her Guglielmo, and then, when the young men for a wager woo each other's girl in disguise, is brought by his evident passion and truth to love Ferrando. The audience, if it listens closely to the music of their duet, has to accept that Ferrando can be in turn in love with two girls, and Fiordiligi with two boys. Truly in love. And the audience has to put the fine love of Ferrando and Fiordiligi into some understandable relation with Ferrando's return to Dorabella and Fiordiligi's to Guglielmo in the final scene when the disguises are removed and the wager done. Mozart in his music makes it plain that love is love however strangely it may alter or even cease. Guglielmo, grumbling in the wedding canon, may not understand what is going on and may wonder that betrayal is so easily glossed over, but the opera's main message is one of love from moment to moment. Mozart's order in this opera is an order of the day only. And human beings have little control over the events of the day. It almost seems as if the Countess is forgot.

At the beginning of his adult career as an opera composer Mozart had thought it necessary, in *Idomeneo*, to invoke a divine solution to human tanglements. Only by the last-moment intervention of Poseidon does the situation achieve resolution with the retirement of Idomeneo and the coronation of the young prince and princess. While acknowledging the fitness of this happy ending the audience must feel that it is only through divine restraint on human passion that order can be achieved on earth. And if Idomeneo is allowed to retire with regal dignity, the mad excitements of Elettra must force an audience to wonder if men can ever live sane and dignified lives without the careful guidance of the gods. But what Mozart had learnt by the time he came to write *Figaro* he did not afterwards forget.

In his last opera, *La Clemenza di Tito*, every expectation of human meanness is contrasted with the actual wonder of human mercy. Though for this opera Mozart returned to the old-fashioned manner of the *opera seria* of his youth, he did not return to the old plot conventions. No god is required to settle the human entanglements which constitute the plot of this opera, there is no threat of hell to keep the baddies in line. Mozart shows an emperor who for the good of his people sends away the girl he loves, and then nobly allows the lady he proposes to make his empress to marry the man she loves, an emperor who forgives all those whom he has discovered in a conspiracy against his life, an emperor who does all this despite, as he says, the force of the stars driving him to vengeance. His people liken him to a god, but Mozart has supplanted divine power by human compassion. The movement away from *Idomeneo* is complete.

It is complete only because Mozart has been able to maintain the faith he expressed in *Figaro*. He presents the audiences of his operas with a progression in realism. What seemed perhaps to many of them an intriguing game in *Idomeneo* – for what was the constant Ilia to them that they should weep for her? – has matured through the testing that Mozart's idea received in the ordeals of *Don Giovanni* and *Così fan Tutte*, until the faith of *Figaro* can be reiterated in *La Clemenza di Tito*. And even at the end some will say that Mozart's belief in the nobility of human life and the supreme value of human steadfast loyalty belongs in the world of fairy tales. Mozart accepts that judgement. He is not afraid to say that through the power of his music life may be a fairy tale and a fairy tale may be life. In his last opera, *The Magic Flute*, set like the *Thamos* of 1773 in an invented Egypt, everything he had come to understand is expressed again. For this final effort to convince his audience he did not shrink from repetition. This is an opera in which everything is meant.

Mozart had by the end of his career wholly accepted the broken character of experience. Colin Davis, the present Musical Director of Covent Garden, has admitted that he feels *The Magic Flute* to be a bad piece dramatically, expecially in the second act:

To have to return to Papageno after you've been through the trials of fire and water with Pamina and Tamino is all very well, but it does become very protracted. Then some of the numbers are so very short. They're perfect, of course, but to string them along with all that dialogue in between is difficult. With *secco* recitative you stay within the convention; with talk you immediately come out of it. Suddenly you have to create a piece as wonderful as *Bei Männern* out of nothing. You cannot accumulate tension.

Mr Davis is a very intelligent musician. And he knows precisely where the oddities of this opera lie. It is, however, always well when considering the work of such a noble genius as Mozart, especially work of his maturity, to consider if the oddities might not be part of the composer's intention. Every element of *The Magic Flute* to which Mr Davis draws attention may be understood as significant in Mozart's design. The composer has prepared the audience for the strange broken incidents of the second act by a flick of the music in the first. Wagner was neither the first nor the last to notice that 'the villain was suddenly changed to a hero, the originally good woman to a bad one', and others have joined him in thinking that this made 'utter nonsense of what had happened in the first act'. But this switch provides a clue for the understanding of what happens in the rest of the opera.

When the prince Tamino first encounters the Queen of the Night and her ladies they have rescued him from a monster, punished the talkative bird-catcher, Papageno, for lying, and asked for help in rescuing the princess Pamina. They have been good in every way. He therefore accepts them as truthful witnesses to the character of Sarastro, the priest-king who has taken Pamina away. He sets off with Papageno to free her from her captor. When he arrives at the kingdom of Sarastro he is brought to understand that the ruler does not fit the Queen's description. Sarastro is a wise and good king. His people revere him as their holy protector against all enemies. So Tamino and the audience are somewhat confused. But they are no more than ordinarily confused, for it is a common experience to find that someone has been mistaken about a stranger, and his actions and motives, especially if the stranger comes from an alien culture with quite different religious rituals. Other men's beliefs and liturgies always look queer from the outside. Here at least is something which may make talk of 'Mozart's masonic opera' relevant. Once the audience has accepted that the fairy-tale events are to be judged in just the way they would judge events in a kitchen-sink drama, or events in their own domestic lives, *The Magic Flute* becomes supremely intelligible. And supremely Mozartian.

In this opera the broken sound of spoken dialogue, aria, and ensemble that Mr Davis remarked on mirrors the broken plot, the isolated scenes, and the shifting characters. The *Don Giovanni* image of a man hunting for yet another woman to give him a moment's physical satisfaction is juxtaposed with the loving incongruities of the duets in *Così fan Tutte* against the background of a strange world. In this world the sexually rapacious Moor has the lady in his power, and yet she is, like the ladies of *Don Giovanni*, never ravished by him. Papageno drives him away. And, hard upon this, the most affecting love song is, as in *Così fan Tutte*, sung by those who are not going to live happily ever after with each other. The princess sings with the bird-catcher. In one scene the effects of both earlier operas are precisely obtained.

It is through the musical characterization of Papageno that Mozart has declared *The Magic Flute* to be an image of our own possibilities. Tamino, the libretto's hero, is not wholly removed from us. His falling in love with a girl in a picture is an ordinary enough experience. His frustration at the fancies of her mother are ordinary too. And so too is his ignorance of what those in power are planning. But there is something a little too romantic, surely, in his accepting such childish tests as the ordeal by silence, for him to be reckoned one of us. And something too heroic in his passing the tests. Papageno's refusal to take such things as part of life, his eagerness for a quick sale of his birds, his innocent boasting of wonderful talents, and his irritation at wiseacres thinking themselves the proper persons to decide matters between him and his girl, is more sympathetic. However impressive Tamino may be to the priest-king Sarastro, the man who boasts, on first meeting the peasant, that he is a prince, is accepted by us as a fellow man only because the music of the first act sets him sharing a part with Papageno. So, at the end, that return to Papageno's affairs after the ordeals of the hero, which worried Mr Davis, is an assurance that the fairy tale does indeed open upon our experience. We too want the familiar contentment that Papageno expects with Papagena.

Mozart was the most generous of all composers. His large mind was, despite his bitter experience of a tyrannical employer, a tetchy father, and a crushing poverty, capable of a sympathy for men which outstretched the limits of religious, political or economic programmes. It was an unhappiness of Ernest Newman's criticism that he made relative so much of what Mozart was doing. 'Virtue, Justice, Humanity, Universal Brotherhood, and all the rest of it' he deemed 'a little fly-blown today,' but the mocking employment of capital letters for such values, the comparison with spoiling meat, and the summoning of modernity to complete the depreciation, are no argument at all when put against the effective power of the music.

Schubert may have had something to say but he never found a way of saying it in opera; Beethoven had one grand statement to make and he did so with magnificent authority in *Fidelio*; Mozart had evidently a great deal to express and continually developed his understanding of himself and others. The great Mozart operas form together a progressive account of the assessment a man of genius made of human life. If any defence of opera were required it would be sufficient answer to point to the achievement of Mozart. For this greatest of composers so evidently discovered in opera the appropriate form for the public expression of his most private understanding. It we are to confront whatever is valuable in the work of the past, and to assess its usefulness in present contexts, Mozart has ensured that we take the art of opera seriously by achieving in this medium the same quality of success as Michelangelo, Rembrandt and Shakespeare achieved in sculpture, painting and plays. He makes their kind of challenge to anyone who would deny the capacity of ordinary men to live noble and heroic lives. He allows each man dignity, meaning, and purpose within the fragmented experience of his common existence, and does so in the conviction that this is the only course for a realist to take.

Perhaps this is a loud claim, and it might be safer to keep to suggestions of Mozart being a great disturber of the peace, a disaffected man in a society ready for political revolution. This was how Napoleon saw him. He famously described *Figaro* as 'the revolution in action'. But he mistook the total character of Mozart's revolution for a mere reorganization of the voting system. In Mozart's revolution each man would learn to look at himself differently and to challenge his own view of himself. Voltaire declared the scene in *La Clemenza di Tito* in which Titus confronts the friend who has conspired against him to be one which 'should serve as an eternal lesson for kings and enchant all human beings', but the Empress Maria Luisa at the first night thought the opera merely 'a piece of German piggishness'.

Opera composers generally have, in their endeavour to elucidate a way to live with some integrity, sought out subjects which put the alternatives of will and wilfulness quite plainly. And, mindful of the requirement that they should entertain if they would have an audience's attention for three hours, they have set their considerations of such matters in strange and attractive contexts. Thus it was that Beaumarchais thought that the Turkish court, 'where despotism prevails', and 'the passions of the great surpass all limits', was the fittest setting for an opera. The wilful tyrant might there be opposed by the sturdy will of a hero. Or, more likely, of a heroine. Under the guise of a fanciful circumstance the European statesman might learn the proper measure of his office, and the people whom he governs learn their proper worth. This is a commonplace lesson. It is taught, for example, in Rossini's *L'Italiana in Algeri* (*The Italian Girl in Algiers*) and in a dozen or so other of those Turkish pieces which clutter the early nineteenth-century stage. But each of the great opera composers has hoped to do more than simply make a political statement. Their energies have been devoted to provoking an audience's scrutiny of how their own lives may be better managed. Mozart's *Die Entführung aus dem Serail* (*The Abduction from the Seraglio*), for example, fulfils Beaumarchais's directive about the location of an action, but, characteristically, he has upturned all expectations of the despotic exercise of whim and the heroic stance of will. Mozart presents a Turkish ruler who is perfectly self-disciplined and of larger mind than the Europeans he encounters. Only in Constanza, the faithful and firm-willed heroine who refuses to marry him, does he find a worthy companion. Mozart's treatment of these two characters must impress the audience with the worth of an enduring integrity in any society.

A REVOLUTIONARY ART?

Lesser composers have known that Mozart was somehow dangerous in the eyes of the authorities and there has grown up an easy tradition of opera being unacceptable to repressive right-wing censors alongside the tradition of opera being most acceptable to extravagant right-wing audiences. The most unlikely composers have somehow got themselves a name for being upsetters of the establishment. Of Beethoven's genius such things were to be expected and his opera is concerned with politics in a grand manner, but of some other, dandier, composers nothing of the sort would be expected. And yet the musical form itself seems to urge them up and over the barricades. Even Bellini found that a duet in *I Puritani* could not be included in the Neapolitan production 'because both love of country and liberty enter into it'.

So clearly was opera seen to offer revolutionary chances that in nineteenth-century Italy composers and librettists were watched by the Austrian or papal authorities lest they should become dangerous men, *les Voltairiens*, and have to be silenced. And it was the greatest of Italian opera composers who was the most revolutionary. 'I want,' wrote Verdi to a friend in 1853, the year when *Trovatore* and *Traviata* were performed, 'I want subjects that are new, great, beautiful, varied, and daring, daring in the extreme.' His very name was shouted as a subversive acrostic by all who looked for a united Italy and an Italian government of *Vittorio Emanuele, Re D'Italia.*

Perhaps Verdi was not intent on establishing himself as the composer of Italian nationalist aspirations, but he was made so by his audiences. At *Nabucco* (1842) the Milanese identified with the Jews under Babylonian rule. The great chorus 'Va, pensiero' was encored as the song of Italians under Austrian domination. At the first performance of *I Lombardi alla Prima Crociata* (1843) the audience identified with the Lombards, the Holy Land was Italy, and the Saracens, Austrians. At 'Today the Holy Land is ours' the audience cheered in the assurance that Verdi was proclaiming the coming united Italy. At the first night of *Attila* (1846) the Venetians rose in clamour at the Roman general's speech to the Hun: 'You take the universe, leave me Italy', though Egio means Italy by 'universe' and Rome by 'Italy'. Perhaps *La Battaglia di Legnano* (1849) was deliberately nationalist. The opera begins with the chorus 'Long live Italy. A sacred pact binds all her sons.' This prompted the audience to wild scenes of patriotic fervour in a Rome which had just expelled the Pope. And at the moment when Mazzini and Garibaldi were in Rome it was certainly provocative to make a grand finale of the dying hero kissing his country's flag. It was at the end of this opera that *Viva Verdi!* was first turned into the patriotic slogan, though it was only after *Un Ballo in Maschera* (1859), that it enjoyed national use. Verdi, however, did not really hope much of politics. He became a member of parliament because Cavour wanted him to do so and he admired Cavour. When Cavour died he left parliament. Political solutions seemed to him as impermanent and ultimately valueless as they did to Mozart. But, unlike Mozart, Verdi did not place any hope in the possibilities of human virtue. It was his conviction, expressed in his operas as in his letters and conversation, that nothing would come of any human effort. The world itself would finally be seen to add up to nothing.

Writing in 1867 to the Director of the Paris Opéra, Verdi said that in making his final revisions to the score of *Don Carlos* he had 'struck out anything purely musical', because he wanted this to be 'an opera which means something'. Verdi's meaning was always, as his mistress, the admirable Strepponi, well knew, that of a man 'not an outright atheist, but a very doubtful believer'. Verdi was, she remarked, one of those who are 'happier believing nothing'. This is a judgement which, of course, we would have to respect from someone as understanding and close to Verdi as she was, even if it were not supported by the music. But Verdi's attitude is revealed in not only the final uncertainty of the *messa da Requiem* written for his political hero Manzoni, nor Aida singing at her death: '*O terra addio, addio valle di pianti*', in which a popular prayer has been subtly turned, nor Iago's progress from the fierce inversion of the *credo* to the proclamation of '*La morte e nulla*', but in his whole musical offering – which prepares us for his letter to the Countess Maffei on the death of a man most dear to her: 'I think that life is the most stupid of all things and, even worse. What are we doing? What have we done? What will we do? After considering all, the answer is humiliating and very sad: Nothing!' '*Nulla!*' echoes from opera to opera in a way that should bring every listener up short.

When he made *Don Carlos* 'mean something', he made it mean 'nothing'. Verdi took Schiller's drama and altered its significant centre. The personal drama of the prince and his father, and of the prince and the queen, is put across satisfactorily enough, but it is evident that Verdi is not much interested in this, and not at all interested in the poor queen. The public drama of politics, of Posa's championship of the freedom of the Netherlands and the Grand Inquisitor's demands for repression in Spain, is presented in rather more exciting music. But it is most characteristic of Verdi's method and interest that he placed at the centre of his music, quite against the drive of the libretto, the man who sacrifices everything and everyone to political necessity, and who, at the moment of sacrificing himself, is wholly a failure. Verdi's difference from Mozart can be seen in the comparison of *Idomeneo* and *Don Carlos*. In Mozart's opera the young prince,

Idamante, thinking his father dead, begins his reign by giving freedom to the Trojan prisoners of war, and, on the return of Idomeneo the king, Idamante's final act is to offer up his life and his chance of happiness with Ilia. Ilia, too, is a giver. She is the one who actually unbinds the prisoner at the beginning. She is prepared for her rival, Elettra, to marry the prince, and she offers her life for his. In contrast Idomeneo is a grabber of life, realm and woman. The god, at the end, rewards the giver. Mozart suggests that sacrifice enriches. Not so Verdi in *Don Carlos*.

In this opera the prince, Carlos, gives up his claim on the princess Elizabetta, whom he loves and who loves him, and she too surrenders everything that can make her happy. She is seen first giving her jewels to the poor, then giving up Carlos, then accepting the insult of the king's exiling her lady-in-waiting. She surrenders everything of home and happiness. Elizabetta gets nothing. Nor does the king who grabs at what he wants. Philip of Spain, like Idomeneo, snatches at his son's bride, then his son's friend, and finally his son's life. But he can keep nothing for himself. His wife does not love him. He mistrusts his friend and has him murdered. When he imprisons his son the people rebel, and his rule of the kingdom can only be maintained by accepting the over-rule of the Church.

At the end of *Idomeneo* Ilia is rewarded by Mozart with her prince and her throne. Self-sacrifice is recompensed. At the end of *Don Carlos* Elizabetta has nothing but her honour and this must, Verdi suggests, be enough for her. Against the cruelties of their own kind, the injustices of institutions, and the chaos of the universe, human beings have to preserve their simple self-respect right to the moment of death. And they must expect such an honourable course to bring about that death. In the early opera *Ernani*, also a tale of Charles V, in which the hero, on the day of his wedding, stabs himself to satisfy a debt of honour to his enemy, a like convention obtains. And it persists to *La Forza del Destino* (*The Force of Destiny*), in which Leonora, the heroine, whose plan to elope with her lover Alvaro is fatally interrupted by her father, and her brother, Don Carlo, who spends his life searching for Alvaro as the murderer of his father and the smircher of his own honour, are bound by a code which Verdi would have the audience respect despite its bringing inevitable unhappiness upon all three of them.

In the original St Petersburg production, on the deaths of Leonora and Carlo, Alvaro leapt from the cliff crying 'I am the spirit of destruction! . . . Let the heavens collapse! Let mankind perish! . . . Extermination! Annihilation!' Though Verdi altered this ending for the La Scala production in 1869 to something gentler, the first version exactly expresses the composer's continuing conviction that only a man's determined preservation of his honour could give him self-respect against the nothingness of the world. It is his reverence for 'honour' that allows Verdi his immense freedom in the presentation of hatred. The ferocity of Rigoletto, of Don Carlo in *The Force of Destiny*, and at last of Iago, is shown as the way in which these characters preserve their identities. Hatred is, in Verdi's operas, a destructive but entirely personal force. In Verdi's view everything is going towards 'Extinction!', and even hatred may seem to offer a man the means to assert himself in the midst of a falling world.

That division of the action into discrete situations each with its separate aria at its centre by which Mozart had in *Don Giovanni* suggested the arbitrary character of action and retribution, the unforecastability and, therefore, the unexpectedness, of the moment when Giovanni is condemned, Verdi makes the paradigm of all human experience. Verdi demands that the audience participate to the full in the cutting up of the action. He invites applause every few minutes so that the story is stopped. Audiences respond to the composer and clap when he tells them to do so. The world of *Trovatore*, *Traviata*, *Rigoletto*, and *The Force of Destiny*, is a world of separate and separated events and actions, devoid of lasting cause and effect.

It is the Verdi operas of the middle years which have contributed, of course, so much to the popular notion of opera as an irrational entertainment. Love and murder and brilliant trills, rape and battle and magnificent arias, constitute, it is generally thought, a rather odd art. It is the intention of Verdi to express his estimate of the irrational world through such odd confrontations. It is the very irrationality of opera which makes it for Verdi wholly realistic. And it is this same irrationality which convinces the audience that opera is properly representative of experience.

Verdi's appreciation of reality, and his expression of it in the waywardness of his operas, is less alien to audiences now than in his own day. In the middle of the nineteenth century the general hope was for a reasonable progress in human affairs. The cry of good men in Italy and elsewhere was for national unity, democracy and just government. It was necessary for those who attended Verdi's operas to represent their melodramatic qualities as either 'good clean fun and fiction', or else as the unfortunate vehicle provided by stupid librettists to carry along the splendid tunes which the melodious Verdi so graciously provided for the singers. The plots, therefore, were generally not thought worth much scrutiny. But Verdi had been stirred by these plots to make the music which so thrilled his audiences. And whatever he found in them should be of interest to those who admit the compelling authority of the music he made for such plots.

The 'absurd' has become in the last quarter of a century an acknowledged literary and theatrical category. Audiences have now become accustomed to accepting a confused and disturbing account as reflecting the inner world of experience. Those who have given their attention to 'the bald soprano' have been readied for anything that the heroine in an opera by Verdi might do or say.

And it is according to the pattern of the great melodramas, of *Ernani*, *Rigoletto* and *Trovatore*, that the last operas of Verdi are most profitably interpreted. That greater coherence of plot and action which some discern in *Otello* and *Falstaff* is itself achieved by an enlargement of the irrational element in the plots of those operas. Verdi accepted gratefully Boito's removal of the first act of *Othello*. Shakespeare had made some effort at the beginning of his play to account for the peculiar arrangement of the characters in Cyprus. He had made it seem plausible that a black man should be placed in command of the Venetian armed forces. And he had, in a famous speech, given such an account of Othello's wooing that it should seem perfectly credible that Desdemona should fall in love with him. Verdi does without such preliminary plotting. All decent explanation is eschewed. Verdi simply starts with the storm. The first note of this opera and the phrases which rush to follow it present the most sudden onslaught upon the ear in the whole of opera. All is disturbance. It is plain that something uncontrollable is happening. The characters are rushed to and fro with the music. Neither Otello nor Desdemona has more than a moment to command our attention before the storm sweeps them away. Only Iago can operate in such a whirlwind. Verdi proceeds to his next intrusion upon Shakespeare's design. The famously horrifying cry of Iago: 'I believe in a cruel God', thrusts its parody of Christian belief straight at the audience. The distortion that this presented to Verdi's first hearers was certainly much greater than we now feel, for we have not all been brought up to recite the Creed on Sunday mornings, but it is still appreciable as a sudden irruption of the unlooked-for. To those who are more familiar with Shakespeare's play than the Apostles' Creed there will at least be the surprise of Verdi's having invented such an important incident without precedent in the original. And Verdi continues to upset things. He brings about the disaster with another unwarranted song. Desdemona's frail remembrance of the girl who went mad becomes her own dirge in this irrational world.

It might be expected that *Falstaff* would not offer much opportunity for anything but fun and frolic. And some have thought of this opera as the final smile of a great and kindly genius. A comforting thought. But it is noticeable that the plot of Shakespeare's *The Merry Wives of Windsor* has been telescoped in a similar fashion to *Otello*. The first gulling of Ford and Falstaff is excised so that Verdi may have greater space for his elaboration of the last act when the wood becomes a malignant demon's stalking ground where Falstaff is terrified and each ordinary citizen deceived until there is no answering Falstaff's question

'Who is the fool now?', unless by some universal admission. These are not dramas composed towards a finale of graceful sanity but rather towards ineradicable madness.

Despite the great range of subject that Verdi deployed in the more than twenty operas of his maturity, it is not the diversity of his works which most impresses. Once he had developed his own style from the aria and ensemble tradition, once he had discovered what he could do with the cabaletta and the stage band, he took every operatic opportunity to convey to his audience his single conviction of the irrationality of the universe. In each of his operas he suggests how sadly admirable are the efforts of the human spirit to make sense of such a universe.

Though there might be many in Verdi's audience who, having been much encouraged by what Mozart had told them in his music, would want a larger acknowledgement of human effectiveness, it would be an impertinence to suggest that so distinguished a musician as Verdi most assuredly proves himself had been unable to see as much of reality as we ourselves do. And at this point it is not really important for us to settle whether Mozart's humane hope is more or less vindicated in experience than Verdi's humane despair. But it is most important to realize that we are only able to entertain such a debate because these great composers have found it possible to express their deepest convictions in opera. The writing of an opera has been for each of them a declaration to their audience of what it is that most thoroughly moves them. The attending to an opera may be for each member of the audience a realization of the composer's meaning.

And it is important to realize also that a composer's meaning, figured forth as it so commonly is in operas of revolution, will almost always lead to a disturbance in our lives. Mozart's vision of human peace, depending as it does on a renewal of generosity in the mind of each human being, is evidently not to be realized unless a great many elements of our present way of living are put aside. His is a radical criticism of things as they are and of us as we are. Verdi's rousing patriotism was more easily understood as a disruptive force in areas where social and political order had been established, and was, therefore, more ferociously opposed by Austrian, Sicilian, and papal governments and their watchful censors, but it too was expressive of a more dangerous insurrection. Verdi's tolling '*Nulla!*' announces the coming end of every man's enterprise. The narrative action of his operas exhibits in diverse situations the single working force of destruction. Ernani, Violetta, Aida and the rest of his heroes and heroines are victims of this oppressive force. No establishment should think it could have saved them.

It is plain that Verdi, however greatly he differed from Mozart in his estimate of what men could accomplish, accepted as wholeheartedly as he did the necessity of expressing himself through a story. The action of *The Force of Destiny*, however clumsily it seems to be put together, is as clearly in narrative form as that of the equally oddly-told *The Magic Flute*. But if the primary design of both these works is to communicate to the audience a sense of the mind of the maker, it would seem that an opera might be successfully composed according to the pattern and structure of the idea itself. An opera might, on the account I have been offering, be structured to express the composer's mind in an immediate fashion, and perhaps only accidentally tell a story. This possible step in the development of opera as declaratory of meaning was taken in brave fashion by Wagner.

A REVOLUTION OF THE MIND: WAGNER

Wagner did not at once realize the possibility of such a shift in opera content. He began, like every other opera composer, with a sense of opera as a form of revolution. And he never lost his sense of the appropriate narrative content. He always dealt with revolutionaries. And such radical men were most naturally expressive of his own temper. It was precisely because Wagner consciously wanted a part in political revolution that he was the composer to realize that opera could be a revolutionary form simply through its presentation of his inner thoughts. Wagner was the revolution in action and composition. 'I intend,' he wrote in his Dresden pamphlet 'The Revolution', 'to destroy the existing order of things.' He was, then at least, of one mind with his anarchist friend Bakunin. This was his belief when he began writing the text for his great cycle on *Der Ring der Nibelungen* (*The Ring of the Nibelungs*). In the twenty years he took to complete this project Wagner's ideas had, of course, developed, but he began with a grim determination that the world of human artifice and guile should be brought to an end.

At the beginning of the *Ring* Wotan, the king of the gods, has in his hand the ashen spear upon which are notched the treaties of gods and men. He has rule by law but he wants power to enforce this. He first attempts to get what he wants by tricking the giants who have built his citadel Valhalla, then by seizing the gold that the nibelung dwarf has stolen from the daughters of the Rhine, and then by keeping the golden ring of power for himself. As the cycle continues we see Wotan desperately trying to find a way of conserving his rule and always failing. He sacrifices his eye for a greater wisdom, and yet has to go wandering about the earth seeking someone who will understand him. Fricka, his wife, scolds his inconstant and ambiguous rule, his daughter the Valkyrie, Brünnhilde, joins in the rebellion of his hero son, Siegmund, and, on his waking the old mother Erda he is told what he has known for so long: his reign is running out. His grandson, Siegfried, breaks the ash spear. It is only when Wotan's order is falling apart that we learn that the spear was made from a branch Wotan had ripped from the world-tree. Law began with the rape of the environment. Gods have power only by destroying order. The ash tree is dying. The final scene of the cycle in *Götterdämmerung* shows how men might live again after the death of the old god and the collapse of his unnatural rule. Wotan's sin is expiated as Brünnhilde gives the ring back to the Rhine maidens. Men are free of god's original sin. But will men make good use of their new freedom, or will they settle down to the same old divine pattern of greed, cunning and violence?

A similar pattern is to be discerned in Wagner's last, and,

perhaps, greatest opera, *Parsifal.* There the young hero, who has at first no name, gradually comes to know himself, to earn the respect of others, to be anointed king of the Grail Castle, to have his feet washed by the repentant woman, and to be received by the knights of the holy order as the man to lead them to a new life, supplanting the old inheritor, Amfortas. Power is surrendered by the dying ruler, and offered to the free hero. What will he do with it? Nietzsche thought that in this opera Wagner had sold out to a fanciful Christianity. But there is no suggestion in the words or the music that Wagner meant an audience to assume that Parsifal would quietly take up the place offered him in the old order. He may not wish to be the guardian of the Christian past. Parsifal's acceptance of Christ-like honours from the weeping Kundry may be taken to mean that he is surpassing Jesus just as he surpasses all other heroes. It may be that Parsifal will sit upon Amfortas's throne, or it may be that he is going to throw over the old conservative order which has proved itself unable to govern. The revolution may be just about to happen. Or it may not.

In Wagner's work there are immediate connections with his political activities – which led twice to his being sent into exile – through the revolutionary narrative content of his operas, and his conception of himself as the maker of the revolutionary art work, to the exposition of his own restless mind. If Wagner remained convinced of the suitability of political and social revolution as the subject of opera, if at the end Brünnhilde and Parsifal offer challenges to our acceptance of outmoded social conventions, he had almost from the beginning appreciated that the importance to him of these narratives of revolution consisted in their usefulness in the expression of his own revolutionary song. In *Rienzi* he had certainly chosen, in this tale of the last tribune, a subject that was expressive of political liberty, but he had not known himself well enough to do it in his own way. He tried to write a grand opera employing every sensational and rhetorical device he had observed in other men's work. But after he had hoped to tempt Scribe to write a libretto on the basis of some sketches he sent him, Wagner looked inward and discovered that he did not need a collaborator. The revolution in his understanding of his revolutionary self had begun, as Wagner said, on writing *Der Fliegende Holländer* (*The Flying Dutchman*). 'From here begins my career as *poet*, and my farewell to the mere concocter of opera texts.' The newness of this course consisted for him in its total innocence of reflection and example. Taking thought played no part in it. 'It was bidden me by my inner mood and forced upon me by the pressing need to impart this mood to others.'

In writing *The Flying Dutchman* Wagner had discovered that his mind might arrange a meeting with other minds at the level of myth. At the suggestion of myth 'the mind is forthwith placed in the trance-like state wherein it shall presently come to full clairvoyance, and thus perceive a new coherence in the world's phenomena'. In his next opera, therefore, he turned to the old folk tale of Tannhäuser, the singer who, caught in the schizophrenic toils of love, was unable to distinguish for himself what he felt, because his medieval world offered him no way of bringing together the languages of Venus and Elizabeth, of animal passion and romantic devotion. *Tannhäuser* accuses conventions of dehumanizing the musician. In many formal ways this is a conventional opera, but in writing it Wagner knew what it meant to write for 'the figure which sprang from my inmost heart'. Perhaps the most startling exercise of will in opera is that in the first act of *Tannhäuser* when the hero's music leads to a tremendous climax in which he cries: 'My good rests in Maria!' Wagner said of his rehearsal with his favourite singer of the part, Ludwig Schnorr, 'I told him that this 'Maria!' must burst forth with such vehemence that the instantaneous disenchantment of the Venusberg and the miraculous translation to his native valley shall be understood at once as the necessary fulfilment of an imperative behest of feeling driven to the utmost resolution.' Tannhäuser commands his world by the power of will. He is at once recognizable as the figure of Wagner himself. The force of creativity within the composer bursts the conventions that had constrained Wagner's expectations of opera. The song contest at the centre of the opera was an expression of his own effort to break into a new music. He could not himself appreciate the full significance of his 'double revolt, as artist and as man'. Only later did he find words appropriate to his experience of communicating through his music not a tale but a mood within: 'I *felt* it then, but did not *know* it distinctly; that knowledge I was not to gain till later.'

It was at another and more famous presentation of a song-contest that Wagner knowingly expressed his appreciation of art as autobiography. *Die Meistersinger von Nürnberg* is clearly concerned with those problems with which Wagner himself had to deal. It is a prolonged debate about the old traditions of music-making and the possibility of breaking into new modes. Walther, the knightly singer, is persuaded at the end to support with his new music a complacent and unimaginative society. He is persuaded by the suave talk of Sachs about German unity, and by his own desire to live with Eva. The moment when he thinks of revolt passes. He is not Tannhäuser. But Wagner does not necessarily approve of Walther's acceptance of the Teutonic flourishes. He may simply be showing the audience how a good musician can be caught by those who run society and used for their purposes. It may be that Hitler did not clearly understand Wagner's intention when he gave this opera the Nazi accolade.

In *Die Meistersinger* Wagner made a direct statement about his own situation: 'In order to enfranchise myself from within outward, that is, to address myself to the understanding of like-feeling men, I was driven to strike out for myself, as artist, a path as yet not pointed for me by any outward experience.' He had had, he felt, to struggle to adapt those conventions of opera which had been designed for the presentation of a narrative to make them serve for his expression of his inner experience. And certainly his determination to express such experience had its effect upon his choice of musical form. Wagner was not, for example, much interested in the possibilities of ensemble singing. Only in the last act of *Die Meistersinger*, when at the ritual of naming the prize-song, Hans Sachs, Eva, Walther, David and Magdalena each voice an understanding of the moment, did he make something worthy to be put alongside the wondrous use of ensemble in the work of Mozart and Verdi. The celebration of his own art led him to see how he might unite all voices in one song. But the ensemble's customary use as a way of expressing the relationship between characters was not of any great interest to Wagner. His musical achievement is rather to be discerned in his command of dialogue. In the great *Ring* cycle the dialogues represent Wagner's turning of an idea in his own mind. Those who, recognizing the interior quality of the great dialogue between Wotan and Brünnhilde as the decision has to be taken about Siegmund's fate in the coming fight with Hunding, have suggested that at this superb moment of *Die Walküre* Wagner is representing on the stage the troubled ambiguities of Wotan's mind, have not quite perceived the music's purpose. Wagner is representing the ways in which the situation and its meaning occur to him. He is thinking about the meaning of his own creation.

Wagner deliberately placed himself at the centre of his operas. The composer took over entirely. The comfort of audience, singers, musicians, and conductors was ignored in order that his encompassing idea should have space and time for its expression. Nothing was to disturb Wagner's concentration upon his own inward music. *The Flying Dutchman*, he hoped, would be given without an interval. He secured that it is impossible to perform *Das Rheingold* with a break. The action of *Parsifal* is continuous, being held together by musical movements which of themselves change the scene. As Wagner's mind moves between castle and woodland so the music and scenery move. Wagner directed in his stage notes that the characters should walk as if in a dream – stepping continually on the same spot as the world moved across the back of the stage. And by what has come to be termed the *leitmotiv* Wagner made his audience aware that what was going on in the opera was not the action of a character or the reaction of other characters, but the working out of the composer's experience of the opera as it shaped in his understanding. These melodies, snatches of tunes, and simple phrases recur in the music independently of the immediate demands of plot and characterization. They recur whenever Wagner wishes the audience to sense with him the undercurrents of his own sensitivity. This is the reality of the opera. And 'the depicting of reality' seemed to Wagner something which, as he wrote to his friend Roeckel in January 1854, 'can only be made understandable by the music'. The music moves forward through the plot and characters, becoming closer to Wagner's inner experience as it develops. The opera is Wagner as he composes. And so the opera tells the audience about him. He sensed that the music revealed elements of his nature of which he himself was unaware.

Wagner, through the exercise of his inner will, brings 'the unconscious part of human nature into consciousness', as he wrote in *Opera and Drama* in 1852. Wagner's concern with his inner life has, however, seemed suspicious to some. Critics have placed a Freudian interpretation on his work. Such men have seized, in their flurry at finding so open a composer, on the incestuous love of Siegmund and Sieglinde, on the Oedipal emotions of Siegfried and of Parsifal; on the Electra complex of Brünnhilde; and on Wotan's dark justification to Fricka: 'My mind is reaching for things that have never happened before.' Wagner was not aiming for anything as trivial as these little complexes. 'In the instruments of the orchestra the primal organs of creation and nature are represented.' The sound is of the sources of his own creativity. His contemplation is fixed upon the springs of his own idea. And he is anxious only how he may control such an idea in an art form. He set 'the clear, specific motion of the heart, represented by the voice, against the wild primal feelings, with their ungovernable urge towards infinitude as represented by the instruments'. The opera is Wagner's expression of his human control of the boundless energy about him and within him. And if his assertions sounded wild to earlier critics now many may admit that Wagner's strangeness, like that of the heroes of the old folk tales from which he drew the necessary images for his feelings, is their own strangeness. (Properly *The Waste Land* twice quotes both *Tristan und Isolde* and *Götterdämmerung*, and

Finnegans Wake quotes the one and *Ulysses* the other.) For many in our culture Wagner has determined the form which myth should take. He seizes his listener and compels him to recognize the forces governing his life. Wagner makes him realize that what happens in the music drama may happen within him.

It may be that the sense Wagner communicates of emotional values derives from some primitive enjoyment of a savage dance, but it develops into something not to be put aside by any snide anthropological categorization. To appreciate his music is to enlarge one's understanding of oneself. In the darkened theatre – which Wagner introduced for the first time at Bayreuth – the music has ever made men aware of the powers within them. At a performance of *Tristan* at Bayreuth in 1889 Chabrier burst into tears and Lekeu fainted. And in 1952, again at a Bayreuth performance of that opera, it seemed to me as the music had its way that I could never have a more erotic experience.

In recognizing the immediacy of Wagner's meaning one may be curious about the composer's continued use of the old distancing devices. Wagner's emphasis on the representation of what happens within himself and his listener became, perhaps, too great for the unqualified success of his own work. Once one has recognized the essential validity of Wagner's exploration of his 'mood' one begins to question the need for those theatrical devices which Wagner retained from the old tradition. Wagner destroyed, by the very force of his revelation of mind, the credibility of the conventions by which opera composers had always hoped to communicate with their audience. What communication there can be, the achievement of Wagner makes clear, must be that of the inward recognition of mythic kinship. The mere telling of a story cannot be expected to do it, certainly not its telling by recitative, aria and ensemble, and probably not by any method common in our culture.

Nor, however, can it be done except through some kind of story-telling. It was, and is, a difficulty for a great number of those concerned with opera to distinguish, among so many Wagnerian changes, the particular way in which he revolutionized the telling of a story. Wagner's realization that the unities of time and space might work against the unity of action had allowed him to tell his story in ways which reflected the inward movement of his mind. His success obscured the pains he had taken to achieve his narrative effect. Not all composers who recognized the wonder of his achievement discerned that Wagner was always careful to tell a coherent tale. Wagner's idea was shaped into a story so that the audience would have a starting point in their understanding of the action. The story would then be presented to them in ways persuasive that it was a myth. And the myth would become a medium by which the composer could communicate experience and his interpretation of it to the listener. There is a carefully orchestrated movement from Wagner's mind to the mind of the individual in the audience. Nothing could have been less like Wagner's method and practice than Hugo Wolf's unconcern with the first staging of *Der Corregidor*. The hapless producer at Mannheim gradually realized that Wolf never cared what was happening on the stage of the theatre because everything remained perfect in his own mind as he listened to his opera with closed eyes. Wolf had no idea of the kind of responsibility a composer has to make his thought clear to the audience. *Der Corregidor* remains static on stage because it never moved from Wolf's contemplative mind. It was not a tale told in the old way but it was certainly not what Wagner meant by 'something organically being and becoming'.

There have been other composers, however, who have appreciated rather more of Wagner's theatrical achievement. And they have wished to convey to the opera audience that the old ways of communication were at an end.

MORE SINGLE SUCCESSES: TCHAIKOVSKY

The announcement of the collapse of the old communication methods is most agreeably to be found in the work of that composer who on his own admission was not hero enough to resist the temptation to write an opera.

Tchaikovsky's success with *Eugene Onegin* ranks, perhaps, with that of Beethoven with *Fidelio*, at least in exemplifying the triumph of a one-off composer. Nothing else, not even *Pique-Dame* (*The Queen of Spades*), came above the level of ballet music, but in *Eugene Onegin* Tchaikovsky did manage to give expression to his ideas. This opera seemed to the composer to be 'the outcome of an invincible inward impulse'. And he himself was so aware that this was the only time he had achieved success that he generalized from the experience. 'I assure you one should compose only under such conditions.' He had evidently listened to Wagner. And what he heard makes it quite unnecessary to allege the composer's homosexuality, as some critics have done, in order to account for the immense power of this opera's single theme: the impossibility of human beings communicating with one another in any outward manner. But it is necessary to testify to his genius in using the most obvious and traditional examples of communication situations to demonstrate this impossibility.

The great scene in *Eugene Onegin* in which Tatiana, the inexperienced girl, writes a letter declaring her love for the too-experienced Onegin, employs one of the oldest opera conventions. Monteverdi's messenger and the letter-writings and deliverings that choke the plots of so many eighteenth-century operas and dangerously complicate the second half of *Figaro* set the pattern for a tradition which continued in the double-dealings of the letter-stealing brother in *Lucia di Lammermoor* and in the ambiguities of the letter-reading in the last scene of *Traviata*; but no one had ever attempted such a fine use of the convention as Tchaikovsky. He made it work for him in a new way. In the work of earlier composers the convention had been popular as a means of developing the plot and transmitting information from one character to another; letters were sent and read, plans hatched and scotched, and at the same time the audience was kept informed of the action. In *Eugene Onegin* the letter-writing scene is designed to make every member of the audience aware that the convention is being used in a peculiar way. The letter is composed – not to give information to a character or to the audience – but to give the audience an insight into the process of letter-writing and the situation facing Tatiana and Onegin. Though the letter is addressed to Onegin, the letter scene is addressed to the audience.

Tatiana sits up through the night composing her letter to Onegin, asking him if he can love her. She pours out an elaborate aria of hope. But it is obvious that the letter will not be successful. Everyone in the audience realizes that Tatiana's hope is misplaced. By the end of the scene one is prepared for Onegin's rejection of her proffered love. No one could be expected to react appropriately to such a delicate declaration.

Tchaikovsky makes it plain that the means of communication are not appropriate. It is not simply a matter of Onegin reading what she has written, understanding what she means and accepting her. Neither of them is ready to appreciate the kind of person that the other is. Onegin's rejection of Tatiana in the next scene is perfectly in character: self-regarding, perhaps, proper, certainly, and indeed suggesting a delicacy which she in her pain cannot possibly be expected to notice. The audience know that these two ought not to be estranged but cannot see how it could be otherwise. There is a strong suggestion that letters are not a good means of communication.

At the party which quickly follows, a cheerful opportunity for village fun, in the midst of Lensky's happiness with Olga, and talk of Onegin's possible marriage, the two friends suddenly find themselves saying things which should not be said, and which they do not mean to say, and end up challenging one another to a duel. The party, which should be a friendly occasion, is turned into an aggressive one. And language, which the characters should have in common, becomes the instrument by which their shared life is pulled apart.

Then, in what is significantly the finest music of the opera, Lensky, waiting in the dawn light for Onegin to come with the pistols, sings of his fear of emptiness, of not seeing the woods again, of losing all he loves. This soliloquy establishes Lensky in the audience's mind much as the letter scene established Tatiana.

They are both quite ordinary people who will never find a way to communicate with others. When Onegin does arrive the situation becomes the complete reverse of that at the party. In this scene it is precisely because they do not say anything when they should, and when they know the words they should say, that tragedy comes. Tchaikovsky's music and its silences indicate just how easy and how difficult it would be for the duellists to throw away their pistols and resume their lasting friendship. They fire. Lensky dies in the snow. The gap in communication yawns again.

Onegin, isolated from everyone, wanders the world and is not seen again until he returns to Moscow and recognizes Tatiana as she moves with assured grace among the guests at a princely reception. She is married. He demands that she talk with him. At their interview he clamours for her to reiterate the love she declared in her letter. But nothing can be the same again. She makes him see that they can never meet. She thinks it is all the fault of his brusque treatment of her long before. He thinks it a cruel return of a long-gone silliness. But the audience have learnt from Tchaikovsky that no other outcome was ever possible from her letter, the party, or the duel. The composer has shown in this opera the inevitable uselessness of every communicative device. If the tragedy had not happened in one way it would have happened in another. Olga living out her life alone, Lensky dying in the snow, Tatiana grown to accept her position in society, Onegin fleeing into loneliness – these are Tchaikovsky's ordinary people. It is only in the fairy-tale world of ballet that happiness and love and understanding can be achieved. Opera for him is about the impossibility of communication between one human and another. The characters are essentially separate beings.

And reflecting on this, an audience must come from *Eugene Onegin* with a sense that if their traditional notions of communication, of letters and parties and talk between friends, have been challenged and, perhaps for some of the audience, successfully challenged in this opera, then it may be that the traditional operatic instruments of announcing the communicatory character of letters, and parties, and talk between friends – the recitative or aria, the ensemble or chorus, the duet or trio – have also been successfully challenged. The letter scene contains the most extended and impressive aria in the opera and has an immense impact in the theatre; the party scenes of peasant festivals, country house birthdays, and urbane receptions, are done with hugely inventive skill, their music gracefully diversified; the conversation that halts between Lensky and Onegin on the duelling ground and crashes to the ground in jagged fragments between Onegin and Tatiana at the end of the opera, is perfectly managed musically. The aria, the ensemble, the duet, each has been given a proper chance, and each has declared itself unable to serve the quite ordinary demands of the characters. Tchaikovsky must have made many in his audience wonder if the old operatic musical devices had ever really enabled the characters to communicate; and must at least have persuaded them that if the devices had ever been effective, then they were so no longer. In *Eugene Onegin* Tchaikovsky pushed the conventions to their limits and attempted to force from them an admission of their inadequacy. But he did all this within the old narrative framework. Wagner, on the other hand, had not intended his audience to doubt the old modes of opera-writing and at the same time remain certain of the value of story-telling.

DEBUSSY

Wagner was a darker magician than Tchaikovsky was able to contemplate. He was, as Debussy called him, 'that old Klingsor'. And intended those coming to performances of his operas to enter by his power a trance-like state in which the story was simply a way of appreciating the myth. Debussy, in writing *Pelléas et Mélisande*, was determined to get away from the spell of *Tristan und Isolde*, but he knew that once he had heard it he could do nothing but work with the Wagnerian concept of the opera as a communication not between characters on a stage but between the composer and the audience in the theatre. Debussy worked plainly with those notions which Tchaikovsky because he was, after all, less intelligent, had only obscurely sensed from Wagner's example. Tchaikovsky had seen that the musical conventions had to be publicly exploded. He had not seen quite how to do this so that the narrative conventions went up with them. He hoped that the audience would perceive the inadequacies of the old conventions of communication, and would then look for a more worthwhile encounter with the mind of the composer. Debussy was less willing to wait on such a hope.

Debussy saw both that Wagner had made it unnecessary to employ the old conventions of opera music and plot, and that audiences had not seen this for themselves. Audiences were still being happily entertained by grand opera stories put together in the manner of Sardou, what Shaw had called 'Sardoodledum'. They were still clapping Puccini's first act climaxes, and asking one another at the interval, 'What happens next?' Debussy took the old music of aria and ensemble wholly out of his design. He wanted to speak to his audiences in such a way that each individual would ask 'What is happening within me?' The man in the audience was to be directly confronted not by the mind of the character as in the old narrative opera, nor by the mind of the composer as in the Wagnerian music-drama, but by the image of his own mind. The action was to take place within him. Debussy prompted his audience to see themselves in the strangely undefined characters and plot of Maeterlinck's play. The audience moved in the mysterious court of the king of Allemonde and felt their lives obscurely changing as they heard Mélisande whisper again her complaint: 'I am not happy.'

The girl's somewhat tiresomely repeated moan is unlikely to sound like a phrase from ordinary life. Many members of the audience will have, of course, memories of those leisured times when they could remark to themselves how unhappy they were, but few will have had the nerve to say this aloud to others as often as Mélisande seems to think allowable, and fewer still will have had the wit and grace to say such a thing at precisely the most devastating moment in a conversation. It is certainly not because Mélisande seems here to be behaving in the way people do behave in 'real life' that we may be persuaded to accept what Debussy is suggesting. Whatever kind of reality there is in the action of *Pelléas et Mélisande* it is not that of a direct slice of life. The composer is hoping that his audience may, by attending to his presentation of his characters' states of mind and will, come to sympathize sufficiently with them to recognize the similarities between the world of the opera and their own inner world, and readily acknowledge its reality. In his assurance that he was attempting to present things as they were Debussy declared his opera to be 'in spite of its dreamlike atmosphere, more human than the so-called documents after life'.

Debussy recognized that *Pelléas et Mélisande* provided him with an opportunity for turning the conventional libretto inside out. He did not simply set the words he had been given: he set new silences. And he made the given situations more mysterious by unexpected gaps in their presentation. No tradition was left unaltered by this great work. Debussy took, for example, the letter convention so skilfully exposed by Tchaikovsky and went one further by presenting letters as a source of bewilderment. He used them in order to confuse not his characters, but his audience. The formal mystery that Debussy creates as the context of all action is much enhanced by the two letters at the beginning of the opera. The first, from Golaud to Pelléas, describing his meeting with Mélisande, is read out in full, though we have already seen the events it describes. The second, from Pelléas's dying friend, is dismissed by a quick reference to the illness of Pelléas's father – whom we have not seen and never do see. The known is reiterated, the unknown is assumed. Debussy's treatment of these two letters is consistent with his intention to create a bewildering atmosphere for the whole action. It all seems so unlike Monteverdi's early use of the letter convention as a means of giving vital information to the audience. And yet in Debussy's letter scene the device is being used in an operatic way. The audience are not meant to be interested in the dying friend or in Pelléas's father. They are meant to be only remotely interested in the actions of Golaud and Pelléas themselves. They are, rather, to concentrate their attention on the more general and immediate problem of how much anyone may learn about another, and to what extent our vision of the world is obscured. So we hear Golaud's version of what happened when he met Mélisande; we have his letter to Pelléas. But it is to be noted that Pelléas does not read it to us. That is left to his mother. Golaud is obscurely present and absent, as is Pelléas. And gradually the audience is brought through the action of this opera to realize that Debussy is suggesting that this is how things always are. It is the final truth about our world as well as Allemonde. Everything is obscurely present and absent to the mind. By the end of *Pelléas and Mélisande* the delicate and frightening mystery of our own ignorance of ourselves and what is happening about us is perfectly figured in the obscurity of the action on stage. We must at the final scene share in Golaud's urgent demand for the truth. What is the truth of the relationship between Pelléas and Mélisande? We have to recognize the finality of Debussy's decision that we should never know. No more than Golaud will we ever have a satisfying explanation. No one who goes to this opera can ever be quite sure when, if ever, Mélisande is telling the truth. Golaud's terrified passion and Pelléas's puzzled innocence are unable to deal with her cry of unhappiness. And no one can go home at the end of the opera with any assurance that his perception of a given situation is accurate. Real life takes on the character of Debussy's art, like Oscar Wilde's suggestion that fields began to look like Van Gogh fields once the painter had shown them how to do it.

Two

Is it for Real?

In setting their operas in mysterious contexts – in the kingdom of the Queen of Night, under the waters of the Rhine, or in the universal country of Allemonde – Mozart, Wagner and Debussy deliberately related music to magic, myth and dream. To some timid critics it has seemed that such a course requires a vigorous defence. 'Opera, unable to imitate reality,' has risen, Rossini proclaimed, 'above ordinary nature into an ideal world.' Opera is, he said in rather bolder voice, 'a sublime art'. Perhaps Rossini thought that he might do the art some good by associating it with the classical authority of Longinus. But to escape the suggestion of frivolity through the bolt-hole of transcendence is not particularly effective. And it is certainly not the way of the great opera composers. They did not consider themselves either escapists or levitationists. It seemed to them that they had been seriously concerned with matters of great human importance. It is because they recognized the relation between myth and the common concerns of men that they employed it in opera. Opera is meant to communicate something of the sublime, certainly, but of the sublime as it is ordinarily found. Not in another world but in this. And it was precisely their placing of the action of opera in the world of magic, myth and dream which alerted their audiences to the immediacy of the action. Audiences recognized and appreciated the music's expression of the strangeness of life. This was the reality of opera.

There are, of course, a great many operas, and written by great composers, too, which are not obviously concerned with matters of mythic import. Not every scene has its apparent goblin, not every grand finale is organized by a kindly wizard. It would be possible to chronicle the stories which composers have selected for their works in such a way that there would appear to have been through the ages a steady progress towards anecdotes taken from that life we lead at the kitchen sink and the bus queue. It would be possible to suggest from this that composers have come to understand that it is somehow easier for those who go in the evening to the opera house to believe in the story they witness if it reflects what they have been doing all day long themselves. Such a chronicle of opera's progress might start from Monteverdi's *La Favola d'Orfeo*, proceed through Handel's *Semele* and Voltaire's *Samson* to *Figaro*, and come to rest with *La Bohème*. It might be difficult for anyone who wished to continue with such an account of opera to get enough examples of more recent opera to make it seem wholly convincing. Modern composers do not generally seem anxious to proceed according to the direction Puccini indicated. But some such history could be sketched. Time and energy would be better spent, however, describing another line altogether. Starting again with *Orfeo*, a development might be suggested through *The Magic Flute*, *Rheingold*, and even *Turandot*, to Janácěk's *Makropoulos Affair*. This series of operas, in which extraordinary elements of divinity, heroism and mystery predominate, continues with the works of a dozen composers writing in our own time. And this choice of subject matter does not seem any less realistic than the other to those who compose operas or to those who attend their performance.

At the musical suggestion of the composers, opera audiences are ready to see themselves in the lost princesses and the liberating heroes, in the mythic personages who act out their dreams. Such a readiness has always been characteristic of those who were enthusiastic about opera. The Sun King was prepared to see himself at least in the gracious Jupiter of Lully's court tale *Phaëton*, if not in the rebel whom the god defeated. Others, less majestical, have even been willing to acknowledge what they have in common with the greedy dwarf, the bullying giant, and the jealous husband. And, now and again, someone may be happy to discover himself in the magic guardian. There was a moment of delight for all the audience recently at the Frankfurt Oper, when, at a performance of *The Magic Flute*, as Pamina raised the knife to kill herself, a young boy cried out 'Don't do it!' For him opera was certainly real. His cry was an exact anticipation of the cry of the genii. In the midst of magic the young boy did the magic thing. Precisely at the moment when he might seem to be caught up in a childishly crude realism the boy was a real sharer in mystery. He had himself become the saviour of Pamina.

And even a less impulsive member of the audience may be expected – precisely because he has been persuaded by Wagner to take seriously Parsifal's struggle amongst the grail knights, the flower maidens and the wicked enchanter to realize his true self – to appreciate the opera as a figure of the composer's effort to make sense of his experience, and, working from this, to appreciate it as a figure of his own endeavour to become a mature human being. Wagner heard, in the intelligible voice of the hero, his own control of those raging forces sounding in the orchestra. He felt that he was exercising a worthy control over a situation which would, if he had not been making an opera, have overwhelmed him. This sense of their own will at work has characterized all opera composers of distinction. If not quite so convinced as Wagner of their own heroic status, they have yet been aware of the necessity to exercise their will strongly if they were to shape the music to an expression of their idea of order. And this is why composers have commonly presented their intentions through stories which direct attention to the same exertions of the human will as they themselves were undertaking. What so many and so diverse composers thought they were about is declared in the titles of their operas: *Orfeo*, *Don Giovanni*, *Fidelio*, *Rigoletto*, *Parsifal*, and *Peter Grimes*. Each title signifies immediately a concern with a distinct and impressive human being. Through these the composer means to express himself. And in these, the composer hopes, the man in the audience will see something of himself.

Opera asserts the interest for all human beings of the individual human being. Each man's situation may be an acceptable paradigm of another's. As the design of the opera story customarily indicates that the composer has originally been interested in the way one human being may believe and behave, so the performance of the opera directs attention to the singular activity of individuals (the composer, the conductor and the singer), and the interior action of the opera occurs within each one who hears it.

That consideration of another's individual effort may well provoke a member of the audience to form a higher estimation than before of his own interest and value. Not all operas have such an effect, but if they do not they are exceptions. Prokofiev's *War and Peace* makes large demands on the concerted effort of the chorus members, and suggests in its action that the grand fates of nations are the composer's proper concern. And, in his *Word about Wozzeck*, Berg remarked contentedly 'no one gives heed to anything but the vast social implications of the work which far transcend the personal destiny of Wozzeck', and on this he congratulated himself: 'This I believe to be my achievement.' But it was the pressure exerted by the Soviet authorities which persuaded Prokofiev to give up his preliminary conception of an opera about the effects of war and peace upon the lives of a very few characters. And Berg certainly deceived himself if he supposed that 'vast social implications' overtopped in interest the destiny of Wozzeck when an audience went to a performance of his opera. If the social theory really had seemed more important than the hero's story then the audience would certainly not have applauded the composer. They would have known that he had not made an opera.

In this context a nice comparison can be made between Verdi's practice and that of a more tedious composer. *Ernani* is one of Verdi's most successful early operas. It has a grand story of love and honour and a dramatically convincing hero who sacrifices the one for the other. Real excitement is engendered in the music as the hero moves forward to his death amid the conventions of a long-gone aristocracy. The story of his singular glory within the confines of an alien culture is made by Verdi a matter for our concern. Ernst Krenek, a century later, in his programme for *The New Music and Today's Theater*, announced that 'shunning the old illusionistic conceptions of history', his opera *Karl der Grosse* 'searches out the true political significance of events'. His work is certainly not convincing as an opera. Successful operas are more personal than that. The individual who, in a world where agencies for the promotion of the greater good and the common wealth abound, is discouraged from thinking too much of himself, may well be startled by opera. Opera encourages self-appraisal.

Such encouragement for a man to take himself as seriously as the heroes of old, amidst the pressures of 'social implications' and 'political significance', is contrary to the general flow of ideas in our time. Those who determine how we should think of ourselves and our environment – social scientists, psychologists, ministers of religion and ecologists – have combined to persuade us that almost our every action exhibits an immature selfishness. And a great many of us have accepted what they say, and been persuaded that it is only by attending to the collective voice that our society can survive at all. We have accustomed ourselves to living in a world which can accommodate only a few great men, and to accepting that we are not of their number. We become used to this subordinate position. But opera demands that we think again. That we think of ourselves.

The variety of opera heroes and heroines and of the circumstance within which they measure out their actions is great enough to suggest that anyone may be such a hero or heroine in the most ordinary situation. The immense stress that is commonly laid in opera on a human being's having to sustain, and being capable of sustaining, his individual integrity in an inimical world, dignifies everyone who responds to this meaning in the music. At its very centre, therefore, opera, concerned with a single human being, turning attention to the sound of the single voice, and heard as an inward comment upon the single hearer, is set against the socially acceptable notion of the 'real'.

THE REAL AND THE CONVENTIONAL

By 1685 Dryden could observe that 'the songish part' of the operas being then performed was carefully ordered according to the model provided by its inventors. He congratulated the art on making so swift a claim, through its tradition of agreed conventions, to being accepted as a serious discipline: 'the first inventors of any art or science, provided they have brought it to perfection, are, in reason, to give laws to it; and according to their model, all after under-takers are to build'. It seemed to him that the seventeenth-century originators of opera had certainly made good their claim to give laws for the art. They had brought it to perfection and were entitled to establish its conventions. It is, however, remarkable that heroic and individualist conventions established in the seventeenth and eighteenth centuries should persist in works produced by composers who are well aware of the changes that have taken place in society during the nineteenth and twentieth centuries. And remarkable that audiences should remain content with these old conventions.

Those who attend a performance of opera are as alert to their circumstances and to the basic assumptions of their society as anyone else. They realize well enough that a composer is saying in his opera something that goes wholly against the drift of modern society, and is using to express his thoughts a set of conventions which are no longer indisputably appropriate. They have as much regard for the esteem of their fellows as anyone else. They are therefore likely to be a little uneasy about the composer's intention. And it might seem likely that they would wish the individualist conventions to be surrendered for others that might at least appear more relevant to modern interests. But, in fact, it has seemed to most a rather less dangerous challenge to the guardians of ordinariness in our society if the composer continues to communicate his immediate references to contemporary conditions through a distancing medium like the conventions of opera. It may be that this desire to maintain the traditional forms of message and medium is the reason why opera houses have to expect empty seats and box-office losses when they perform modern pieces. That characters in denim or nothing at all will sing in the conventions of blues or pop, that they will sing of kitchen sinks and bus queues, that they will come too close for comfort, and thus involve the audience in something directly revolutionary may be a fear common to those who stay away altogether, or who rise indignantly at the interval never to return. And composers should realize from what their predecessors have accomplished that they do not need to break the conventions in order to announce the immediacy of their intent. The art form itself provides enough immediacy.

It is at any rate clear from the history of the art form that a member of an audience may more enthusiastically and wholeheartedly sympathize with the intent of a composer who shows him a mythic figure rather than an individual character in a naturalistic plot. The Siegfried who forges the sword of freedom, defies the old god, and wakes the beautiful girl on the mountain side, has commonly been accorded the identifying sympathy of student and stockbroker, while the muddled fellow, so like their ordinary selves as others see them, who stumbles through the domestic misunderstandings of *Götterdämmerung* has not. Or not so easily and fully. And in lesser matters, too, an audience may not be prepared to welcome the familiar. There was a great deal of laughter at Bayreuth at the centenary performance of the *Ring* in 1976 when Siegfried came on in a neatly fitting dinner jacket. It appears that it is more likely for us to see ourselves in a character when the action of the opera is clearly happening somewhere else and at some other time. No one had laughed at the Siegfried of the previous opera in the cycle when he appeared in his Robin Hood costume.

The more distanced the presentation of the opera action is, the more acceptable will the action itself be. The structural conventions of opera, the patterning of aria, ensemble, and chorus, are, paradoxically, instrumental in persuading those in the audience to accept what is happening on the stage as a convincing metaphor of what goes on in their lives. Exemplars from the history of the art form and present desires for a tangential way of approaching the difficulties of experience, come together in a generally unspoken justification for aspects of opera which might be supposed to be self-evidently absurd. Those who ordinarily use language to express themselves do not find it at all odd that *Trovatore* and

Traviata should use aria, duet and ensemble as a means of communication between characters. The conventions of the sung word permit all sorts of things to be expressed and to receive due attention which in other circumstances would be thought not too dull or too complex but too personal. The conventions are precise instruments by which the composer can address us directly and intimately. Those who manage aria and ensemble better than others have been accepted as giving the most affecting vision of reality. Like Wallace Stevens's shearsman, Verdi plays 'a tune beyond us, yet ourselves'.

ARIA AND ENSEMBLE

The aria presents the perfect means of advancing the action through the revelation of character. If a composer can use it correctly to support the action of his opera he is well on the way to making contact with the audience. The aria in opera can be more forceful than its counterpart in a Bach cantata. The cantata remains at a stage from which opera progressed through the energetic and exemplary work of Mozart. The great arias of the Christus in the *St Matthew Passion*, for example, sound 'operatic', as the BBC commentators suggest each Holy Week, only because they are set in the context of the contemplative stillness of the other vocal parts. They would not sound so if placed in the progressive story-line of an opera that moved in the manner of *The Magic Flute*. Conversely the orchestral processionals of that work, so like some passages of the *Passion* that they must be developed from them, are only just brought within the bounds of opera through their function as parts of Mozart's narrative design.

The aria is the instrument by which an opera composer expresses the individual will of a character and by which he hints to each member of the audience the possibility of the triumph of individual will. An opera composer sacrifices such an instrument only if he thinks himself bound to do penance for some enormity. And those who have been most concerned with the representation in opera of life as it is have not disciplined themselves to work without the aria. Leoncavallo, for example, did not allow programmatic verism to prevent his giving his tenor one of the best chances in the theatre of an uproarious ovation. '*Vesti la giubba*' is, though it lacks the perfect shaping of some of Mozart's achievements, a great aria. Audiences love it. So do tenors.

The composer who attempts to present a character without using the aria will soon find himself confronted by an irate singer. In 1669 an opera called *Genserico* had to be supplied with several extra arias to please the various members of the cast. And the composer who favours one character with too brilliant an aria will soon find himself under attack from the singers of the other parts. In the 1916 version of his *Ariadne auf Naxos* Strauss makes experienced fun of the theatrical manager, who, on the strength of his influence with the composer, promises the tenor 'Two of her arias [will] disappear', while he whispers to the soprano that the composer is 'cutting out half of his'. Singers in the first hundred and fifty years or more of opera delighted in embellishing their arias. And audiences were for a while delighted by these graceful additions to the evening's entertainment. Composers, observing the singers' freedom and the audience's pleasure, learnt to make a place in their tunes for the singers' embellishments. The performance came, through the popularity of the aria, to represent an alliance between composer and singer, the librettist falling from public view. 'Music soon,' wrote Voltaire, 'had its own language and expression and its own situations; all independent of the poetry.' Composers quickly realized from the singers' success that the aria was their way to communicate directly with the audience. 'Often the orchestra rendered emotions that were no less vivid than those conveyed by the actors.' The most famous example of the exercise of that power of the composer which Voltaire noted regretfully occurs in the second act of Gluck's *Iphigénie en Tauride* of 1778. While the librettist has given the character a relaxed and self-confident text: 'Calm comes again to my heart', the syncopation of the violins against the tune carried by the voice makes the audience aware of quite other feelings also at work in his heart. The composer's command of tempo, harmony and orchestration has been enlarged to include characterization and mood. The aria has become the communicative instrument for anything the composer wishes to say in his opera.

As with the aria, so with the ensemble. This convention of characters singing together, but not necessarily singing the same words or melody, provides opportunities for the composer to effect the most graceful moments in the opera house. The ensemble was not so quickly developed as the aria. Neither of the great early Italian librettists, Zeno and Metastasio, gave much encouragement to their composers to write ensembles, and seventeenth- and eighteenth-century composers themselves, except perhaps Scarlatti, appreciated very little of the ensemble's virtues. It was some time before composers appeared who appreciated the opportunity to write music which revealed their characters' differing responses to a situation. Handel had moments of structural illumination, in, for example, his use of the aria to forward the action in *Giulio Cesare*, yet he only rarely saw the possibilities of the dramatic ensemble. Nor did critics applaud what success composers did achieve in this medium.

Corneille, like most of those attending their first opera performance, was much puzzled and indeed aggrieved by the ensemble convention. Thinking, mistakenly, that the object of singing a phrase was simply to provide information for the audience, Corneille saw only obfuscation in the workings of the ensemble. Nothing that the audience had to know could be put into the ensemble: 'on account of the confusion created by the diversity of voices pronouncing the words simultaneously, they would have caused great obscurity in the body of the work if they had to inform the hearers of anything important'. The objection is logical and quite reasonable. And yet the experience of opera audiences does not support Corneille's notion. The exhilaration felt by members of the audience as an ensemble mounts in intensity counter-weighs any objection. As in all else, Mozart was quicker than his predecessors in realizing this.

When in 1781 the young Mozart took up the tale of *Idomeneo* that Campra had made into an opera in 1712, he had to put up with a deal of advice from Raaff, the sixty-five-year-old tenor who was to take the title part. And this advice was generally that the composer should provide yet another fine aria for Idomeneo. Singers very rarely recommend the writing of ensembles: they take a longer time to rehearse and offer only a share of the applause. Raaff wanted a nice solo where Mozart had made a stupendous quartet for the leading characters in which fury and despair, love and resignation were expressed in individual, pairing, and ensemble singing. Happily neither at this time nor later in his career did Mozart listen to individual singers' objections to the ensemble form. He went on working at it until he came in *Così fan Tutte* to its perfect mastery. It took Mozart less than ten years to effect this transformation of the structure of opera. He made the ensemble the peculiar operatic instrument of the composer, and an undisputed convention of opera.

Mozart made it unmistakably clear that through this convention of several characters singing at once a composer may set forth, almost wholly unaided by any of the librettist's arts except perhaps those of rhyme and assonance, a simultaneous demonstration of the several attitudes among the characters and of his own intention. The ensemble can articulate more than one kind of statement from the composer. It may be used to suggest both the harmony of characters in agreement and the tugs and tensions of their differences. Everyone in the audience knows well that there have been times when his and others' minds were in accord and times when they were privately in discord. Everyone knows, too, that no playwright has managed to express either this simultaneous agreement or this disagreement. The ensemble allows the composer a psychological and a social realism denied to all other dramatists. The ensemble is, as Auden remarked, 'the crowning glory of opera'. Every great opera composer since Mozart has understood this and made the most of his opportunity.

There follow hard upon Mozart's demonstration of the versatility of the convention the stupendous quartet at the entry of Leonora in *Fidelio*, the grand ensemble of the first act of *Die Meistersinger* in which Wagner manages the dozen voices of the

Mastersingers, and the quintet of the third act of that opera which is the paradigm of the formal ensemble, and the generous variety and freedom of Verdi's ensemble inventions.

Verdi described Shakespeare as 'a realist by inspiration', and himself and his contemporaries in the opera house as 'realists by intention and calculation'. In making a proper claim for his kind of operatic *verismo* Verdi was, perhaps, too hard on some of his contemporaries, and, certainly, much too hard on himself. Verdi is properly famous for his command of ensembles which offer the audience a sense of the reality figured in the action of his operas. Verdi is the master of ensemble. He achieves the effect that Weber described: 'The ensemble, revealing several aspects at one and the same time, can and should be a Janus head to be taken in at one single glance.' Examples of Verdi's success with this form so abound that they may be taken from any of his operas. There is a dashing and amusing ensemble in *Un Giorno di Regno* in which everyone offers the false king a different explanation for what is happening. This opera, written in 1840, perfectly suggests Verdi's immediate mastery of the convention. And the first act of *I Lombardi* in 1843 gave the audience promise of a great evening with its ensemble announcing the characters' apprehension or delight at the prospect of the villain's revenge. Verdi's control of the ensemble situation developed with experience. Perhaps the most complicated of his ensembles occurs in *Don Carlos* when, while the Eboli expresses her remorse for suggesting to the king that his wife was false to him, the king acknowledges the injustice of his suspicions, Elizabeth laments her friendless life in an alien country, and Posa determines that the time has come for him to sacrifice himself for the good of the people. But of all the splendid uses of this convention in his work none has had more compliment than the final quartet in *Rigoletto* (1851), '*Bella figlia dell'amore*', in which the dying Gilda and Rigoletto, her tormented hunchback father, sing in ignorance of the rakish Duke and his latest conquest, the inkeeper's sister, who are enjoying a moment's pleasure. Verdi told the original singer of Rigoletto, Felice Varesi, that he never expected to better that quartet, and Victor Hugo, from whose *Le Roi s'Amuse* the opera had been taken, said in his stall at the first Paris performance: 'This is marvellous, simply marvellous! Ah, if I only could in my play make four people talk simultaneously in a way that the public would understand the words and varying sentiments.'

Verdi suggests at once the diversity of his characters and the singleness of their doom. There is some rightness, therefore, in the old staging of such things with the four singers ranged along the footlights, for by this device the audience may appreciate both the isolated characters of the story and the singers united in the music. The peculiar thrill of such an ensemble, and indeed the peculiar thrill of opera, is that the more a member of an audience is aware of the convention being used with skill, the more likely is he to respond to the emotional communication of the composer, and the more likely he is to discern the reference of the composer's work to his own circumstances.

VERDI'S MELODRAMATIC REALISM

Tchaikovsky thought that the plots Verdi chose made it impossible to take his characters seriously. 'The feelings of an Egyptian princess, a Pharaoh, or some Nubian, I cannot enter into, or comprehend.' He thought almost all Verdi's great operas too contrived and stagey, and quite a number of opera-goers have echoed his sentiments, however prepared they were to suspend their disbelief when confronted with *Traviata*, *Rigoletto*, or *Trovatore*.

Yet what seemed implausible to Tchaikovsky and those who have his notion of realism, has seemed entirely likely to others. Certainly Verdi did not think himself eccentric when he presented his audience with the incidents of these operas; he was simply offering a set of crudely realistic events which they would recognize as bearing a relation to everyday life. The distinctive character of his opera-writing lay in his power to persuade people to look at events the way he looked at them. Perhaps his sympathies were wider than Tchaikovsky's – that is likely since he is a much greater composer in every way. At any rate his personal experience fitted him for understanding how both the rough and the subtle insults of society might hurt a girl who, though she delighted and pleasured a multitude of respectable persons, could not herself be reckoned respectable. In *Traviata* in 1853 Verdi put a contemporary situation on the stage, taking some joy in shocking those respectable grumblers of Busseto who had snubbed his mistress, Giuseppina Strepponi. His opera touched so closely on contemporary social matters that the Venetian management, with no hint of irony, dressed the piece at its first performance in costumes of the France of Louis XIV, thus distancing its uncomfortable contemporaneity. Verdi was not at all pleased. He wanted his audience to realize how nearly the action of his opera touched their lives. Once he had brought them to realize the relevance of his operas, however, they became worried at the possible effect of his work. Verdi boasted of his breach of convention in making a hunchback clown the hero of *Rigoletto*. The authorities were more worried by Verdi's presentation of a duke as a rake and a wastrel. This breach of operatic convention seemed to his contemporaries to hint at a desire to upturn social conventions. *Rigoletto* had a hard time with the political censors in Italy because it disturbed the social order. Everything was too real for his audience. And if the famous incident of the baby being thrown on the flames in *Trovatore* has seemed far-fetched to Verdi's audience, it cannot have seemed far-fetched to the composer. Verdi, when a baby, had himself been hidden in a church belfry by his mother as a troop of Russian marauders riding through Le Roncole cut down women and children. In a time of police chiefs and political prisoners, of massacres and marches, revolutionaries and tyrants, there is not much which is thoroughly unreal and unlikely.

Verdi's continuing popularity is in large part due to the fact that what happens to the girl, the vengeful fool, and the gipsy happens to many whose economic and social circumstances are quite removed from those presented in the opera. Realism in opera, as in any other art, is not a matter of kitchen sinks, or not of kitchen sinks necessarily, it is rather a matter of presenting a human situation in which an audience may recognize their own emotional possibilities. When Rigoletto pleads for the restoration of his daughter a man in the audience does not have to imagine himself the jester of a Renaissance court in order to recognize in himself Rigoletto's frail hold on happiness and the irrational nobility of his capacity to love. It was because Verdi was aware of our capacity to see ourselves in others however different the context, that he could afford to ignore superficial realism. He was content again and again to change the setting of his opera plots and the social context of his characters. His alteration of *Un Ballo in Maschera* from the Sweden of Gustavus III to the Boston of a colonial governor is only the most famous of his bows to the censor on matters which seemed to him not at all important. Move *Carmen* from Spain or *Madama Butterfly* from Japan and the illusion would collapse because it depends more upon external circumstance than upon integrity of characterization. Verdi realized that men and women of any country or clime could be pushed into the strangest situations by love and hate and accident and scheme. Everything is possible. But there is for everything a recognizable cause within the caprice of destiny. The final scene in *Rigoletto* when the hunchback tears open the sack to find not the dead Duke but his dying daughter is in itself as bizarre as anything in opera. But it is perfectly credible. An audience may see how it has been caused. And, as the situation is ever explicable, so the characters are ever capable of appreciating the situation and its explanation. This is an important and peculiar element in Verdi's presentation of the world.

Verdi understood his relationship with the man in the audience to be a meeting between men of honour who have determined to face the facts of a fearsome world. His music, communicating such a determination, shapes characters who have a continuing appreciation of what is happening around them. They recognize the terrors of events and their own part in them. There is nothing in Verdi's operas of a kind with the escapist resort of Donizetti's most famous piece. While the mad Lucia di Lammermoor is trilling brilliantly in her blood-stained dress, most members of the audience will delight in the composer's inventive mastery and the singer's command of fine musical phrase, but few are likely to feel even a passing sympathy for what sorrow has made of a human being and may make of them. The plight of Donizetti's heroine does not touch them. Verdi is intent on making the audience realize how closely they in their ordinary proceedings may come to a state like to that of his characters. So he does not distance them from the character by projecting an image of madness.

It is precisely because Rigoletto is not allowed to find refuge in madness that his suffering is felt with such immediacy by those in the audience. Verdi certainly did not intend his audience to identify with those who were so frightened by the world that they retreated into madness. Even the poor gipsy Azucena of *Trovatore* whose mother has been burnt as a witch, who has thrown her own baby son in a crazed mood upon the flames, and whose life is ending in a dungeon, is not driven into madness. Verdi wrote to his librettist, 'I do not want her to be mad at the end', and more insistently, 'Do not make Azucena mad. Overwhelmed by care, grief, terror, sleeplessness, but she is not mad.' For Verdi, the only mad people were those who would not exercise their own will, who sought relief in the acceptance of another will: who sought it, for example, in religion. Poor Strepponi's efforts to convert him were laughingly rejected with 'You are mad.' He himself did not, she admitted, need anything beyond the human.

A SLICE OF LIFE

Tchaikovsky was not alone among composers in thinking that Verdi's plots of kings and slaves and hunchbacks and courtesans represented a retreat from the realism of *Carmen*. From such thoughts came an attempt at a new form of opera for which the claim was made that it alone was properly '*verismo*'.

Verismo is first of all a literary term originally coined to describe the style of Zola's novels. In Italian literature it applies primarily to the short stories and novels of two Sicilians: Luigi Capuana and Giovanni Verga. In his several attempts at opera Zola was unlucky with his collaborators. His librettos were subtle and imaginative examples of a controlled realism. Verga was happier, at least in one arrangement with a *verismo* composer. He achieved some operatic fame when his short story *Cavalleria Rusticana* was made into one of the most famous *verismo* operas by Mascagni. As in literature so in music Italian *verismo* derived from a French model. Bizet's *Les Pêcheurs de Perles* and *Carmen* were its earliest exponents though certainly there were earlier hints in Grétry's eighteenth-century *opéra-comique*, in the great original *opera buffa*, Pergolesi's *La Serva Padrona* of 1733, and further back still in the low-life interludes of Cavalli and Monteverdi.

Probably the first *verismo* opera of the modern kind was put together by the Polish composer Stanislaw Moniuszko. *Halka*, written in 1846, is a tale of a peasant girl's betrayal by a nobleman and her decline into insanity when he abandons her. In this, as in other early *verismo* operas, there is a certain amount of social comment. Moniuszko's hero, the faithful peasant Jontek, who would save Halka if he could, was offensive enough for the opera to be banned by the authorities for some years. So the first real stage success of the new realism deals with blood and revenge among the poor, and *Cavalleria Rusticana* was followed by an opera which is often coupled with it: Leoncavallo's *I Pagliacci* (1892).

Leoncavallo wrote his own libretto from an incident which had happened in his district when he was a boy. Truth was to be put most truthfully on the opera stage. His opera starts with a singer appearing before the curtain to announce in a prologue that the action the audience is about to witness is 'a true story'. And at once the difficulty of writing *verismo* becomes plain. The composer has had to resort to a theatrical device, a prologue, to present a slice of life, the truth. And Leoncavallo's piece continues in this ambivalent manner. The intention and the form are continually opposed. So much of this opera is simply the old conventional material: happy peasants chime perfectly in a church bell chorus; the impassioned and Verdiesque principals declare their loves and frustrations in stirring arias and duets. Leoncavallo deceived himself if he thought that these constituted a new realism just because the peasants and the lovers were part of a past he had himself experienced. And it is when he exploits the oldest conventions most shamelessly that he achieves his finest effect. It is the artificial *commedia dell'arte* entertainment, with its pastiche gavottes and minuets, which comes across most powerfully. The communication of passion is more successfully managed, even in *verismo* opera, when the composer is working within the framework of acknowledged conventions.

If it be true that *verismo*, as Grout declares, presents 'a cross-section of life without concerning itself with any general significance the action might have', then its presentation in opera form is not going to utilize the particular qualities of that medium. Chances of presenting such slices of life have generally been taken by competent second-rate novelists rather than by opera composers. It is perhaps significant that Galsworthy was enthusiastic about Leoncavallo's achievement in *I Pagliacci*, esteeming this 'one of those rare operas in that the story takes complete possession of the music'. Galsworthy's comment was evidently that of a professional story-teller, and he concentrates upon the carefully controlled progress of the incidents of the plot. The music was, it seemed to Galsworthy, obedient to the mood of events. I am not at all sure that the peasant chorus or the clown's broken aria are quite so obedient as Galsworthy suggests, but his remark points to a more important characteristic of *verismo* opera. Leoncavallo's method of story-telling implies an abrogation of the opera composer's opportunity to say something about his conception of existence. If the story takes control of the music, so that the music has to serve as well as it can the mere narrative sense of the text, then what becomes of opera as the expression of the composer's view of life? For it is plain that a view cannot be offered to an audience without some selection and interpretation of reality.

Perhaps it is because Verdi had so evidently not been content to present 'a slice of life' that those most dominated by his example and memory were the most eager to present themselves as working without philosophic intention, without the suggestion of a coherent view of the world. The effort, of course, to compose a work of art without announcing through that work a sense of the world's structure, is hugely demanding. Art is so evidently a comment upon experience that its very nature has to be frustrated if such an opera is to be made, or even to seem to be made. The greater the effort the shorter the course must be. The examples of Mascagni and Leoncavallo suggest that *verismo* is most satisfactorily contained in a one-act framework, and Puccini's *Il Tabarro*, equally an opera of low life and passion, is equally short. Puccini, however, did attempt to stretch the form to full opera length. *Madama Butterfly*, *La Bohème*, *Tosca*, *La Fanciulla del West* (*The Girl of the Golden West*) and *Turandot* were each designed as *verismo* opera.

He evidently thought himself capable of great things. And certainly he was the maker of some of the finest melodies ever offered for an audience's diversion. It is his carelessness of so many possibilities of the opera form which seems to prevent his being thought a great opera composer, however much it has to be admitted that he is a popular one. Puccini never seems to realize that through the composition of an opera he can say something as suggestive and stimulating to human thought as other men might through the writing of a treatise or the passing of a social reform. He does not respect his medium sufficiently. He does not expect from it any hint of the possibilities of human life.

Puccini hoped to bring a coarse naturalism into the opera house, and at times, as during the bloody card-playing in the bar in *The Girl of the Golden West*, he is certainly successful. But more often realism, when extended over the length of a three or four act opera, collapses into mawkish tear-jerking, like the condemned Cavaradossi's farewell note to Tosca, soppy sentimentalism like the flag-waving child in *Butterfly* or horror-comic melodrama like the torture of Liù in *Turandot*. Some of his tunes are marvellous but Puccini does not offer much more than tunes. Of course he took the craft of opera seriously. His correspondence about *Turandot*, for example, shows that he took immense care over the structuring of an opera. But when the Puccini operas are examined they do not offer the same rewards as do those of Mozart, say, or Verdi.

What Puccini offers is severely limited in time and place and interest.

He is a 'realist' composer, passing the whiskey in *Tabarro*, *Butterfly* and *The Girl of the Golden West*, and delighting in creating snatches of local orchestral colour for the Bohemian world, Japan, China and Frontier America. But the way in which the pretty pieces of tune and orchestration which decorate *Butterfly* – the American anthem and the Japanese tinkle – are applied to the surface of musical mannerisms common to *Butterfly*, *Tosca* and *Turandot*, serves only to make such snatches seem forced and unreal. Whatever the programme and the costumes suggest Puccini is again presenting his audience with Italy and with wholly Italian music.

Puccini was equally limited in the kinds of feeling he could experience. The limitations of Puccini's psyche are immediately evident in the limitations of his operas' version of reality. In no other opera form is the audience so confined by the personality of the composer as in *verismo*. Puccini's audiences have to stay within his bounds. Like Massenet, the composer of operas which told of Manon, Thaïs and Cleopatra, Puccini took great delight in the idea of the repentant sinner as heroine. But while Massenet became President of the French Academy, Puccini's interest in penitents never seemed quite respectable. His way of telling his stories seemed to his contemporaries to be decidedly odd. The peasants of Torre del Lago nicknamed him '*il maestro cuccumeggiante*', 'the man who makes harlot music', but Mosco Carner observes that in comparing Puccini's presentations of his heroines 'with their original models in the relevant novels and plays, we are struck by the extent to which the composer sought to transmogrify his fair sinners into shining little angels'. Certainly Puccini guarded them from too explicit sexual reference. The scene of Scarpia's attempted seduction of Tosca is much less fierce in the opera than in Sardou's play. Puccini protected his frail heroines and he tortured them with a horrific sadism. His biographer suggests, as an explanation for this treatment, that for all their 'unworthiness' the composer felt unconsciously 'that his heroines were in some way rivals of the exalted mother-image. He may even have identified them with it to some extent, so that loving them carried with it an incestuous implication'. The heroines would, therefore, be seen by Puccini as both romantically lovable and guiltily associated with what he himself called his 'Nero complex'.

It is general in *verismo* opera to deal with women who have in some way shut themselves out of society. In *I Pagliacci* an adulterous travelling show-woman, in *Cavalleria Rusticana* a jilted village spinster, and in *Tiefland* a street dancer married off to a shepherd to conceal the fact that she has been the village landlord's mistress. These are evidently doomed girls. But it is peculiar to Puccini that it is the woman alone who is punished and given no hope of a better time after punishment. In *I Pagliacci* both the heroine and her lover are caught in disaster; in *Cavalleria Rusticana* the man who has wronged the heroine is killed; in *Tiefland* the shepherd punishes the girl and then accepts her as his wife. But in *Butterfly* the heroine is cheated of everything and finally kills herself; in *Tosca* the heroine, having been made to listen to the screams of her lover under torture, is cheated out of her promised freedom with him; and in *La Bohème* Mimi's death in the chill attic is drawn out with many a heart-rending run of chords. A comparison with the death of Violetta in Verdi's *Traviata* shows what may be achieved with a different kind of realism. There is no salvation possible in a Puccini opera, not because the world is terrible, as Verdi believed, but simply because Puccini is a sadist. At least he is a sadist as far as his treatment of the heroine is concerned. Sometimes the hero is freed from his past: Pinkerton goes back to America with his wife and child.

This kind of analysis may explain what is going on in Puccini's work, but it is interesting only in so far as Puccini himself is interesting. And the 'meaning' of his operas is not what accounts for his interest as a composer. This is almost entirely due to his being able to write good tunes. I must own to being one of those Mr Kerman, in his elegant essay on *Opera as Drama*, scorns for being 'awed by Scarpia's chords or touched by the *Vissi d'arte*'. Puccini is a perfect example of Thomas Mann's idea of the artist as 'magician'. The audience is charmed by his tunes into accepting all kinds of strangeness and insignificance. The significance of *Tosca* or *Butterfly* stops if not at Tosca and Butterfly then at Puccini.

That an opera reveals the psychology of its composer is not, of course, prejudicial to its being a great opera. There are a number of discerning critics who have seen in Wagner's work aspects of his psychological make-up. But it is a characteristic of Puccini's psychology that it is self-destructive, claustrophobic and trivializing. He had evidently concluded that it was difficult enough to make a sound musical structure, properly alternating lively and solemn melodies, solo and ensemble situations, without bothering overmuch about meaning. In 1889 in a Milan theatre he saw a performance of Sardou's melodrama, *Tosca*, and, though he knew only a few words of French, when he heard that Franchetti was thinking of making an opera out of the play, he seized the libretto for himself. Puccini worked hard at the construction of the *Te Deum* scene, the torture of Cavaradossi, and the final leap, until everything added up to an evening of 'real theatre'. In *Tosca* he has managed to make a struggle for political and personal freedom into an opportunity for delicious singing and melodramatic twists. What was supremely important for Beethoven has become simply a piece of theatrical business. Again, when he saw an American play in London in 1900 though he understood very little of the dialogue he knew at once that *Madama Butterfly* would offer him just the right opportunities for his kind of opera. And, though this opera was a total fiasco at its first performance in Milan in 1904, he was quite right. It does have all the elements of popular art. From the second production in Brescia three months later it has held its place in the repertory of every opera house. But for those who ask such questions a short answer can be given to 'What is this opera about?' Indeed the only appropriate question at the close of *Butterfly* is 'Did you cry?'

Puccini was often described as Verdi's successor. *Manon Lescaut*, Puccini's first popular success, appeared in the same year, 1893, as *Falstaff*. And there are some superficial similarities between

Puccini's operatic material and that of Verdi. The frail lady, dying of consumption in a garish Parisian setting, is common to *Traviata* and *Bohème*; the pomp of an imagined East decks out *Aida* and *Turandot*. But what Verdi did vigorously from strength, Puccini did sentimentally from weakness. It seems to me that audiences are generally at least as likely to 'identify' with the characters presented by Verdi, whom *verismo* partisans are prone to describe as 'melodramatic', as with those of Puccini. The popularity of *Bohème* and *Butterfly* is akin to the popularity of romantic novels. These operas, of a high melodic calibre, are fine for a sentimental weep but hardly ever mistaken as being 'like life'.

Composers who have attempted opera since the days of Puccini *verismo* have generally not accepted even his best work as exemplary. They seem, indeed, in some ways to have gone back to Verdi's methods.

Though the grander sweeps of Verdiesque orchestral blare, thrilling aria, and conclusive ensemble, are no longer, it seems, available to modern composers, Verdi's concentration upon the mental states of characters remains paradigmatic for most of his successors. These have generally not been content with the well-made play as a model for opera structure. Rather they have developed and transformed for their newer purposes the Verdiesque presentation of characters whose intensity of feeling and will in a destructive world has determined the course of life for themselves and others. The declaratory aria by which Verdi alerted his audience to how forceful a character's response to the situation might be, to how strongly willed a course of action might be, has been developed in recent operas into an instrument for the revelation of diverse conditions of mind and will.

One of the features of early *verismo* was the location of the action in an ordinary and modern setting. *Traviata* and *Carmen* owed something of their shocking character to the contemporaneity of their setting. Puccini had, in hope of a greater wonder, escaped to exotic surroundings, to Japan and China and the Wild West, but others came back to the earlier consideration of what might be going on in the lives of quite ordinary men and women in quite ordinary circumstances. They had thoughts of a *verismo* that would take into account the real power in ordinary life of quite strange symbols. The *verismo* of Bruneau's *Messidor* was not simply concerned with a village's need for adequate irrigation, but with the imaginative force of such symbols as harvest and Eucharist and gold, an imaginative force so great that in the mind of the peasant woman, Véronique, the refining machinery becomes a ballet of gold. The old *grand opéra* convention of the Paris theatre is appreciated as *verismo*. And in the heritage of Verdi it is a *verismo* of the mind. The ballet reveals the thoughts and feelings moving within Véronique. What goes on inwardly has been recognized as the proper stuff of opera. This is the new realism.

A NEW REALISM

The new realism is intimately related to opera before the late nineteenth- and early twentieth-century *verismo*. That relation of opera to myth and dream which had been discerned, intuitively, without any of the precision of the modern sciences of such things, by Gluck and Mozart and Wagner and Verdi, is now quite deliberately revived in the work of a number of modern composers. The curtain rises regularly now to disclose a singular unconscious ambitious to be accepted as the collective. There is scarce an opera written by a major composer – and to have the persuasive power that leads managements in these cautious days to risk so much of their money declares a man to be a major composer – which does not at some moment or other require a member of the audience to accept some of the action as going on either within a character or, rather more impertinently, within himself.

The realism of modern composers is not, of course, precisely that of Verdiesque opera. For one thing the *verismo* experience was not without some effect even on those composers who were convinced of its ultimate failure. The *verismo* movement had at least reinforced the Mozartian suggestion that a serious opera could deal with characters who belonged to the middle and lower classes of society. And, with the disappearance of aristocratic influence and patronage in the world the composers knew, this was a most useful suggestion.

THE NEW HERO

In early opera, as in Greek tragedy, the hero or heroine was someone who had a space in which to exercise his will. Kings and counts, fighters and high priests were shown properly using their power and affecting everyone around them. The action of the plot depended on the behaviour of such powerful individuals. Monteverdi turned down a suggestion from the librettist Striggio for a new story on which they could collaborate, with the solemn rebuke: 'the music required by such a plot is altogether of too low a level and too close to the earth'. Striggio had been rash enough to suggest an opera on *The Marriage of Thetis and Poseidon*. Busenello's *La Prosperità Infelice di Giulio Cesare, Dittatore* and Metastasio's *Regolo* show that in the beginning librettists thought that it was necessary to give the activity of will an epic framework. Every member of the audience accepted that Caesar could exert his will over the world surrounding him. The presupposition that only the impulses of a man like him were important was common to composer, librettist and audience. That the will of a relatively ordinary human could be exercised in any way that was important was a thought that could only occur to Mozart, and that only he could express. Gradually Mozart shifted attention from important to lesser political figures: from Idomeneo, king of Crete, to Almaviva, a Spanish count, until by a turn of his music we discover that a mere servant, Figaro, can determine events around him; after achieving this it was possible for Mozart to reveal with renewed vitality and an acceptable sympathy the perplexities of an emperor. *La Clemenza di Tito* is not the celebration of a powerful political figure whose whim decides the destiny of many, but of a generous man.

It is a measure both of the resistance among audiences to such a democratic notion and of the vitality of Mozart's mind that in the years that followed his death even that great humanist Beethoven could only put across his idea of universal brotherhood by placing at the centre of his opera an important political prisoner and his wife, who at the end are shown to be friends of the Minister of Justice. Ordinary folk can only express their hope for freedom and applaud when they are given it. *Fidelio* is not an opera which encourages the opera-goer to think himself important. Nor are the generality of operas in the nineteenth century more encouraging. Wagner and Verdi returned to the traditional use of tales of gods and emperors.

There is evidently a deal of truth both in relation to customary plot and character and to the forms of aria and ensemble, in Kurt Weill's remark in *On the Composition of 'Dreigroschenoper'* (1929), that 'Opera was founded as an aristocratic form of art, and all operatic conventions serve to emphasize the sociological nature of the genre.' It is, therefore, an indication both of the attractions of the form and its resilience that composers have recently successfully turned the conventions to bourgeois use in the story of the housewife in *Kata Kabanova*, the private soldier in *Wozzeck* and the shepherd in *Tiefland*. And Richard Strauss, who certainly has a claim to being a realist composer, contrived with *Intermezzo* to shock a number of his friends by too obviously depicting his domestic clash of wills with his wife. Each of these lesser characters is dignified by the attention of music to the expression of her or his will.

A difference in the hero demands a difference of form. Modern opera's interest in men more like Papageno than Idomeneo has led to composers looking more seriously at the *opera buffa* and the *singspiel*. If E. T. A. Hoffmann, the author of the tales that Offenbach set, was correct in his idea that the essence of *opera buffa* lay in the intrusion 'of freakishness into everyday life and the confusion which results therefrom', then almost every modern opera belongs in the *opera buffa* category.

More important than their shifting of the social status of the leading characters of opera, composers have lately begun to employ characters lacking the strength of mind and will of the old heroes and heroines. Operas today are more likely to deal with inadequate members of society than with those who have command of themselves. This is a major difference between past and present opera. The old form of opera was shaped by the efforts of those who lived in a time when men were expected to celebrate reason and progress. The composers who controlled the form of opera were themselves men of great intellect and will, who knew that they could achieve something with their talent. The conventions they devised may well, therefore, accommodate a sense of the absurd, for they were generous enough in their sympathies to see that this is often 'a mad world my masters', but such conventions more easily express the possibilities of a man mastering the madness for a while and making something of it.

In the nineteenth century things had begun to fall apart. If the late eighteenth-century opera is an art celebrating that which is achievable by the force of will – the 'catalogue song' of Giovanni's conquests, the confident estimate Figaro makes of the Count: 'Little Count, you may go dancing, but I'll call the tune' – nineteenth-century opera was an art of will frustrated. Wotan wants universal power but his universe is burnt about him. King Philip wants the obedience of his son, the love of his wife and the rule of Spain, but he loses them all. Opera is here presenting that mistrust of human capacity felt by so many nineteenth-century artists. The wonders of progress and the growth of empire had not prevented them from considering the feebleness of man's efforts to improve and govern himself. This was an anxiety given forceful expression by Tennyson in the bitterness of *Locksley Hall, Sixty Years After*. And a greater disillusionment has appeared in recent years. It is a commonplace of criticism that after the Second World War, after Korea, after Vietnam, nothing on the stage can be as disjointed, as painful, as absurd as life itself. We are used to feeling confused by the world around us. And this is a new predicament for opera composers as it is for all artists.

Donizetti had shown his heroine mad, Bellini had shown his heroine sleep-walking, but neither had explored more than the fringes of what a human being may experience once control has been lost. Wagner came nearer to presenting human beings who did not know what was happening to them in the world. But he insisted on their recovering full consciousness before the end. Sieglinde may be driven mad by Hunding's carrying her off from her burning home and Siegmund's rescuing her in a transport of love, but she is brought back to sanity before she dies to preserve Siegmund's son and sword. Siegfried may be drugged and mystified into an unconscious betrayal of Brünnhilde but he is given a moment's understanding so that the world may make sense to him before he is killed. Tristan does not, at the beginning, understand himself at all. Even at the climax of the second act, when King Marke asks him for an explanation of his apparent treachery he simply says, 'I cannot tell you.' But in his great soliloquy in the final act Tristan moves from total despair to an acceptance of his responsibility for what has happened and a readiness for death. He brings himself back from the brink of madness and declares of the fatal potion, 'I myself, it was that brewed it!' Verdi had equally refused to allow his characters to capitulate to the excesses of their own passion. They are always able to appreciate what they have done. Even Azucena knows what is happening around her. The burning of her mother, the hideous mistake about her baby, the war, the torture and the dungeon, cannot deprive her of her wits.

Verdi's determination to preserve opera as the expression of those who remain sane in the face of the *nulla* they experience, has not been maintained by composers of later opera. Composers have realized that if they would now compose 'a tune beyond us, yet ourselves' they will have to attempt rather stranger things than Verdi essayed. There have recently been operas which, by deliberately taking their plots beyond the point Verdi thought appropriate for opera, have presented characters whose situations have driven them into insanity. The suggestion that there are resemblances between modern opera and the work of Donizetti is a tempting one, but it will not quite do. The madness of Lucia is not sufficiently seriously explored for it to be thought a forerunner of modern musical treatments. The pressures applied to Wozzeck, for example, or to Kata Kabanova or Peter Grimes are carefully delineated so that the audience realizes that they are strong enough to destroy these characters. And the music has been made to express these pressures and this destruction. Every shaping of the music in *Wozzeck* is designed to shatter our expectation, to put us in a mad world in which captains and doctors are perverted sadistic monsters and camp followers repent their faithlessness. What happens in the tale seems mostly the result of impersonal accident rather than of human arrangement. The one character who is presented as altering the tone of things is the Fool. In the compass of a part no longer than thirteen notes, he redirects the action. His 'Joyful, joyful . . . and yet it reeks . . . it reeks . . . of blood' is a crisis point. By this short set of musical phrases the composer gives a twist to the opera. Madness is in charge and the music says so. Berg ranges from one musical medium to another, confronting the twelve-tone conventions with those of Wagner, so that the audience is never sure which is the standard. There is no standard. The music is the madness.

Wozzeck is concerned with a man driven mad by the world's ordinary procedures. In this it was prophetic of what opera has come to say. But this change in opera was not immediate. In *The Rake's Progress* (1951) Stravinsky hobbled between views of the world and of the asylum. At the start of the opera, and for much of its action, a devil is required to confuse Tom about the nature of the world. Ordinary things are right enough; it is Tom who gets them wrong. But when he is finally certified he is given first a most beautiful ballad melody to sing, and then a magnificently formal duet with his true love, Anne, suggesting that his madness is a return to the lost world of Venus and Adonis. There is every encouragement at this penultimate moment for an audience to question whether his mad world is not more gracious and ordered than the city beyond the walls of Bedlam. But Anne's inevitable return to that city with her protective father makes the contrary suggestion, and makes it in the music as well as the libretto: the Bedlam world will not do any more. *The Rake's Progress* is ambiguous in its assessment of the world's sanity and of the old opera conventions' usefulness to a composer who would present contemporary reality. Other composers have since become less doubtful.

It now seems to a number of composers that their characters' sensations are too complex and obscure to be articulated in the bold sound of the aria and ensemble. In the main recent composers have thought it part of their profession to resist the allure of the old conventions and to make a more distinctly individual sound. The aim of such composers is to communicate more personally with their audiences, but it is not at all times obvious that the resulting music is attractive to an audience, and many among those who support the enterprise of opera were grateful to Sir William Walton for producing in 1954 what was evidently 'a singers' opera'. *Troilus and Cressida* offered singers a new chance to delight audiences with the declaratory aria, the love duet, and the ensemble of conflicting reactions. In large part Walton succeeds in his usage of the conventions. The sound is mostly good to hear even though sometimes it seems that one has heard it before, not only in Walton's own work but in Puccini and, most particularly, in Britten's *Peter Grimes*. But Walton has not employed the conventions for their usual job. The great Verdi structure was designed to show the action of an individual of some distinction in demanding circumstances. The sensitivity of the protagonist in a hostile situation was fitly expressed in the large ways of the aria, so that the audience might come immediately to understand what was going on within the protagonist, might sympathize and realize the similarities between his situation and their own experience, and thus be made aware of what might be going on within most other human beings. All this depends on the composer quickly and with authority establishing the interest of the protagonist for others. And this Walton has not managed to do in his music. Troilus is not much more interesting than Diomede; both of them receive attention only so far as they provoke a response from Cressida. Though Cressida has some lovely wide-melodied music, even she is not placed clearly enough before the audience to prompt the necessary interest. The attempt to make a *leitmotiv* out of her red scarf fails because of the insubstantial musical expression of its meaning. The scarf remains a skilful device in the libretto. And indeed too much of the opera remains in the libretto. Hassall's text is of such interest that Walton seems often to be doing not much more than setting it to music. The action is in the words, not in the music; so that however much Walton works within the nineteenth-century structural conventions, the effects of aria and ensemble are not achieved. This opera does not provoke an audience to any further appreciation of experience. The libretto directs the music to the singular life of Cressida. In performance the lines which count are those in which she expresses her hope that someone will enter her loneliness. At various points her father, her friend and her lover discard her. 'I close my arms and so shut out the world' sings Troilus, but he is not near when she needs him. She is then, as ever before, 'Alone'. But her cry is not our cry. It is not an articulation, as it is in *Peter Grimes*, of each human being's irreducible loneliness. It is simply that no one is looking after Cressida. At the end, therefore, when Diomede and Troilus both have rejected her, and an ensemble of great skill is staged, her suicide is simply a sad spectacle. The opera fades and we, untouched, go home.

There is a moment of inarticulate tableau in Tippett's *The Knot Garden* which the composer says cannot become an ensemble because whatever is going on inside the characters and in their relations with each other is not yet understood enough for them to find such expression. Tippett determines that if he cannot speak he will, as Wittgenstein suggests, keep silent. Many another modern composer discovering that the ensemble will not serve his purpose has thought, contrariwise, that he will make a different noise.

That shift from the old conventions of Verdi's opera to an appropriately disturbing modern noise which shall be expressive of our peculiar madness, is nicely exhibited in the operas of Hans Werner Henze. He began with a setting, in *Boulevard Solitude* (1952), of that old romantic story of Manon Lescaut which had attracted Massenet, Auber and Puccini, though Henze jazzed it up quite a lot. His *König Hirsch* of 1956 was again based on an old tale which, though not as operatically popular as the Manon story, has the distinction of having been considered by Brahms as a subject for an opera. However, Brahms restrained his desire in this matter and left Tchaikovsky's notion of heroism intact. Henze, in taking up this strange tale of metamorphosis and metapsychosis, realized the possibilities of opera's relation to mystery and magic but his movement among such strangenesses was somewhat unsure. The spells were clumsily managed, perhaps because he still refused to learn from Wagner how such things may be done. With *The Prince of Homburg* in 1960, Henze made a direct entry into the world of dream. The opera is a working-out of the prince's prologue vision of himself, until at the end we appreciate the significance of the wreath, the golden chain, and the bride he had seen in his dream. In this opera the world of ordinary political and military affairs is brought into harmony with the world of dream. All is unified through the integrity of the young prince, who, on refusing a pardon because the sentence of death passed on him by his father is wholly just, finds his vision realized. The old opera convention of the hero achieving some order in the world for himself is renewed. This is an opera recognizably akin to the great Verdi celebrations of honour but it is at the same time urgently of its period in finding fascinating the hidden strengths of such honour. Henze shows his audience how the civilized code may have links with the free-ranging fairy tale.

Henze did not stay with this structure of folk myth and madness and social manners. He went on to question even the integrity of what dreamers and poets can offer. *Elegy for Young Lovers* in 1961, though it is conducted by folk song, aria and ensemble, questions the old conventions. Not only is the poet hero most evidently an anti-hero of some unpleasantness, but the mad lady whose visions have inspired him is suddenly confronted by outside reality, and becomes a sane and sharp commentator on what is going on around her. Henze seems to be saying that it is not through dreams and visions that the world may be understood, and that we would do well to distrust the poets who express such things.

What was there for Henze to do after this? He himself said in

1970: 'I feel opera is finished.' It was finished because the conventions were no longer viable: 'the major musical and technical problem is the disintegration of those traditional means of expression that are essential to the making of an opera'. And, like all distinguished opera composers, Henze discerned the intimate connection between the way in which a composer puts an opera together and the view he has of society. The disintegration of those conventions 'heralds the decay of present society'.

Henze, however, had also remarked to his interviewer that 'the basic idea of putting drama to music is not finished'. And in 1976 he presented Covent Garden audiences with the portentously entitled *We come to the river*. Here the *Wozzeck* position is restated. It is the ordinary world around the General, the world of politics and finance and war, which is mad, and which puts the central figure into a madhouse as soon as his sanity and humane kindness are detected. As the exploration of madness has continued in modern opera it has become apparent that the conventions of the opera form are of less and less use to the composers. And audiences are properly restive at what they are being asked to hear and pay for. People are getting bored by so many shaven heads and irritated by so many irrational leaps from note to note.

We come to the river is definitely not an opera in any previously agreed sense. It is not the three bands on stage, the percussionist running and the organist walking among the characters, or action taking place simultaneously on more than one part of the stage, or the general indistinguishability of what is being sung, or the instrumental noise, which deny this work the name of opera, though they militate against it; nor is it any lack of serious intention, for, however simple his view of a depersonalizing society, the evils of war, and of the inability of anyone but the blind to perceive this, Henze certainly has a solemn notion in his head; nor is it any incapacity of the composer to present affecting incidents: the shooting of the deserter, the shooting of the peasant woman at the river and the shooting of the Governor outside his office are all nicely managed if somewhat noisily and smokily. It is most centrally Henze's main character's total lack of substance which prevents this work from being an opera. It is impossible to be interested in the General. It is impossible, indeed, to believe, from the poverty of the musical invention for his part, that Henze is interested in him. No work can deserve the name of opera if it does not engage one's attention for what is happening to a human being of large enough sympathy for one to feel a sense of identification. Of course such a work may be 'putting drama to music'.

Wagner had begun by writing operas. 'Let us take it again from the Meyerbeer triplet,' said Siegfried Wagner at a rehearsal of the *Rienzi* overture. But Richard Wagner had soon realized that he wanted to do something different. And in announcing this difference he declared himself to be writing 'music drama'. Cosima Wagner led her husband's disciples into talking of 'music drama' long after Wagner's death. But Wagner was not a stubborn man. He recognized what he was doing even in *Parsifal*. He came again to talk of his works as opera. It may be that his example will be followed by the modern opera house, and we shall be rid of 'putting drama to music'.

That opera may be returning was faintly signalled in a work that had its first performance in Munich in the same month that *We come to the river* was performed in London. Josef Tal's *Die Versuchung* was rather less attractive to the ear than Henze's piece, though certainly it was easier to make out what the characters were saying. Crudely philosophic in its suggestion that gold, god, power, and sex are likely to corrupt the innocent, and very thin in its characterization both of the corrupters and of the innocent, this work just managed, in the last moments of its performance, to justify its composer's calling it an opera. For while for the most part of the evening no character had come across as more than a pasteboard figure, one, doubtless with some significance called Johannes Kolumbus, did towards the end inspire some interest in his condition. Surviving the experience of living in the asylum where a corrupt dictator keeps his political opponents and cast-off mistresses, he sets out, as he had at the beginning, in hope of a free world. There is some small sense here of man being able to deal with experience. There is, therefore, some small hope that aria and ensemble, those classic means of expressing man's ability to understand himself, will return. And, with more hopefulness than is provoked by a study of Tal, some have discerned in the work of Tippett, the composer who understood the meaning of ensemble sufficiently well to know when he could not use it, such a return of opera.

Tippett began in the world of myth and symbol. The main characters of his *The Midsummer Marriage* are involved in an elemental ritual. Mystery 'seems much nearer than expected'. Even the rough mechanic, Jack, has dreams. The opera moves on to the Jungian ground of *anima* and *animus* and is an exploration of what, in these terms, integrity may be said to consist of. The marriage of Jennifer and Mark becomes symbolic of an inner harmony not unconnected with what Verdi had in mind in the last scene of *Aida* or Wagner at the close of *Parsifal*. Tippett's opera represents a proper control of those forces which Henze allowed to get out of hand in *The Bassarids*. It is a control exercised through an acceptance of the world of myth within each human being. Tippett's next opera, *King Priam* (1962), seems to begin in a similarly mythic mood, but as it proceeds is revealed as a denial of the possibility of that controlled existence which his first opera suggested. In *The Midsummer Marriage* Jennifer and Mark had had to understand the secret forces at work in themselves and each other before each could properly choose the other. And they had managed this at last. In *King Priam* every choice is seen to be an illusion. Priam's choice of his son's death is frustrated by the shepherd who rescues the baby Paris. And this is a paradigm of all choice. Paris cries infatuatedly in his desire for Helen: 'O Gods, why give us bodies with such power of love, if love's a crime? Is there choice at all?' At the burning of Troy Priam accepts Helen, who has never made a choice, as his final companion. It must seem at the end of this opera that however aware a man is of the workings of the world and however anxious he is to do something, he has no effective will. Everything in the conventions of opera goes against the representation of such a theme. The rejection of aria and ensemble must here be followed by a rejection of all singing if the theme is to have formal support. For the very act of singing, requiring such control of mind and body, defies every suggestion of human impotence. As Auden once remarked: 'Every high C accurately struck demolishes the theory that we are the irresponsible puppets of fate or chance.' Those who witness such a precise command will be unlikely to accept any notion of human effort being worthless. The performance will itself militate against the composer's message.

And Tippett, being a most honest composer, seems to have realized this. If he is indeed able to exercise control in music then it must be possible, just as it was possible for the elemental forces of *The Midsummer Marriage* to be brought into human harmony, for men to understand and operate amongst the metaphysical forces of *King Priam*. Nature and Fate must be controlled in a peaceful way of life. In *The Knot Garden* (1970) he attempted an elucidation of how this might be managed. He begins with a version of the imperative 'Know thyself', reminding one of the concluding section in *A Child of our Time* where he had set going a fine ensemble piece from the sentence 'I would know my shadow and my light'. The encounter of Dionysus and Apollo within the activities and passivities of men is, in *The Knot Garden*, presented with confidence in man's power to command these forces within himself. And to command these same forces when they confront one another in public places.

Faber and Thea, at the beginning of the opera, are enduring a marriage. He is the maker from the city, she the tender of the garden. Their ward, Flora, is disturbed by their antagonisms and fears that Faber will break out in a sexual attack upon her. So they have sent for Mangus the analyst to treat her. He begins by treating them and their guests. He ends by realizing that he himself is not as ordered a man as he had thought. Each character in the garden starts in a muddle, given order only by the anxious hope that 'I'm real somewhere'. And each one knows that integrity is not to be achieved by denying any part of themselves. The forces must be brought into balance. 'Angels have fought angels,' sings the tortured Denise, 'I'm a two-way man,' sings the homosexual Dov,

'Sometimes I dream I am a boy,' sings Flora, 'and then I am a girl again'. Within the muddle of their lives, expressed in a jumble of musical quotations from miriad sources – Schubert and blues and protest song – each finds a distinct integrity which is expressed in a particular musical idiom. For a moment each may centre a world on his individual music. 'Under the influence of Dov's music,' so runs a stage direction, 'the rose-garden begins to form.' But none can sustain the world for long alone. On Mel's tapping Dov on the shoulder, the music stops, 'the garden fades'. The wonder of Mangus's work is that at the end each is capable of entering an ensemble. Indeed the process that Mangus initiates may be understood as the making of an ensemble. It is through art that human beings may discover themselves and this is the chief impression that the work makes. The analytical stuff does not in the opera sound vastly convincing as an instrument for sanity, nor need it do so. What works is the music. The music is the therapy.

In his latest opera Tippett suggests and presents music as the controlling resource of brave men in an unordered world. *The Ice Break* of the northern rivers is an image of the release in society of forces which may enrich or destroy us. The ambiguity of Community and Mob is shown in a slogan world of East-West and Black-White and, in echo of the Odyssey, Generation-Gap confrontations. Tippett has sometimes succumbed to the temptation of a slogan libretto. But generally music restrains him. And does so in a strictly structured form. The opera begins with the unintelligibilities of an airport loudspeaker, and develops through dislocations of sound and character in the first act. The second act starts with a jumbled music for four singers that aspires to ensemble but leads only to further musical confrontations, a race riot, and the disruptive noise of the police siren. The third act rises in hesitant phrases of self-doubt through the hallucinations of drug-taking into 'an alarming but healing ritual' of rebirth. But the mythic fades like the politcal slogan and the paradise garden. Music survives. And perhaps humanity. The eloquent song of an understanding 'O much deeper' is the composer's final reaching towards the real.

Three

Do the words matter?

Tippett's realism is peculiarly that of a composer. His endeavour is to invent the musical terms in which the vital motions of his characters may be expressed. His achievement consists in his so often compassing such invention. A member of the audience, if he had no knowledge of the English language, would not, even if he attended most carefully to the changing sound of voice and orchestra, be able to discover all that Tippett intends. He would be in the wrong if he concluded that the sound alone could tell him all he needed to know. Tippett's text may often be barbarous in its language and deserve more chuckles than any verse of Wagner, but it is quite evident from his music that he wants his audience to hear and ponder his words. Those who suggest, under great provocation, that he should not have written his own libretto, are themselves witnesses to the effort Tippett has put into making his audience notice the text. No one could, on hearing Tippett's music, think him a heedlessly arrogant man. It is, therefore, something of a puzzle why so sensitive a composer should elect, despite his having few gifts that way, to shape the words for his operas. His musical determination of what is heard in the opera-house prompts a consideration of what place the librettist has had and should have in the scheme of opera, and in particular the relation of his work to that of the composer. This is a complex matter. It is best to begin with some simple statement of obvious truth and importance. And it is best to begin, as the king ordered, at the beginning.

It has been general in the history of opera for the librettist to be responsible for the original idea, the theme and plot of a piece. This is still the custom. Szymanowski said of Iwaszkiewicz's outline for *King Roger* when he received it in the post: 'The rough Sicilian sketch dazzled me immediately.' At the start of a rather more satisfying work, Richard Rodney Bennett responded as quickly to Beverley Cross's synopsis for *The Mines of Sulphur*. But such promptings, however properly acknowledged by the grateful composers, do not after all add up to any large responsibility for the opera in performance. No one thinks of those earlier authors, from whom Shakespeare took so many of his plots, as being responsible for the distinguishing virtues of his plays. And there are few who think that Shakespeare himself was responsible for what Verdi managed in *Macbeth* or *Otello* or what Boito did with *Amleto*. And there is enough evidence to suggest that composers have only accepted the promptings of librettists if there was already something of the sort stirring within themselves. At least composers often suggest that this is how it happened. Szymanowski says that he responded to the *King Roger* idea because it was 'a sort of revelation of some mystery of my own'. Richard Rodney Bennett had, some time before he met Cross, been wanting to write an opera that would be 'violent, pestilential, sinister'. And in the sense that such a prompting of their own ideas was all that they required from a librettist, some composers have thought it enough for a librettist to give them a start and leave them to finish the opera. Weber, for example, was so anxious for a librettist to give him a good beginning that he advertised in the *Allegemeine Musik-Zeitung* in March 1813 for a text ready to be set to music, inviting 'the poets of Germany' to 'post off their manuscripts in a parcel' to his address in Prague. The librettist was to pack up his words, send them to the composer, and wait for the finished opera to be advertised on the theatre bills. 'I cannot read the libretto,' wrote Hugo Wolf in the excitement of his discovery – for the second time, at the first he had not cared for it – of *Der Corregidor*, 'without being seized with a musical fever.' But when his flattered librettist suggested a revision of a scene in the text which Wolf now regarded as wholly his own, she was rebuked as insufferably impertinent. 'Who the deuce put this monstrous flea in your ear?' he demanded.

Things are, as both these composers discovered, a little more complex than such a simple view suggests. The relationship between composer and librettist is not so easily confined to the beginnings of the opera. It becomes, usually, a collaboration. Verdi was ever sending suggestions for new lines and situations to his librettists. Weber is said to have demanded twelve rewritings of the libretto of *Euryanthe* from Helmine von Chézy. And Hugo Wolf would have done better to have talked the structure of the opera over several times with his librettist before committing himself to a text so dramatically unsound. It must have come as a proper shock to Wolf to discover that others were interested in the work of the librettist even after he had taken control of the piece. After listening to his enthusiastic account of the wonders of his opera the Kapellmeister of the Vienna Opera was careful enough to say 'If the text is only half-reasonable we shall certainly perform it.' There is certainly a deal of rashness in the assumption that the librettist is scarcely of more importance for the success of an opera than the stage-manager or the backer. But in what does his precise importance consist?

That the librettist should provide something even half reasonable has not been the universal expectation. 'The principal intention of the songish part,' said Dryden, 'is to please the hearing rather than to gratify the understanding.' The words might be anything singable. Addison suggested as the first rule in the making of an opera that 'nothing is capable of being set to music, that is not nonsense'. Corneille would 'have nothing sung that is necessary for the comprehension of what is going on', and he suggested that every time there was some necessary information about the plot's twist or the characters' development, the actors should break into speech. According to him, therefore, the librettist had a chance to make his meaning clear to the audience, or even to make the composer's meaning clear to them, only when the composer bowed out for a while and left the actors speaking. The librettist on this plan would have his moment only when the audience was likely to lose interest and to think of other things while waiting for the next tune to turn up.

Such a method of production was indeed tried in the French

theatres with predictable results. In Rousseau's experience no audience would stand for such unpleasant to-ing and fro-ing, composers observed how eagerly they were waited for, and managements consequently cut the dialogue passages; operas, therefore, became more and more unintelligible as the plots became less and less articulate. But the audience was better pleased because opera became an exhibition of fine tunes and brilliant singing. If we go to such an obscure entertainment as opera has become, Rousseau remarked, 'we need to be distracted by the manner in which it is sung'.

So the librettist might well come to see himself as a slight and unimportant assistant in the making of an opera by the composer and its realization by the singer. 'Some hunt, some drink, some play cards, some busy themselves with intrigues, and I,' wrote Beaumarchais ruefully, 'I, who do not care for any of these things, write a modest opera.' But, like many another librettist, Beaumarchais harboured a larger ambition than such remarks suggest. In the preface to the printed version of *Tarare* in 1790, he declared, 'If I could crown the work with a great philosophical idea – even in giving birth to the plot – I am sure that such a spectacle would bear its fruits and intelligent people would be grateful for my work.' A similar hope of making the audience look for a moment at the world in the way they suggested impelled a great many of those who put their wits at the service of the opera composers.

Composers have, however, been unwilling to allow librettists such a share in responsibility for the characer of an opera. During the composition of *Seraglio* in 1781 Mozart told his father, 'I have explained to Stephanie the words I require for this aria', and announced that he 'had finished composing most of the music for it before Stephanie knew anything whatever about it'. He thought that in such an *opera buffa* 'the music reigns supreme and when one listens to it all else is forgotten'. He did not mean that the libretto could be of indifferent verse. Rather the contrary. He meant that the librettist in the *opera buffa* tradition had learnt to work according to 'the composer's idea for the whole'.

He demanded from poor Stephanie a total re-working of the plot of Acts II and III of *Seraglio* so that he could place an effective quintet at the end of the second act. Stephanie did as he was told and Mozart wrote home happily 'Everyone abuses Stephanie. It may be that in my case he is only very friendly to my face. But after all he is arranging the libretto for me – and, what is more, as I want it – exactly – and, by Heaven, I do not ask anything more of him.'

Mozart, equally, had his way with the more experienced and famous da Ponte who wrote the librettos for *Figaro*, *Don Giovanni*, and *Così fan Tutte*. This exotic man, the son of a Jew, studied long enough at a Catholic seminary to call himself an Abbé, was ordered to quit first Venice on account of adultery, and then Vienna on account of his satiric witticisms, became a London music publisher, taught Italian at Columbia University, and died an American citizen in 1838. He was capable of anything. Da Ponte has been overpraised by a good many critics and underpraised by a few reactionaries. Certainly he was not the equal of Mozart. He was not a creative artist of any great merit. But he did have a knack of putting together from diverse sources a libretto with which Mozart knew he could work. And that was a significant talent.

Da Ponte was the prince of adaptors. He took the best from other men's plays for his librettos, and even *Così fan Tutte*, for which there is no single direct source, depends on his pulling together ideas from several earlier plays and operas, and includes an aria taken from Metastasio's *Demetrio* with only one word changed. Perhaps here, as in his other works, the only element peculiarly his own is a moral ambiguity particularly in relation to sexual adventures. But it is not that element, however pruriently nineteenth-century critics might point it out, which dominates in the operas Mozart composed. Whatever Mozart felt about da Ponte's hectic life and ribald humour he did not give him control of those moments in an opera which were most decisive in the determination of tone and effect.

In the middle of *Figaro* there are some uncomfortable moments:

when the Countess listens too delightedly to the page's love-song, or when she refuses too complacently to forgive her husband for suspecting her of yielding to Cherubino's singing. At such moments the audience may feel that there are no accepted norms by which to judge her actions. But there is no hint in the music of such an ambiguity in the final scene when even though it is obvious from the libretto that da Ponte fancied that the Count would not long remain faithful, the Countess pardons her repentant husband in music which reconciles all the differing elements of the opera. Again, in *Così fan Tutte*, a situation which the librettist thought amusing is taken much more seriously by Mozart, and through his music the audience begins to realize that the love affairs and emotional entanglements of the four young people are not simply matters of fun. Mozart makes the work his own. By dictating the tone of his operas, commanding a text which suited his purposes, and ignoring it if it expressed ideas which went against his intention, Mozart made an opera of whose success the librettist had to take what share the composer allowed him.

And yet, perhaps not paradoxically, the librettos that da Ponte made for Mozart are much more effective than those he produced for Salieri, Storace, or Martin. Those who are asked for less give less. And they know what they can expect from lesser men. When the librettist Casti provided Salieri with the text for the theatrical in-joke of *Prima la musica e poi le parole* in 1786, he was content to sketch a scene in which the composer and the singer happily conspire to deprive the despised librettist of every innocent success until at last they have rendered his words into melodious nonsense.

Schikaneder, despite the experience of collaborating with Mozart over *The Magic Flute*, seems not to have learnt to judge his work by composers' reactions to it. Beethoven had a long-drawn controversy with him in 1803 about *Vestas Feuer* during which the composer asked the librettist 'to have the verses and the contents of the libretto corrected and considerably improved by someone else'. In vain. 'It was impossible to persuade this fellow, who is so infatuated with his own opinion, to do this.' When it came to making alterations in *Leonora* Beethoven was more circumspect. He rewrote the text himself, and then wrote to his librettist, Sonnleiter, asking for approval of his reduction of three acts to two, remarking in a footnote, 'There is too little time or, in order to convince you, I would have sent you the libretto with this letter.' The poor man had simply to accept whatever Beethoven had done to his text. He was not even shown the finished version.

ROMANI, BELLINI AND THE BEAUTIFUL WORD

The independent dignity of the librettist had been eroded all through the second half of the eighteenth century, as managers of opera houses began to employ house writers. These literary hacks were content to bring out a libretto which satisfied the demands of a conservative audience. They made something conventional to which a composer might set a few new tunes and refurbish others. Together a complacent author and composer would prepare entertainment in which a singer might become the delight of the audience for a night or two. In such conditions few early nineteenth-century librettists could establish a name for themselves, and the only one amongst all those working for the Italian opera houses who could make a recognized claim to literary or dramatic distinction was Felice Romani, who held a sinecure in the papal tobacco monopoly and could, as result of his financial independence, afford to make demands on the opera-house managers. Romani may well have thought that he could resurrect the old dominance of the librettist. He was the last successful writer in the classical manner, seeing himself as continuing a great literary tradition as he put together the preface to yet another libretto. Or rather the theatrical tradition of the librettist's control of the opera, because he very soon discovered a style of his own quite distinct from that of earlier men. Romani was the master of a lively verse, which, while seeming to disregard all the formal niceties of regular rhyme scheme, stanza form and line length, was beautifully apt for his dramatic purpose. On receiving a Romani libretto the composer was expected to rejoice that the task of shaping the plot and creating the characters had already been completed for him. The composer was simply expected to provide melodies appropriate to the Romani words. Indeed Romani was equally famous for the melodious quality of his verse and thought perhaps that this provided a directing inspiration for a composer. There was a time at the height of his fame when he was besieged with commissions from composers and managers. This confirmed him in his notion of himself as someone in total command of the opera form. But such success rebounds upon itself. Romani just could not write enough librettos to satisfy the demand. He was notorious among composers for his delays in delivering his texts; and his belief in his effortless superiority as a poet making him careless of their complaints, they eventually lost patience with him.

For a while, however, Donizetti and Bellini and half a dozen more of their contemporaries queued for Romani librettos. Bellini, however, was never quite as conformable and biddable as the great librettist expected. He saw that Romani's librettos were often far too prolix, lacking that simplicity and brevity which he, like every competent opera composer, demanded. Yet in 1828, when he was composing *La Straniera*, or such scraps of the libretto as had reached him, Bellini, on being offered another librettist in Romani's place, replied that the alternative would 'never, never, be able to versify like Romani, and especially not for me, who am so bound to good words'. And good words Romani could certainly supply. 'That,' Bellini declared, 'is why I must have Romani.' But their collaboration was fraught with disputes even about Romani's words. Bellini seems to have been a good judge of how far to push Romani. He once sent back a passage to the librettist for re-writing but the second version was so much less to his liking that 'in order not to tire him, I'm using the first'. And then there is another tale of Romani being forced after four rejected attempts to write words for a melody Bellini played him on the piano. And sometimes even

Bellini's skill was not effective in managing the great man. 'That blessed Romani has not given me anything for six days.' There were all sorts of good excuses for Romani's failure to provide a promised scene. During their collaboration on *Zaira* in 1849 Romani got in a scrape with the Parma police for wearing his offensively liberal moustache, and this gave him a new excuse for the delay in bringing his verses to Bellini. And when the whole thing was indeed finished Romani placed at the head of the libretto offered for sale on the first night a declaration that he had been rushed into producing a botched job. Those who had paid their money in expectation of a grand experience were naturally furious at being offered something self-confessedly second-rate. *Zaira* was not a success. And on their agreeing to try again with an *Ernani* for Milan in 1830 Romani seems to have gone off at once to write the libretto for the Donizetti *Anna Bolena*, and then to have put aside *Ernani* for the second time to adapt *La Sonnambula* from a scenario by Scribe. Bellini seems to have been quite content with this change of plan. But relations between the two were not wholly peaceful for long. Bellini, after the disaster of *Zaira*, had become rather nervous, and at the dress rehearsal so badgered Romani to write new verses for his soprano that the librettist stormed out of the theatre. The great success of *La Sonnambula*, however, kept the two men happy enough to work on *Norma* for La Scala in 1831.

Only in *Norma*, and then perhaps only by accident, did Bellini manage to write an opera whose dramatic action was carried along to a satisfactory conclusion. In this opera he effected in a wholly musical manner an exciting forward movement. Each aria contributes to the development of the action and what is, in other operas of his, mere display, has become in this work purposeful while remaining no less brilliant. Bellini himself recognized the musical character of his opera's success. Not in Romani's verses but in the precision of Bellini's arrangement of recitative and aria, and in the appropriate invention of his orchestration, lies the unique power of *Norma* among his operas. Bellini must have recognized, also, that he had exercised more control over the libretto of this opera than Romani had ever previously allowed him.

Wagner saw *Norma* as the Italian opera which brought the form nearer to the ideal of Greek theatre than it had ever been before. He even composed a bass aria and chorus after the style of Bellini which he thought a singer of taste would be pleased to insert in a Paris performance. What attracted Wagner to this music was, as he said on a visit to Naples in 1880, that it is 'all heart, closely, intimately linked to the words'. But the relation of the music to the words of the libretto was not simple. Certainly it was not just set to the original verse. Bellini had sent back the text of *Norma* again and again. Always he wanted the librettist to prune his verses. He got at last a splendid libretto of direct and forceful verse, interesting characters and consistent style. He got from Romani a great design which had been shaped until the self-sacrifice of the central action directed the whole text. And Bellini's music moved forward with a reciprocal dramatic energy. Romani liked the finished work but he did not care to be so hard driven. He complained of Bellini's roughness. And the gossips irritated them both by seizing on these complaints. But in October 1832, thinking about an opera on Christina, Queen of Sweden, for the Teatro La Fenice in Venice, Bellini could still describe Romani as 'my expert and favourite poet'. They decided on a new subject. Romani had just finished writing librettos for Donizetti and Mercadante, and had promised further librettos both to them and to Coccia and Majocchi. He just could not find time to put together the kind of careful libretto that Bellini demanded. In December the Venetian police had to summon the librettist to work on the text. Once Romani was in Venice and settling down to the work, he was pestered by Donizetti waiting for his promised libretto in Rome. Donizetti began to lose patience. He asked his friends to help him find 'a theatrical poet who is less of a rascal than Romani about keeping his word'. Caught between two such demanding men Romani again produced a botched job for Bellini. On the failure of their Venetian *Beatrice Tenda* Bellini was as exasperated with Romani as Donizetti had grown to be.

A newspaper war broke out between the two and their supporters, with each party accusing the other of having ruined the piece. Bellini's men attacked Romani for his inability to get a libretto to a composer on time. Romani sent letters to the Milanese and Venetian papers suggesting that Bellini had spent in the arms of the soprano the time he should have spent at the piano. Though in 1834 Bellini – in the midst of struggles with another Italian librettist, Pepoli, possessing a contract offered by the Madrid management for a couple more operas, and wondering whether he might not write an opera for Paris to a text by Scribe – wrote to Romani asking him to write the libretto for a new San Carlo opera, the two men never met again. Bellini died in 1835. In his obituary notice Romani puffed himself handsomely as the encourager of the young man's talent, and as the man who had set him great tasks which brought out his genius. Of the *Beatrice Tenda* quarrel he said merely that 'this was a brief time of discord of which we both came to be ashamed'.

There is something in Romani's claim. He did inspire Bellini to make a glorious sound with his music. But he was perhaps the worst sort of librettist for the young man to have met. Bellini had immense lyric gifts. He could make beautiful melodies of the most breath-taking wonder. And he knew it. He knew that his music could create a beautiful moment. And he knew that he was most often moved to make such beautiful sound by the words Romani offered him. But Romani offered no more than words. He did not force Bellini to consider how an opera should be structured. So Bellini wrote stupendous melodies for scenes which were often quite rubbishy. His operas generally have no shape. They shift from sensation to sensation. A greater librettist, a man who had something to say, would have made Bellini think more about what he was doing. So, paradoxically, though Romani came to be thought by Bellini as simply his assistant in the business of making an opera, Romani was in their collaboration responsible or, rather, could have been responsible had he had enough time and energy to spare for such things, for all those elements of plot and character, of structure and tone which composers and librettists had disputed over for the previous two hundred years. Bellini was so much concerned with his power to demand neater words from his librettist that he did not see how little he was influencing the meaning of the opera. Romani was so concerned with getting enough words written for so many composers that he did not have time to put in much of a meaning. Opera became during their collaboration a sensitive and luxurious sound, words and melody, and not much more.

SCRIBE, VERDI AND THE THEATRICAL WORD

Italian audiences made it plain to Bellini that they had come to the opera house for the song and the singer. French audiences at the Paris Opéra, while not despising such delights, had learnt to be more demanding. They had come to expect something of a more stunning character than the simple pleasures of a fine melody or a sustained high note. All sorts of things had to be brought together for their entertainment. Quinault's less than happy design for the *Triomphe de l'Amour* had long ago established the ballet as a required diversion in the midst of French opera. With the corps of dancers the management had to engage a great number of chorus singers. And the development of the large opera orchestra is a peculiarly French responsibility. The Venetian theatres, in the past as in the present, were beset by financial difficulties and not at all likely to encourage composers to write for a fourth bassoon or another desk of 'cellos. But in France the management's possession of a royal or republican monopoly ensured a deal of financial aid from the state. Chorus and orchestra grew enormous.

By the second quarter of the nineteenth century French audiences were prepared to accept every kind of elaboration and decoration in the opera house. They were ready for Eugène Scribe. Scribe was the master of large sweeping subjects, historical pageants, and astonishing ballets, against which melodramatic twists of human action were displayed. Scribe's librettos are the paradigms of *grand opéra*, that peculiarly French institution of subtle *préparation*, through a multitude of lavish details, for the *scène à faire*, the climactic scene. Scribe set a fashion which was followed not only in opera but in spoken drama in France for most of the nineteenth century.

Scribe was a man of the new regime. He had been born in 1791. Combining with Meyerbeer and Auber he produced marvel upon marvel for the French. Certainly it was 'for the French'. Scribe aimed as much at a popular success as his predecessors at the court had aimed at royal favour. In everything except his conviction that the librettist should be the chief partner in the enterprise, he was wholly unlike Romani.

Scribe is a librettist of the new breed. He effected for a while a command of opera that Metastasio had possessed and Romani hoped for, but he accomplished his triumph in quite a new way. He represents a wholly different aspect of the librettist's influence in the opera house because he used wholly different instruments. He is the first librettist to control opera production without making any claim to be a poet. He was a librettist of stage-effects rather than of verses. Bringing his audience the startling sight of the Council of Constance, or the St Bartholomew Massacre, or the court of Gustavus III, he set them wondering at the spectacle and the situation rather than at the words. Scribe managed again and again to make his audiences accept opera as an epic art in the grand manner which Busenello had attempted. His historical subjects were intended as presentations of huge issues in world history. Through opera a man might hope to understand how the world came to be as it is. This was a large subject and the only one for which Scribe really cared. He was not much interested in the actual words of the libretto. He simply wanted to have control of the action. He let Meyerbeer do as he liked with the words, and when the composer asked for more verses he simply handed the job over to the house hack. And in his collaboration with Auber he quite often wrote scenes to fit the music that the composer wished to include. He was ready to do anything for a quick effect. He was even ready to listen to advice. His famous effect in Meyerbeer's *Robert le Diable* of a ballet of unfrocked nuns was suggested by the scene designer who thought it might look interesting. The skating ballet in *Le Prophète* was inserted because the sport was at that time very popular among those who made up the audience. He let the tenor Nourrit write the words of his own aria in *La Juive* in 1835, and was pleased enough with the result to hand over the grand climactic duet of *Les Huguenots* for him to write the verses in 1836. Scribe's operas move from climax to climax. They are full of effective wonders. Scribe had no interest in saying anything. He was not even interested in his plots making sense. And generally, therefore, they did not. The fact,' wrote Wagner in 1879, 'that the happenings in *Robert le Diable* and *Les Huguenots* may be intelligible to none but the inmost circle of initiates has much in its favour.' And yet, of course, audiences came in great numbers to applaud their librettist. The operas were commonly ascribed to him and not to their composers. And, when even Wagner was not above stealing some of Scribe's grand effects to decorate his own work, it is not surprising that Meyerbeer was content to allow Scribe to have his way.

Though Beethoven is well known to have wanted to write an opera on the subject it was Meyerbeer who was thought by Goethe to be the only composer, other than Mozart, fit to make *Faust* into an opera. This was no mean tribute. And Meyerbeer certainly was peculiarly fit for theatrical writing, he knew just how the music of an opera should be put together, and how an audience should be brought to its feet applauding. But his life was dominated by a dread of failure. Among his many talents that of rousing the audience to loud huzzahs at the melodramatic close of his music was his only surety of happiness. He had to have success or else be plunged into black despair. If the price of success was obedience to Scribe then he would be obedient.

But if Meyerbeer was content to serve Scribe in public, and Wagner to steal from him in private, not all composers were so obligingly flattering. It was not at all surprising when a collaboration for an opera concerned with, most unsuitably, the Sicilian Vespers was arranged by the Paris Opéra between Scribe and the most imperious of contemporary composers that ructions occurred. The Opéra's contribution to the Paris Exhibition of 1855 was several times in jeopardy. Verdi was not used to accepting a librettist's opinion on the structuring of an opera. Once Romani had lost his position of power this ceased to be the Italian habit. It was certainly not Verdi's.

The two men were not of entirely differing opinions as to what was required for an opera to be a success. Scribe's emphasis upon the general tone, the forceful emotive phrase, and his theme of a heroic but hopeless struggle against a clerical establishment, as presented by him in the crushing of the Prophet, the Jewess and the Huguenots, were parallel with Verdi's concept of stage action and the scenic word and with his demonstration of the meanness of spirit of the Egyptian priests and the Spanish Inquisitor as they dealt with Aida and Don Carlos. Composer and librettist were agreed in the main on content and method. And indeed the Paris Opéra invitation was in many ways welcome to Verdi. The great historical subjects which delighted him had unnerved the political censors in Italy. They had been ever ready to suspect him of stirring up revolution against the settled order of their society. But in France the old royal tradition of great spectacle had been revived together with the monopoly of the Paris Opéra, and historical subjects were popular with people and government. Everyone looked forward to greater wonders each season, though there was some doubt whether anyone would ever be able to beat the effect Spontini had achieved with real horses in his *Fernando Cortez* in 1809. For a composer who loved to set such subjects as *Attila* or *I Lombardi* the opportunity of working with such resources was a grand one, no more to be rejected by Verdi than by Rossini or Donizetti. So the Paris managers might have expected that the collaboration would proceed smoothly.

It is paradoxical that Scribe, who through thinking little of the libretto's words had loosed his hold on the delineation of character, should not have got on with Verdi who had determined to present the characters of his operas solely through his music. But the reverence Scribe had received before he came into contact with Verdi had not prepared him for the commanding approach of a composer accustomed only to obedience and applause. And Verdi, though he was prepared to receive suggestions from the librettist on the starting idea for their opera, the incidents of the plot and the words of the text, was also prepared to reject the librettist's suggestions on these matters if they did not accord with his intentions. With most other composers Scribe had been quite content to let them do the hard work of fiddling with the text as it was a chore that did not attract him. But once Verdi had insisted on his having complete control of the text, Scribe thought differently about such matters. He demanded control of his own words. There was a great deal of trouble.

What Verdi demanded from a librettist was a total abandonment of any pretension to order the structure of his opera. When Verdi was preparing to work with Scribe he knew that the Frenchman was a librettist who needed only a little discipline to become exactly the collaborator he needed. But Verdi could not control Scribe. So he ignored the man and concentrated on his plays. He was happy, for example, to take Scribe's play *Gustave III*, tighten its structure a little, bring out its key words, simplify its characters, and make out of it *Ballo in Maschera*, worrying not at all about the discordances he had set up by rearranging Scribe's verses. This was how he treated all his librettists.

Verdi knew what he wanted of a librettist. The librettist was first to suggest to him the shaping idea for the opera. Verdi was convinced that no opera could be his kind of success unless it expressed a suitably worthy idea. From this beginning words and music would take their inception and development. The initial idea would determine the course of the action and the character of the music. So the librettist's second task was to provide Verdi with a text from whose straightforward design the audience could get hold of the idea. The librettist was above all to give the composer scope to impress the audience with his meaning. The libretto was to put its emphasis on certain words given to the librettist by the composer who would then set them as signposts in the music to direct attention to the dominant emotion of each particular scene. It is with the device of the 'theatrical word' or *parola scenica* that the operas of Verdi's maturity are peculiarly associated. Evidently it is a device which belongs with those traditionally the business of the librettist.

Verdi worked with words as well as with music. His appreciation of literary matters is shown not only in his care for the works of Shakespeare but in his exactly appropriate regard for the lesser virtues of Schiller and Hugo, and for the poorer work of Scribe. Verdi took to himself not only the composer's right to criticize a verse as improperly long or short, or in some way unsingable, but the librettist's right to determine the proper rhetoric of a scene. Verdi believed that the words were his, and that they were present in the libretto only because they were expressive of his idea. What is true generally of all the words in the text is, of course, particularly true of the 'theatrical word'.

Though in the great opera rush of the mid-seventeenth century Italians had spent money on *cereni* – librettos to be read by candle-light in the auditorium during the performance – Stendhal was happily surprised when he found that the early nineteenth-century Venetians were content to get a rough outline of the plot and a key word of an aria and then to settle down to hear the music. 'Two words,' Stendhal learnt, 'are enough to tell us that the hero is sunk into depths of despair, or else that he is winging across the infinite spaces of happiness – that is all we need to grasp.' Stendhal's Venetian ladies would seem to have embodied the characteristics of Verdi's ideal audience. Verdi was always alert for the *parola scenica* which he defined to Ghislanzoni as 'the word that puts the situation in the proper relief and renders it clear and obvious'. If the theatrical word were not discovered and made plain to the audience the scene could not succeed. He wrote to Ghislanzoni in the midst of the librettist's work on *Aida* that in the latest batch of dialogue 'the theatrical word is missing, or if it is there, it is buried under the rhyme and metre and, accordingly, does not emerge as clearly and markedly as it should'. Therefore it all had to be re-written.

Generally each scene would have its own word which would

express its dominant emotional interest: *love*, and *honour* and *revenge* are common. But sometimes Verdi envisaged a whole opera as expressive of one theme, and then the scenic word would recur from situation to situation. *Rigoletto* is probably the most famous example of an opera of the continuing word.

Rigoletto was in the first stages of composition called *La Maledizione*. It was the curse which gave shape and purpose to the opera and Verdi made this plain to the administrator of the Fenice when he was sent the libretto as it had been revised by the Venetian censor: 'The old man's curse, so terrifying and sublime in the original, has now become ridiculous because his motive for uttering the curse does not have the same significance, and because it is no longer a subject who speaks in so forthright a manner to his king. Without this curse, what scope or significance does the drama have?' With the curse, however, as we now have it, the opera moves along from the first act to the last, from the opening curse of the wronged noble to the final destruction of the hunchback and his daughter. *La maledizione* sounds through the music towards a stupendous climax.

Verdi did not, of course, claim to be the inventor of this useful device. It had long ago been perceived in works of dramatic literature, and most appropriately in a play which had its part in the history of opera. Diderot as early as 1757 had noted in Racine's *Iphigénie* that the pathos of his writing at a particular moment in the drama depended upon the repetition of '*c'est le sang ... c'est le pur sang d'un dieu ... d'un dieu vengeur.*' But Verdi was exceptional among composers in recognizing such dramatic instruments. Few had anything about them of his literary sensitivity. In the works of earlier opera composers Addison had heard 'the most beautiful graces, quavers, and divisions bestowed upon "then", "for", and "from"'. And Grétry, in his *Reflections on Music* in 1789, had noted that 'the Italian loves music too much to give it fetters other than those which are self-imposed; he willingly sacrifices the beauty of his language to that of the song'. No such nonsense was permitted in Verdi's operas. In a letter to Piave about *The Force of Destiny* in 1864, the composer commanded him not to end lines with '*che*', '*piu*' and '*ancor*', and to have enough care of sense not to take twenty-five syllables to say 'the sun is setting'. The weight of words and their placing in the line was a matter of great concern to him as he worked at his music and he would not put up with the inappropriate. The distinction between language and song is not one which in Verdi's work has anything like its earlier strength. His belief in himself as the single artificer of the opera was expressed in the coherence of all its parts. From the character of his idea there emerged the character of each part. Everything in the final version of the opera came out of the composer's idea and found its recognizable purpose in the disclosure of that idea.

Verdi wanted a librettist's obedient assistance in realizing '*opera a intenzione*', that form in which the composer had imagined the action. This had been his established policy with all his writers. For *Ernani* Verdi had provided Piave with an outline of each scene and told him to make the necessary verses. Piave, a man of humble charm, appears not to have resented Verdi's imperious manner, and produced a very serviceable text. At moments it was excellent. There is a scene in Act III when the king, coming from the tomb of Charlemagne at the signal that he has been elected emperor, is greeted by the conspirators' cry '*Carlo Magno Imperatore*', to which he replies 'Charles V, you traitors!' This antithesis is put to brilliant use later in the scene. Pardoning Ernani, the new ruler attributes his clemency to his ancestor: 'Glory and honour to Charlemagne', to which the chorus replies 'Glory and honour to Charles V'. This is a good example of the kind of simple and effective writing that Piave gave Verdi. Easy to set to rousing tunes, Piave's verses were all that Verdi could require. He was retained, therefore, by the composer for *I Due Foscari* in 1844 and *Macbeth* in 1847, *Il Corsaro* in 1848, *Stiffelio* in 1850, and most celebratedly, for *Rigoletto* in 1851 and *Traviata* in 1853. As their collaboration continued, Verdi more freely expressed his determination to be the dominating partner. He wrote to Piave in May 1844 when the librettist was working on *I Due Foscari* suggesting 'Work yourself into a proper state of feeling and write some beautiful verses.' Though for this opera Verdi appears to have been satisfied, when he looked over Piave's *Macbeth* libretto Verdi was not happy about a couple of scenes, and, with the self-effacing Piave's permission, he got another poet, Maffei, to write some new verses. Ironically the Maffei scenes were judged failures and Piave got all the blame. He does not appear to have complained of this unfair treatment, remaining, it seems, content to do anything the master required of him.

The 1853 libretto for *Traviata* was put together only after Verdi had sent him scurrying to and fro to alter almost every phrase. And Piave's experience of the same imperious behaviour over *Simone Boccanegra* in 1857 was repeated for Boito when he was commissioned by Verdi to produce a second version of the libretto for that opera in 1881. It was even rumoured that Verdi had written the *Simone Boccanegra* libretto himself and just put Piave's name to it. Verdi neatly killed the rumour by remarking how contented he would have been to write such good verses, but that he had been thought capable of such a thing is a sign of how well-known his behaviour towards librettists was.

And even when a libretto was finished Piave could not rest assured that it would not have to be revised some years later. Verdi had required a great many revisions of his verses for *The Force of Destiny* for the 1864 revival. Piave had been asked again and again to do better, 'retaining as far as possible the words I sent you, but turning them into better rhymes'. His compliance however did not completely satisfy the scrupulous Verdi as for the 1869 production, after Piave had suffered a stroke, further revisions were made by Ghislanzoni on Verdi's orders.

Verdi's concern with the words actually witnesses to his appreciation of the librettists who worked with him. He was absolutely convinced of the necessity of their getting the words right, for it was for the precise words of the final text that he wrote. When the political censors proposed alterations which left the verse rhythms intact, he replied: 'If anyone says to me I can leave my notes as they are for this new plot, I reply that I don't understand this kind of thinking, and I say frankly that my music, whether beautiful or ugly, is never written in a vacuum, and that I always try to give it character.' Only if the words were right could the music be properly expressive of the idea within the action. And Verdi drove his librettists hard in order that he could write the proper music-drama.

It must have been with somewhat ambiguous feelings that his librettists had so often to admit that Verdi was a man of finer dramatic intuition than they. He had need only of someone to put his ideas into words. Though Verdi was greatly concerned with the idea and the words, he did not care much about the formal quality and quantity of the verses. He wrote to Ghislanzoni that 'if the action demands it' he should at once 'abandon rhythm, rhyme and stanza'. It is evident that Verdi did not have a poet's interest in language. He was not much bothered about the usual concerns of librettists. And, in order for him to have his way, he needed the services of a peculiarly accommodating type of librettist. Verdi was fortunate in his knack of discovering just the men to collaborate with him in his enterprise. The young Piave did exactly what he was told and managed to seem pleased to do it. Ghislanzoni was willing enough to let Verdi tamper with scene after scene: Verdi even polished off *Aida* with a few quick lines of his own in place of the poet's work. And just when Verdi needed him there appeared Arrigo Boito.

Boito was an industrious craftsman who wrote more librettos than there were composers to set them, or, if they got set, than there were theatres to mount them. In his spare moments, to please his mistress, Eleanora Duse, he provided her with translations of *Romeo and Juliet* and *Antony and Cleopatra*. Boito was, like Verdi, a great admirer of Shakespeare and, again like Verdi, an admirer who wished to put the playwright's work on the opera stage. Boito had begun his career by making a *Hamlet* libretto for Franco Faccio in 1865, and this early text shows signs of that genius for opera construction which so endeared him to Verdi. The great moments in the story are put in quick relation to one another with immense delicacy. This is a gift that he possessed right to the end of his career. He was unable to control his own operas but anyone can see that the libretto of *Otello* is a masterpiece of obedient compression. Even those who do not share their opinion can appreciate what some critics mean when they talk of the opera as being a greater theatrical experience than *Othello*, and a large part of the credit for this must go to Boito. The librettist cut out the first act to give himself room to make Iago, after whom librettist and composer had first thought to name the opera, a credible agent of catastrophe. The famous *credo*, in which Iago proclaims his devotion to a lord of chaos, is a development of the main idea of the opera and not a decorative piece of rhetoric. Verdi appreciated what Boito had offered him and gave this open declaration of the force which drives Iago, and thus the force which drives the opera, the most splendid resonant music. He was particularly pleased that when *Otello* was performed in London in 1889 although the critics disapproved of the omission of Shakespeare's first act 'they don't criticize your Iago's Creed'. The *credo* is entirely appropriate within the structure of the opera. It is demanded by the form of the action which Verdi had chosen. It would not fit the play or the character as Shakespeare wrote them but it holds the opera together in masterly fashion. Iago may be less human in *Otello* but he is more effective operatically as the driving demon of the action.

For it is a world of demons that Boito inhabits. His own ironic *Mefistofele* at the start of his career, the development of Iago's inversion of all truth and faith, and the terrifyingly drawn-out nightmare scene at the end of *Falstaff*, lead at last to his *Nerone* in which the burning of Rome is meant to be symbolic of the end of the world in hopeless confusion. '*Tutto crolla*', 'all crumbles', is the cry that rises from that confusion. Nero is enveloped in a catastrophe to which he has been driven by unrelenting Furies whom he has himself unleashed through the murder of his mother and his dealings with the wizard Simon Mago. Nero's tragedy is that he has to survive within the End. He cannot be set free of the eternal confusion that he has brought upon himself. This is a hellish scene far more effective than any other in opera history. *Mefistofele* took more than six hours to perform on its first night at La Scala in 1868. The occasion was a famous failure. But, even in the severely cut version now in the repertory of the New York City Opera, it is possible to recognize a frightening power of self-destruction. In the *Nerone*, which was never performed in Boito's lifetime, a universal destruction is invoked. Perhaps the *Re Lear* he planned with Verdi, but never wrote, would have overtopped even these horrors. Perhaps, therefore, it is not altogether a misfortune that they could not complete this project. It might have offered audiences more of reality than humankind can bear. But what, then, could they bear?

WAGNER, WAGNER AND THE UNIVERSAL ART-WORK

It seemed from the bizarre entertainments of French grand opera that audiences would receive with delight almost any product of exotic fancy, any monstrous distortion of plot and character, any irruption of ballet, engine or trombone, and, with these, any convolution of ordinary linguistic usage. The words, whenever they could be distinguished by the listener, came disjointedly across in unaccustomed sequence and with unaccustomed stress. It was not expected that the sung word should relate, as if it were a part of some spoken phrase or sentence, to those which came before or followed after it.

It was to the relation of operatic song to ordinary speech that the most famous of nineteenth-century librettists addressed himself. It seemed to Wagner that he ought to take stock of the ways in which this relationship might be formulated.

Wagner recognized that Mozart had exercised a care for words which was not commonly discernible in the work of later composers. Mozart had established a precise balance between meaning and melody. It is difficult not to be impertinently crude in describing any of Mozart's elegant devices but it is a common thing in the operas of his maturity for the voices not to take up a melody proceeding in the orchestra until he had made sure that the audience has been told plainly what is going to be sung. This care for meaning can so delay a vocal entry that sometimes in

Figaro it seems as if a vocal recitative were proceeding above an orchestral aria. Wagner often talked as if Mozart had worked separately on words and music, and had by setting them alongside one another both allowed them distinct value and presented the audience with more than one view of an operatic situation. 'The dialogue becomes all music,' said Wagner, 'whilst the music converses.'

The clarity of the dialogue music could only be maintained as long as the words were given something at least very close to their spoken value, and as long as phrases and sentences were arranged according to the patterns of speech. If the characters had to sing verses which because of their obedience to formal demands in the music were not recognizably related to human speech then Mozart's careful structure would be ruined. Language, character and plot would collapse together. Mozart's successors had foolishly transferred the melody from orchestra to singer and achieved the present confusion of nonsense.

Wagner mocked the way in which Marschner in *Adolf von Nassau* brought a rhythmic accent down on a trivial phrase, and the way in which in order to keep his rhythms going Weber in *Euryanthe* uncaringly altered the emphases of the librettist's sentences. 'This sort of thing,' he said, 'leads the hearer away from any serious attention to the words.' And in *Der Freischütz* he found hilarious examples of the composer's melody making it impossible to discover the sense of the words. Wagner was exasperated by the easy way in which their indifference to the ordinary structure of language led his contemporaries to an equal carelessness over the integrity of their characterization in an opera. He was astounded at the quiet acceptance by opera audiences of characters who expressed themselves in wholly incredible words, of Prussian majors who sang in exactly the same wholly unlikely terms as French peasants and Cypriot queens, of 'love' and 'dove' and 'awful destiny' and 'divine decree'.

And the abandonment of verse and characterization had been succeeded by the abandonment of the reasonable plot.

The grand opera effects of *Robert le Diable* or *Les Huguenots* were evidence to Wagner of what happens when a composer of execrable taste commands the services of a competent librettist. The collaboration of Meyerbeer and Scribe seemed to him to have consisted chiefly in the razing of everything a librettist might call his own and the erection upon these ruins of a music whose greatest 'effects' were wholly without identifiable causes. Wagner offered a famous analysis of the central scene of *Le Prophète* in which the hero, urging his followers to storm the ramparts of the enemy city, compelling them by his own enthusiastic words to share his urgent love of freedom, his sense of the divine within men, is suddenly, as Nature declares herself a sharer in his exaltation, illumined by the brilliant sun. This, he says, is a scene in which a critic must recognize Scribe's truly poetic imagination. But Meyerbeer does not recognize the inner causality of the action. The divine for him is a hymn-tune, the sunrise is an engineer's triumph, the hero is a tenor in romantic costume. All is cheapened into quaint melody and a pretty effect. And in these days, even in the richest international houses, the audience is unlikely to enjoy much of an engineering spectacle. At the Metropolitan Opera's production of *Le Prophète* anyone who had but a moderate acquaintance with the piece would have missed the miraculous sun altogether. The only place now for Meyerbeerish effects is in the outmoded parades of imperial pageantry at the Trooping of the Colour where *Les Huguenots* march bold as brass can make them. At that royal ceremony, of course, no one sings a word. And even in the opera house, then as now, the audience, getting nothing but melodrama and prettiness, think it right to be grateful to the composer for his effort to make from the dull work of the librettist an evening cheerful with song.

How, then, may the librettist resume his dignity? It is evident that whatever he does must be acceptable in musical terms. The librettist must work in awareness of the music. This is not necessarily a demand for all librettists to be, like Metastasio, capable of humming for their words some little tune of their own composition. Rather the librettist must appreciate what it may mean for a word to be sung, what may happen to speech when it becomes music. If he appreciates that he may through the making of a word for music burst the barriers of expression which contain the spoken word and say something more powerful than speech he will know how great is his responsibility not to waste the opportunity provided by opera. He will appreciate the care required in the selection of an idea worthy of such expression. He will search diligently within himself to discover whatever it is he holds most dear, for only that is worthy of song. Only that demands song. Wagner thought that most librettists produced a rhyme-ridden verse that could only become nonsense when shaped into musical phrases governed by a different structural principle. He required that the words should be seen to have achieved their own sense only when set by the composer. The librettist must not hope by literary devices – by rhyme and metre – to produce a language worthy of the explosive idea within. He must rather prune his language until it says in bare terms what he feels, and at its intensest it must be apparent that only by the raising of this pure language to the succinct expression of the musical tone can this feeling be made public. The language of opera represents an emotional enlargement of the word according to the possibilities of a sharply focused tune.

Wagner turned inside out Voltaire's remark that 'What is too silly to be said has to be sung' and declared 'what is not worth singing a poet should not bother to say'. The librettist should set to work on 'a real, heartfelt drama'. The scenes would then at least mean something for him and have, consequently, the power to inspire the composer to make 'some really dramatic music'. It would be difficult, of course, to persuade a composer of the artistic integrity of the librettist's work. That precise expression of the idea which demands its appropriate musical tone may be taken up by an insensitive composer as if it were merely a set of words which he may according to his arbitrary desire allot to notes.

But, anyway, where was such a librettist of integrity to be found? Gradually Wagner came to realize that he was himself the only librettist for his purpose. Though Schumann seems to have told Wagner that the libretto for *Lohengrin* could never be turned into an opera, he never found any other writer who could shape a libretto according to his needs.

In Paris Wagner hoped that he might have an opportunity to write an opera for the French, and he had some dealings with Scribe about a libretto. But Wagner had already become used to writing his own words and Scribe cannot have entertained the proposal wholly seriously. At any rate in 1849 Wagner was writing to Liszt from Paris that he could never write operas of Scribe's *verre d'eau* sort. 'A libretto of Scribe or Dumas, I cannot set to music.'

Wagner's consciousness of the single language articulated by verse and music led him to see that such driving forces should be expressed not by poet and musician; not by different minds, but by one, the musicianly poet, the poetic musician. Such a man would be driven by the power of these forces to make something that presaged the future. He wrote the enormous poem of the *Ring* and as he wrote the music shaped itself.

In putting his own librettos together Wagner took over those elements of Scribe's structure which he had admired beneath the silliness of Meyerbeer. He took Scribe's conception of a total experience of words, music, production and opening night glamour, and refurbished it all for Bayreuth. The customary elements of the Scribe plot – the hero faced with almost insurmountable difficulties, the pressing forward of an exciting action, the confrontation of the hero with a powerful antagonist, the confusion effected by misunderstandings between the hero and those who should be on his side, and the echo in each section of the action of the moving idea of the whole – occur not only in the later works of Sardou and Pinero, but in each of the Wagner operas. Even in his last opera, *Parsifal*, Wagner employed the old conventions of French grand opera of which he had in his earlier criticism written with such disdain. In his review of Halévy's *La Reine de Chypre* Wagner had made fun of the French fashion of making people behave like flowers, in *Parsifal* if he was not doing exactly that, he boldly made flowers behave like people; in a notice of Auber's *Les Diamants de la Couronne* he had laughed heartily at the caves of Portugal wherein Scribe had set the action, in *Parsifal* he placed the Grail castle on a mountain in Spain, and indeed nothing is more evidently Scribesque than the vaguely historical-religious structure of this consecratory opera.

Wagner was not, of course, wanting merely to write French opera in German. He had ambitions to fulfil the promise of earlier German opera in a peculiarly German manner. He thought of himself as continuing the national work of Weber. There is certainly something prophetic in Weber's remark about the destiny of German opera. It was to be 'a fully rounded and self-contained work of art in which all the ingredients furnished by the contributing arts disappear in the process of fusion and, in thus perishing, help to form an entirely new universe'. This is an apt description of Wagner's 'universal art work', or at least of his expectations. And so far as he actually accomplished the task he had set himself, he did so by choosing freely from the devices employed by earlier composers of whatever nationality. Wagner was a great plunderer. He was, as Debussy said, 'a great collector of clichés'. And a brilliant renovator of those clichés. The *leitmotiv* which makes its first appearance in Monteverdi's *Il Ritorno d'Ulisse in Patna* (*The Return of Ulysses*) and is struggling for maturity in Schubert's *Fierrabras*, is made Wagner's own instrument in the revelation of the thought behind the speech, and the unconscious behind the thought. The Metastasian exit-aria which had so selfishly been twisted into a show-stopper by eighteenth-century singers was stretched to fill the scene of Wotan's farewell to Brünnhilde, and then stretched further to make the final scene of *Götterdämmerung*. The ravings of Donizetti's heroines and the long unrepetitive melodies of Bellini are antecedents of the astounding mad scene in *Tristan und Isolde*. And, reaching back to the elaborate court spectacle of the earliest opera librettists, he demonstrated his delight in transformation scenes of woodland to palace, in flying goddesses winging their way between earth and heaven, in rainbow bridges and collapsing towers.

Perhaps his most original treatment of an old device is in his use of silence. In earlier times librettists often left a character silent and inactive on the stage. Juno in Monteverdi's *The Return of Ulysses*, for example, is kept waiting around with nothing to sing because the composer could not think of anything he wanted her to say for the moment but could not send her off because she would be needed later. Wagner makes a virtue out of his characters' silence and inactivity. The silent regard of the Dutchman and Senta when they first meet in her father's house, the silence of Lohengrin upon which the whole plot turns, and the silence of the lovers, Eva and Walther, on the morning of St John's Day, lead to the great silence of Parsifal throughout the first Grail ceremony in the mystic castle. This is a silence so difficult for a singer to maintain, so intense in its effect and so easily marred by lapsing into just standing there, that Melchior used to walk off the stage and come back only when he had to sing again. Wagner made of silence a vital attentiveness. His characters are as appreciably moved as they consider in silence the quality of their experience as they are when they launch into a stirring expression of that experience. There are moments when Wagner is the librettist of 'operas without words'.

There are moments, too, when his words sound like the merest punning doggerel, assonantal nonsense of the highest degree, as if he were failing to write a musical *Finnegans Wake*. But Wagner can commonly manage to produce the words he needs for his music. The doggerel occurs because he means the musical sound to take at that moment a greater share than usual in the communication of his feelings. There are plenty of other times when his verse does a beautifully precise job and when the listener can hear Wagner's exact intention in the words. Wagner can perfectly well manage dramatic language in a way which is recognizably effective according to established conventions; and he can make these conventions serve his peculiar purpose by using them to proclaim the revolutionary character of his art, and to reveal his own mind as the area within which the action takes place. In *Die Walküre*, for example, the discovery that Sieglinde and Siegmund are twins is made to the audience through the imagery Siegmund uses in his wooing – long before the lovers recognize their kinship. Siegmund declares Love to be the bride and sister of Spring. And at Sieglinde's replying: 'You are the Spring for which I longed', the image has done its quick work for the audience. This is all nicely done in the way of the old librettists. Later in the opera an audience will hear something new in Wotan's announcement to Fricka, his wife: 'You only understand convention, my mind is reaching to what has never been done before.' The audience must hear at this moment both Wotan's acceptance of the lovers' incest as an instrument in his great purpose, and Wagner's own determination to revolutionize art. And later still they must hear in Wotan's self-explanation to his daughter Brünnhilde, 'I talk to myself when I talk to you', Wagner's declaration that the dialogues of his operatic form are representations of the debate that goes on within his own mind. Wagner's librettos are artistic achievements of some magnitude, for in precise images they reveal not only the tale but the teller.

WAGNER AS PARADIGM

Staginess and splendour combined in awesome proportions made Wagner the dominant composer of the nineteenth century. Everyone knew it. When Verdi made his own independent discovery of how to use a suggestive and recurring melody as a hint of what was going on beneath the surface rhythms of an opera, a great many critics supposed that he had stolen Wagner's *leitmotiv*. It seemed quite natural to them that every composer should emulate Wagner. And while Verdi was justifiably furious at the impertinent suggestion, many contemporary composers were quite ready to copy the great German. So were many of those who came later. Responding to the challenge of Wagner's towering genius a great many composers – far more than were suited by talent for the enterprise – had a go at making an opera and thus establishing themselves as serious musicians. Wagner had made it compulsory to try out the form. The Wagnerian sound was heard in even a Spanish story. 'Without *Die Meistersinger*,' Hugo Wolf wrote to his librettist, '*Der Corregidor* would never have been composed.' A similar acknowledgement might have been made about Schumann's debt to *Tannhäuser* in *Genoveva*. Such things show how compulsive was the desire of composers quite incapable of the task to make a Wagnerian opera.

Perhaps the most charming product of an opera composer's veneration of Wagner is Humperdinck's *Hänsel und Gretel*. The young Humperdinck was a *répétiteur* at Bayreuth and gained there the immense distinction of being co-composer of *Parsifal*. The stage-manager had demanded a few bars more of music in which to effect the transformation scene. Wagner refused to add a note. But, during a sultry break in rehearsal, Humperdinck produced seven bars which satisfied composer and stage-manager and which, though now no longer required, remain in the score. Humperdinck remembered *Parsifal* in writing his music for the angel guardians of his wood children, and *Die Walküre* in his witches' ride. This composer makes, too, one connection between Wagner and Richard Strauss. The lament of the shepherd at the close of Humperdinck's *Königskinder* (*King's Children*) prepares in a nicely Wagnerian manner for the melody and the orchestral tone of the final exulting duet of Strauss's *Ariadne auf Naxos*.

Wagner himself remarked that his influence might be noted not in the music of his contemporaries but in their choice of subjects from medieval tales, the Edda and the rugged Northern narratives. Reyer, for example, set his *Sigurd* among the Nibelungen. When he first drafted the libretto of *Die Meistersinger*, in the summer of 1845, Wagner knew that the Norse tales and the Arthurian legends were not thought fit for the modern stage. When Walther is first asked to sing for the Masters of the singers' guild he wonders what subject they would like to hear: 'Siegfried and Grimmhilde?' he suggests, 'The story Wolfram sings of Parzival?'. The Masters do not care at all for these suggestions. The musician hero of the opera, however, is Wagner's representative of the new world of story that is to be opened by his work.

The Masters are also much more interested in the structure of the music than the action of the narrative within the song. The tapping of the marker does not signal a wrong turn in the tale but an offence against the musical conventions. Wagner tried to bring musicians to take the libretto seriously. And a good many composers have learnt from him in this matter.

Composers have mostly found, however, on concerning themselves with the words, that their literary ability was inadequate to the task of writing the libretto. So, paradoxically, Wagner's insistence on composers giving greater attention than before to the words of their operas led to careful composers taking no chances with either their own phrases or those of others yet untried. As a result there was a move towards setting already proven plays.

A goodish number of composers have attempted to work out an opera from already finished plays of established quality, not in the Verdiesque manner of adapting the grander scenes, but by a faithful following of the complete text, or as much of it as the length of performance will reasonably permit. There have been mistakes in this matter, too, of course. Pizzetti's *L'Assassinio nel Cattedrale* (*Murder in the Cathedral*) should never have happened, and Strauss's use of Wilde's *Salome* is not much more creditable, but Debussy's success with *Pelléas et Mélisande* is in large part due to his care for the text he took from Maeterlinck. And within so unwagnerian a frame as the already-made play, and despite writing in conscious reaction to *Tristan und Isolde*, Debussy produced an opera that bears myriad traces of Wagner's critical influence. He himself admitted that he had had to tear up pages of his music because 'the ghost of old Klingsor' kept returning to haunt him. Maeterlinck's play seems to have been for Debussy that text demanding music for its full expression which Wagner had declared the proper libretto. Working faithfully to the essential doctrine of Wagner's opera criticism, Debussy found for himself a most personal way of making manifest vaguely but not insubstantially the dimly layered meanings of Maeterlinck's play, a way which yet employed many of the wizard's peculiar spells to achieve a rich musical texture. And Debussy appreciated Wagner's silences. His delicate employment of pauses in the action and his quickening of such silences by the small and low significant gesture are tributes both to the master's discoveries and to the later composer's individual talent. Though *Pelléas et Mélisande* could not be bettered in its own manner, it is a pity that Maeterlinck's view of what was proper did not allow him, when asked a little time after he had given Debussy permission to make his opera, to let Puccini set the play. We should then have had a perfect opportunity to compare the kinds of things that can be done with a text of modern literary integrity. We would have been able, too, to see how diverse the influence of *Tristan und Isolde* could be on later operatic presentations of love. For Debussy certainly was hoping to make something to put alongside Wagner's celebration, and Puccini might at Maeterlinck's prompting have managed that love-duet to eclipse the second act of *Tristan und Isolde* which he had planned but never wrote for the climax of *Turandot*.

The success composers have had with ready-made plays must act as an encouragement to them to ask for the collaboration of established playwrights. But the undertaking is fraught with possible misunderstandings and demarcation disputes. It is a rare playwright who is willing to subdue his literary invention to the demands of the music, and rarer still for a humble enough playwright to be so appreciative of what has to be done that he is precisely sensitive to the composer's need for words that demand to be sung; it is even rarer for a writer of such understanding to be content to make a text which is not fully complete until it becomes music. He will generally want to be recognized as poet or playwright rather than as librettist. And a composer's asking a playwright for a libretto does not mean that he has given up his old claim to the final command of the opera's structure. After all Wagner himself when he came to write the music of *Götterdämmerung* did not hesitate to go quite against the tone of his poem 'Siegfried's Death'. And he was always prepared to set a pretty piece of doggerel if it would help along the musical movement of a scene. Nothing in Scribe is quite so foolish as the river maidens' cry '*Rheingold, reinesgold*', 'Rhinegold, pure gold', but it fitted nicely the balanced harmony of Wagner's musical design. Wagner as librettist had not felt himself displaced from public attention by Wagner as composer. His art's coherence as a whole was due to his ability to unite the two artistic roles in his own person. He could not know what difficulties might occur if the relationship of librettist and composer were attempted by men of comparable talent.

STRAUSS, HOFMANNSTHAL AND THE ELEGANCE OF FORM

Probably the most effective working-out of Wagner's hopes for a universal artwork in which the librettist and the composer should contribute in a distinguished but not distinct manner is to be seen in the partnership of Richard Strauss and Hugo von Hofmannsthal.

Strauss's orchestration was grandly Wagnerian at almost every point, and required as many players, even adding a few for whip-cracks and slat-strikes. The composer might have spent his time and energies in devising even louder and lusher sounds had he not attended intelligently to the counsels of his librettist. And Hofmannsthal might have journeyed further and further into the realms of elf and symbol if it had not been for his acceptance of Strauss's commonsense cautions. Strauss developed the musical possibilities of the Wagnerian enterprise in collaboration with a librettist who could not bear 'the intolerable erotic screamings' of Tristan and Isolde. Together they produced the most impressive body of operatic work of the twentieth century. Their operas, with those of Mozart, Verdi and Wagner, form the staple of the international repertory.

Like the great Austrian dramatist before him, Franz Grillparzer, who approached Beethoven with a libretto, Hofmannsthal was aware of the distinction of the composer with whom he worked. And though Hofmannsthal had really no understanding of, and not much liking for music, Strauss soon appreciated the exceptional quality of Hofmannsthal's work. On being recommended by some well-wisher to take a look at a play in the Scribe tradition Strauss wrote cheerfully to Hofmannsthal that 'Sardou's (*horribile dictu*) *Ninth Thermidor*' if used as a libretto would doubtless prove another '*sujet à la grand opéra*', and he got a sympathetic reply, 'Yes, some things are absolutely out of the question nowadays, *Thermidor*!' Their common understanding of the possibilities of the form is a wonder of opera history. They acknowledged one another as men of talent and encouraged one another, though not always in the most temperate manner.

The way Strauss dealt with Hofmannsthal's *Elektra* gave the playwright an indication of what he was going to have to put up with if they went on working together. Strauss was ferocious. Hofmannsthal accepted his ferocity. Strauss took what he thought to be the elemental emotions of the play and gave them free rein in the orchestra. When composing *Salome* he had simply turned the play as it stood into an opera libretto, matching decorative vulgarity with decorative vulgarity with an impudence which is almost superb. He was as careful of the obscenity in Wilde's grandly debauched play as Debussy had been of the mystery of Maeterlinck's eerie fatalism. But Hofmannsthal's play had to be treated differently. The playwright's peculiar virtues resisted immediate translation into libretto form, and Strauss insisted on almost every part being changed to accord with his musical intention before it was acceptable to him.

First Strauss shortened the play considerably. Hofmannsthal courteously tried to think through the play from the composer's point of view and wrote suggesting a further cut of 'the brief interlude of the cook and the young servant'. The pair of them wondered together whether they might not leave Aegisthus out altogether, but Strauss wrote finally that 'he is definitely part of the plot and must be killed off with the rest'. However, the whole scene of Aegisthus's entry had to be rewritten by Hofmannsthal to Strauss's directions in order to concentrate the musical effect, and then, in consequence of this rewriting, the scenes which followed had to be reshaped, and then again, the final scene had to be done anew for the opera's conclusion.

Strauss, evidently, forced the pace of the collaboration. He was always making new demands on his playwright. For *Elektra* he wanted 'a great moment of repose' during which he would 'fit in a delicately vibrant orchestral interlude' so 'couldn't you insert here a few beautiful verses?' He even complained as the playwright worked to fulfil this order that Hofmannsthal did not seem to understand his need 'for material to work at will towards a climax'. And, perhaps the most dangerous thing he could have done, and certainly something to have outraged a lesser man, Strauss sent Hofmannsthal some suggestions of what might be added to the verses the playwright had offered him. Hofmannsthal, it must be remembered, was then a famous man himself, and justly considered the best dramatist living in Austria. He put up with the suggestions without a murmur, and received next a demand from Strauss for a simultaneous duet for Elektra and her sister Chrysothemis, for which he was asked to provide nothing but recapitulatory waffle, 'nothing new, just the same content, repeated and working towards a climax'. Such demands must have been rare in Hofmannsthal's experience. It is not thus that a deliberate author makes his plays, and though he may not have accepted Strauss's remark 'You are a born librettist' as 'the greatest compliment to my mind', Hofmannsthal must have agreed that, whatever the general artistic case, for him, in his collaboration with this demanding and wholly musically-minded man, 'it is much more difficult to write a good operatic text than a fine play'.

Hofmannsthal's experience with Strauss over the making of *Elektra* into an opera taught him a lot about the relationship between librettist and composer, and about what happens to a man who lets a musician get hold of his play. He decided that before Strauss would be allowed to set his next play it would have to be performed, as he had written it, 'on the ordinary stage'. What Hofmannsthal habitually enjoyed was the dramatist's command of character and dialogue. He liked rounding the characters and diversifying their language. And he recognized now that the composer might well want to reduce the complexity of the verse so that he could take charge of the characters and give them shape through the music. Hofmannsthal cherished his command through the verse of that psychological revelation which made writing a play an exciting enterprise. He found that Strauss wanted that pleasure for himself, and that he was unwilling to appear even chronologically second to the playwright. Strauss objected to the play being performed as a play before he had presented it as an opera. He could not bear the thought that the audience would already have an idea of the characters and a grasp of the drama, and would see his work as a version of the dramatist's. He expressed this attitude in crude terms which Hofmannsthal found it easy to refute. Strauss told Hofmannsthal that he could not accept the idea of an audience knowing how his opera ended before they saw the beginning. Hofmannsthal quickly pointed out that once the first performance had been given everyone would know the ending anyway. And that knowing the ending had not prevented people attending some operas again and again. And further that dramatically there is some excitement in both watching an action unfold and knowing what is going to happen. But of course Strauss was not simply complaining about the loss of his surprise finale. He wanted the play for himself. He wanted it as a libretto and not as a play, so that he could make it his own. Finally he told the librettist that he doubted whether, 'if spoken', the play would 'have anything like the effect that, as an opera, it is *bound* to have'. Hofmannsthal held his ground, however, and offered the play to Max Reinhardt. He told Strauss that 'we should never have arrived at a useful opera libretto – which I trust we shall still get – had I not first worked out this plot in the form which is my own, namely as a psychological comedy in prose'. Only after he had had control of the drama could he understand its structure well enough to make it into a libretto for Strauss. After all, Hofmannsthal remarked, Mozart had been pleased to find hints for his musical treatment of Figaro, Susanna and Cherubino in Beaumarchais's play. Strauss was not persuaded. Nothing came of all this talk of an opera about Casanova, and Hofmannsthal, anxious perhaps to get Strauss away from thoughts of that piece, sent him a scenario for what became *Der Rosenkavalier*.

The scenario was quickly followed by a draft of the first act. Strauss was delighted. Hofmannsthal wrote nicely that he was not sure if he had not gone too far in his 'disregard of operatic convention' and accommodated himself too little 'to the needs of the singing voice'. As their correspondence continued Hofmannsthal let Strauss know that he was delighted to be ranked with da Ponte and Scribe. He followed this happy compliment more dangerously by making a suggestion of a purely musical kind: 'Do try and think of an old-fashioned Viennese waltz, sweet and yet saucy, which must pervade the whole of the last act.' To Hofmannsthal's full acknowledgement of being this time not a playwright but the supplier of lines and phrases for a libretto, Strauss replied contentedly, 'You're a splendid fellow. When do I get the rest?' If Hofmannsthal was content to liken himself to one of Mozart's librettists, Strauss was quite prepared to treat him accordingly. He wrote next for 'some more text', saying nonchalantly that 'the music is all ready and I only need the words for accompaniment and filling in'. Hofmannsthal, growing bolder in his relationship with the composer, then suggested an alteration in the music, daring to remark that 'Wagner does such things with marvellous nicety'. On the other hand when Strauss, quite wrongly as most producers feel, insisted that no one in the audience would look for a motive for the Italian intriguers' change of sides between Acts II and III, Hofmannsthal replied with a warning, equally unnecessary it might be thought, that Octavian and Sophie should not be allowed in their love duet to burst into 'a Wagnerian kind of erotic screaming'. So Strauss must have felt that at least in some things he was capable of a greater nicety than Wagner.

From such discussions developed total confidence. In the end Strauss was told by Hofmannsthal, when some new verses for *Der Rosenkavalier* were in question, that he 'found it rather agreeable to be bound in this way to a given tune'. The composer and librettist had found a way, each working with exceptional distinction at his share in the common task, to make with the other a sensitive comedy that ranks with *Figaro* in both its sensitivity and its comic qualities.

It is impossible for a man to attend even a perfunctory performance of *Der Rosenkavalier* without experiencing an enlargement of his powers of human sympathy. It is impossible while listening to the music not to feel the urgency of the words. In this opera at least it is necessary to be closely acquainted with the text in order to appreciate both the words and the wonder of what Strauss has been inspired by them to create. And it is impossible for anyone of whatever age or culture not to realize that in this opera the matter presented is directly relevant to their situation. The theme of the gap between generations and the difficulty of transferring power from old to young, which had puzzled Mozart and Wagner and amused Donizetti and Rossini, is handled here with probing delicacy. The Marschallin is forced in the midst of her affair with the young count to confront the lines reflected in her mirror, and the ruffianly Baron Ochs is forced to resign his claim upon the young girl and her dowry. And neither for one moment loses the audience's sympathy, despite the tender handling of the love between Octavian and Sophie and the wish each member of the audience must have for them to find happiness with each other. What in Mozart is a matter for terror, in Wagner a matter for exultation, and in Donizetti a matter for fun, as they present Idomeneo, Wotan and Don Pasquale, is for Strauss and Hofmannsthal a matter of delicate inevitability. A member of the audience easily feels sympathy with every character in *Der Rosenkavalier*, and understands their behaviour, whether sad or amusing. A good deal of confusion can be caused in *Idomeneo*, the *Ring* or *Don Pasquale* if the older generation are presented too sympathetically. However powerful an audience's feeling for the Marschallin and the Baron there is never a danger of it being too great for the structure of the opera. Indeed unless the Marschallin is shown to be properly loved by Octavian and Sophie at the end no audience can feel sure that the youngsters are truly in love themselves.

This was not the only long-standing problem of opera construction to which Strauss and Hofmannsthal found a solution in their partnership. In *Der Rosenkavalier* the old difficulty of how to hold comic and tragic elements together within the boundaries of one opera without having recourse to a separate sub-plot – a problem which threatens to pull even *L'Incoronazione di Poppea* and *Die Meistersinger* apart – is perfectly solved by the creation of the characters of Octavian and Baron Ochs. And so confident did Hofmannsthal feel of their powers together that he next invited Strauss to collaborate on an opera in which the meeting of *seria* and *buffa* characters and incidents is organized not by setting them side by side in one plot but by taking two plots and involving each set of characters in the other's action. In *Ariadne auf Naxos* (*Ariadne on Naxos*) Hofmannsthal takes a conventional story from the old opera books, the *Arianna* tale of the girl deserted by Theseus on his way home from Crete, and places it within and without the games of the *commedia dell'arte.* Almost everyone has been astounded at the technical demands Strauss makes on the leading *buffa* singer, much greater than those made on the grandest grand opera heroine; some critics have thought the piece too elaborate and brittle in its intermingling of the artistic genres, but for me this is one of the most splendid pieces in the repertory.

Strauss first set about composing an *Ariadne* when he and Hofmannsthal decided it would be pleasant to present a *divertissement* for Max Reinhardt's production of *Le Bourgeois Gentilhomme.* It was to last half an hour. The final version, lasting much longer than half an hour, is one of their greatest operas. They turned the slight tale of Ariadne's lament at being abandoned by the caddish Theseus into a marvellously subtle exploration of what it means to be in love and be loved. The faithful Ariadne longing for death, the fickle Zerbinetta enjoying a set of flirtations, the innocent Bacchus who discovers his own divinity only when he realizes that he is loved, may bring many thoughts home to Strauss's audience. They offer a choice of ways of being human.

The structure of *Ariadne auf Naxos* is designed, like *Fidelio,* to lead the audience very gradually through a sequence of ever more demanding responses into an appreciation of what the librettist and the composer wish to tell them. The audience finds itself at first confronted by a *singspiel* in which there is a large quantity of talk; this breaks unexpectedly into arias of great beauty, and then, as the music becomes more delicately complex, the scene becomes more obviously a revelation of what is going on within the characters. The first scene displays for the audience the muddle backstage as an opera company – the nervous composer and endlessly bickering tenor and soprano and the manager trying to get better terms for his employees – prepare a performance of an old-fashioned Ariadne piece, while, at the same time, a tumbling troup of harlequinade comedians congregate round their leading-lady, Zerbinetta, and plan their evening's antics. The confusion is doubled by the announcement that since the hour is late and everyone is going to demand payment for their attendance at the party, both groups are to perform on stage in one amalgamated action. But, says the poor composer, Ariadne must appear alone upon her desert island, 'she is the symbol of Mankind in Solitude'. He at first refuses to comply even for the fifty ducats that, as the manager reminds him, he is to be paid. But the wiles of Zerbinetta lure him into snipping and cutting at his music until there is room for her dancing. She has told him that it is she, as she twirls upon the stage, who is 'the loneliest girl in the world'. At the beginning of the second act we are on-stage. *Ariadne* begins. The opera singers attempt to tell the old tale of Ariadne deserted upon Naxos; the comedians chime in with snatches of fun and dance, interrupting the smooth progress of the lamentable opera. Strauss has given Zerbinetta such stupendous music that, as she rouses the romantic Ariadne from her distress the audience must be persuaded that there is a meaning for them in her cajolery at least as much as in the heroine's steadfast love. At last the power of love, just as Zerbinetta said it would, indirectly leads Ariadne to welcome the god, and all ends with Bacchus and his bride's triumphant realization that they may be divinely happy. 'Only now doth life begin for thee and me.' The opera persuades us that love may be stronger than death and may reveal the eternally divine within us. 'My godhood wakes within me through thee.' In this opera's telling of the myth, Dionysus, at least in his Roman guise, is a god to be welcomed. Zerbinetta makes her own apt comment on Ariadne's transformation, seeing it as relating to her own experience: 'When a new god comes to woo, we can only accept in silence.'

Strauss has realized that the story allows him to say something that will be appreciated by both Ariadne and Zerbinetta and the audience. He rejoices in his own graceful power of invention. The music transports the hearer to that island where he may discern some new truth about himself.

Critics have repeatedly attacked the librettist's lack of understanding of the musical scope of opera. Romain Rolland wrote to Strauss in 1924 of his regret that Hofmannsthal should 'too often lack a sense of theatre' and clutter his plots with philosophic notions of no musical interest. Ernest Newman described the piece as 'the most interesting failure in the whole history of opera', and, in 1936, thought it most unlikely to establish itself permanently in the standard repertory. But he admitted that he came to every revival with renewed curiosity. Hofmannsthal, it seemed to him, was 'mastered by symbolism'. And in 1964 William Mann in *Richard Strauss*, his authoritative critical study of the operas, allows that he has made 'some rude remarks' about 'Hofmannsthal's misuse and misguiding of Strauss'.

Newman supposed that Hofmannsthal had made a great mistake in weaving 'a philosophical interest' into the meeting of the flirtatious Zerbinetta and the young Composer. The theme was not, he thought, developed in the action of the opera. In this he was mistaken. In the matter of *Ariadne auf Naxos* at least, Hofmannsthal and Strauss were appreciative of the same symbol and its meaning. William Mann remarks that Hofmannsthal 'meant the Composer as a self-portrait'. Hofmannsthal must have felt a trifle uneasy when Strauss wrote to him wondering whether the Composer might not have a little affair with Zerbinetta, but not too serious, and 'he must not be too lifelike a portrait of me'. Each saw himself in the artist who is misunderstood and yet inspired by the practitioner of a different art form.

The working-out of this personally urgent theme in both parts of the piece gives it a dramatic, musical and, if the critics will have it so, philosophic, unity.

Certainly Zerbinetta does not meet the Composer again. Once the prologue of backstage tantrums is over there is no place in the structure of the work for the Composer to see her again. She leaves him for the performance. But he has a moment of wonder before the *Ariadne* begins. He sings in triumphant self-discovery, 'Music, Music is the Holy Art'. This image persists in the mind because Strauss has given the Composer here some of his most splendid music. The image of a man realizing his own possibilities as a result of the declaration of another human being, of some girl who does not understand him but is saying that she loves him, is so strongly impressed on the mind that it can be recognized again in the equally impressive music of the final situation when the mourning Ariadne welcomes the young god. Strauss took immediate and telling advantage of Hofmannsthal's readiness to leave the structure to him. He turned Hofmannsthal's mirroring of the two incidents into a triple progression.

The music announces in the first part that the young man is stirred by the fickle soubrette Zerbinetta to appreciate the wonder of being a Composer. In the second part the young god acknowledges to Ariadne that 'my divinity wakes within me through thee'. This is a tribute of one collaborator to another, even if couched in rather patronizing terms. And it hints, in terms exactly appropriate to opera, at a matter of great philosophic interest. It hints at our customary puzzlement that we should be changed by those with whom we converse: that with one person we should be dull and mean, and with another, who sees us differently, we should be witty and generous. Strauss and Hofmannsthal here make their opera comment upon matters which confront social scientists when they talk of role-playing, systematic theologians when they talk of justification, and existentialist philosophers when they talk of 'bad faith'. But the music must move between these moments. And in between, however, Strauss has elaborated the part of Zerbinetta until, quite out of

Hofmannsthal's original design, she demands the audience's total admiring attention. Zerbinetta is the free and exciting musician who berates the foolishly pensive word-spinner, Ariadne. The display of Zerbinetta's almost wordless song removes the audience's sympathy from the duller heroine. From Hofmannsthal to Strauss. Just for a moment, but quite decisively, the music announces the composer's command of the opera.

It may be, as Rolland suggested to Strauss, that the librettist brings off his pastiches so well that he ends up taking them seriously, but Hofmannsthal's absolute control of artistic form enabled Strauss to give a civilized coherence of elements from the very first operas – the lament of *Arianna*, the wordly wisdom of *Didone Abbandonata*, and the epiphany of the god in almost all of them – with elements from the *opera buffa* of the old Italian companies, combined with the nineteenth-century vocal diversions of Donizetti, and the twentieth-century fondness for mixing spoken dialogue with song.

In his peculiar command of form resides Hofmannsthal's importance as a librettist. Hofmannsthal worked hard to obtain that professional mastery of the librettist's skills which characterizes his contribution to the partnership. He became so assured a librettist, as he had become so assured a playwright, only by applying his genius to the craft. Every opera of their collaboration exhibits Hofmannsthal's precise appreciation of what was possible within the frame that they had chosen. This was a liberating, not a confining, comprehension. He came to understand so thoroughly the possibilities of the form that he could discover opportunities for Strauss's musical exploitation which librettists before him had not seen. Sometimes, it seems, his invention surprised even himself. When Hofmannsthal wrote to Strauss that he thought he might have accommodated himself too little to 'the needs of the singing voice' he knew that Strauss needed little encouragement to find for himself the complementary possibilities of that voice. And, though Strauss would not have relished its being remarked by his critics, gradually Hofmannsthal brought the composer to appreciate the precision of their craft. That the music of *Salome* modulates into the music of *Arabella* and, indeed, that of *Capriccio* is in no insignificant way due to the tasteful exercise of Hofmannsthal's formal discipline.

Of those formal elements of opera which serve to secure a design from beginning to end, and subject individual delights to the overall demands of the work, none was so precious to Hofmannsthal as the defining image or symbolic gesture by which a scene might be delicately placed in the whole work's expressive structure. At the start of their collaboration Strauss was not at all sure what to do with this instrument in opera, but gradually Hofmannsthal educated him in the use of the dramatic gesture. This was a matter in which Hofmannsthal understood Wagner better than Strauss. The *Ring* manages well enough, as Herr Friedrich has recently pointed out in his programme notes for the present Covent Garden production, with three properties, the ring, the spear, and the sword. These change hands, and their transfer is the action of the drama, they change relation and their change brings about the resolution of the action. Hofmannsthal admired this economy. He had in his plays attempted some such coherence of gesture and he guided Strauss to a sensitivity to such simple significances. The Marschallin sets Faninal's mind at rest about what he is to think, and what the neighbours will say about his daughter's marriage to Ochs being broken off, by simply allowing him to lead her to her carriage. We see what it means to him to be seen with her. Perhaps Hofmannsthal rushed Strauss too quickly into symbols with his libretto for *Die Frau ohne Schatten* in which nothing happens unless it happens on several levels of the imagination, and in which every action is symbolic in more than one way. Strauss felt somewhat cramped by such surroundings. But in the wholly naturalistic context of *Arabella*, their last collaboration, Hofmannsthal made a great effort to bring the action to its resolution through the quiet effectiveness of a symbolic gesture.

Arabella is a pretty miss, the girl who turns men's heads at a party, and who dreams of a man who will somehow be unlike all those who pursue her and who will yet, of course, want to marry her. Mandryka, the stranger who comes to ask her father for permission to marry her, is all she could wish, but, with a misunderstanding of Wagnerian subtlety, Mandryka thinks that she has been unfaithful to him on the evening when they have agreed to marry. The misunderstanding is cleared away, but, in opera as in life, it is clear also that the two young people have to come to terms with their own mistrustful natures. Somehow they must learn to love one another as they are and not as they have dreamt each other to be. Arabella grows up faster than Mandryka. She teaches him to be loyal to those around him. But how is she to teach him that she has forgiven him and that he has entered into a pure loving relationship with her? Hofmannsthal has placed very early in the opera Mandryka's peasant story of the village girl bringing her lover a glass of water on the night before their wedding to show her pure love for him. The gift is a symbolic gesture of great beauty. And Hofmannsthal has retained this image all through the libretto in preparation for the wonderful moment when Arabella comes down the stairs to the wretched, puzzled, and frustrated Mandryka, carrying the glass of water. The gesture brings everything to a perfect conclusion. At least it did for Hofmannsthal. All through their collaboration he had been working towards this delicate moment, and had employed the symbolism of water in many places which required the audience's understanding of a perfect relationship where husband and wife lived lovingly together. In *Elektra* the demonic fancies of Elektra had prevented her from appreciating the beauty of family life for which Chrysothemis had longed. She could not understand her sister's desire to take her children by the hand as she walked through the village to the well. In *Die Frau ohne Schatten* the Empress and the Dyer's Wife have only been able to achieve happiness and drink from the magic fountain once a generous acknowledgement of other people's dignity has been made. The drinking of the fountain water is possible only because the Empress has refused to grab happiness at the expense of others. In *Die Aegyptische Helena* only after Menelaus has recognized the unreality of his dream of a wife and carried the real Helen homewards across the sea to be what he calls *vollvermahlt*, 'truly married', is a resolution of the opera possible. Hofmannsthal had conceived the gesture of water in *Arabella* as a gesture of maturing love. Strauss, however, was not enthusiastic about such gestures. He began tentatively, saying that he was 'getting less and less keen on that drink of pure water', he hinted that some journalist would count up all these water scenes and write something about 'Hofmannsthal has water on the brain', and wondered whether something quite different might not be arranged from 'this somewhat childish symbolism'. Hofmannsthal knew that his gesture had to be part of the opera or there would be nothing of substance for him in the design. 'I do not think,' he replied, 'that I shall be able to find anything better.' Neither his imagination nor the collection of Slav customs he had been using in his research for the opera could suggest a more useful symbol. The gesture was the only one which could take place in a village and in a city hotel. Anything else would look unnaturally staged, as if Arabella wanted to make a theatrical effect instead of a simple loving gesture. She could, of course, kiss Mandryka, but this would fail to exploit all the wonder of the moment. 'A kiss she cannot carry towards him, she would simply have to walk up to him and give him the kiss; the other implies the most bridal gesture in its chastest form, and it can be followed by the kiss which thus gains solemnity, something that raises it out of the ordinary.' Hofmannsthal died before the completion of the opera. Strauss set the scene as he had written it, but his music at this point does not have that climactic wonder for which Hofmannsthal had hoped. The composer did not quite accept his argument. And unless the composer is convinced the music will not convince the audience. The final gesture almost fails. But Strauss's free decision to do as Hofmannsthal had thought right at this point is conclusive evidence of his admiration for the librettist's share of their work.

If Auden, in his note on the libretto he and Chester Kallman provided for Henze's *The Bassarids*, says plainly that what they wrote 'will not be judged for its literary merit, if it has any, but for the music it has produced from the composer', it is yet the case in the partnership of Strauss and Hofmannsthal that the composer meant the librettist to be heard – despite those cartoons which show him clamouring for more noise from the orchestra lest the singers become audible.

In his last opera, *Capriccio*, written in 1942, over a dozen years after Hofmannsthal's death, Strauss made a final acknowledgement of what he had learnt whilst working with the great librettist. Through the formal device of a discussion about the nature of opera itself, held in the elegant salon of a chateau near Paris at the time of Gluck's reform, Strauss was able to present various concepts of his art, and in particular to suggest to his audience a view of the proper relation between words and music. At the end, though each has had a moment when it seemed that the other would have to yield the primacy, Strauss offered no way of resolving their rivalries. But he did offer a hint of how he came to hold this irresolute position.

Strauss reminds his audience of the greatest scene of his collaboration with Hofmannsthal. The Countess in *Capriccio*, when all the guests have ceased their wrangling and gone home, gazes at herself in her mirror. We see and hear again the graceful Marschallin as she gazes at the first wrinkles reflected in her dressing table mirror. The first act wonder of *Der Rosenkavalier* is brought again to mind. We know again the total effect that words and music had once made. In the earlier opera Hofmannsthal's invention of the ceremony of the rose and Strauss's invention of the early eighteenth-century waltz had been expressions of their total confidence in the complementary talents that they exercised together. Each element had found its proper place in harmony of the whole. But in *Capriccio* a subtle change has occurred. A curious nostalgia and curious puzzlement have taken the place of the previous confidence and comradely sureness of touch. In a context deliberately reminiscent of earlier operatic success, the Countess confesses that she cannot decide which art should be accorded greater dignity: poetry or music. Nor can she decide which man she loves more: the poet or the musician.

In this scene Strauss is making a final bow to his great librettist. He declares what sort of a person he is by this delicate gesture. It is a charming irony that it is by precisely such a gesture as Hofmannsthal had so often urged upon him that Strauss makes his clearest self-revelation. Nothing so finely declaratory occurs in the cruder narrative of his deliberately autobiographical opera, *Intermezzo*, for which he had himself written much of the text.

While he was working with Hofmannsthal the practical problems of putting an opera together had been resolved in a partnership of equal talent and authority. But at the end of *Capriccio*, by his generous acknowledgement of Hofmannsthal's genius, Strauss is admitting his puzzlement about the ultimate definition of opera.

Four

How did it begin?

In the *Capriccio* discussion of the nature and possibilities of opera, the poet, the composer and the impresario consider subjects that might delight the Countess. 'How would you like *Ariadne on Naxos*?' asks the poet. 'Too often done before,' she replies, though the impresario thinks the tale 'such a good opportunity for a lot of long lamenting arias'. The composer remarks that he 'would find *Daphne* much more pleasant'. And the rest agree that music might well manage even the girl's transformation into a tree. But they agree, too, that nothing can be done with mythological subjects any more. 'We'll be having the Trojan War next,' says the Countess's brother, and he goes on to suggest that poet and composer 'write about ourselves'. They are urged to take their afternoon's conversation, 'all that occurred here today', and make an opera out of it. Strauss is here enjoying a complex game. While his characters are demonstrating how irrelevant the old Greek legends look to those who do not understand their meaning, the composer is enjoying reminding the audience at *Capriccio* in 1942 of his *Ariadne auf Naxos* of 1912, and his *Daphne* of 1938, and, at the Trojan War remark, his *Die Aegyptische Helena* of 1928. They are to note that his career has been one in which the modern relevance of the classic stories has been finely demonstrated. Strauss has shown how such stories may in music become 'about ourselves'.

Strauss had not always been aware of such things. He had not always been aware of the subtle relation between music and myth. That was revealed to him by his librettist. And at first he was suspicious of the mythic motion Hofmannsthal made. Gradually, however, Strauss came to appreciate Hofmannsthal's talk of myth's availability for the composer who would say something of modern relevance. And he came to be as enthusiastic for this mode of revelation as his colleague.

When Hofmannsthal explained the story of *Die Aegyptische Helena* in 1928, hearing that the plot began in the house of a princess, the lover of Poseidon, Strauss at once interjected, 'Does Poseidon appear?' The reply came, 'No, Poseidon does not appear. No gods appear at all. In fact, take everything as if it happened two or three years ago, somewhere between Moscow and New York.' Hofmannsthal knew that Strauss would realize that the classic story was concerned with modern questions.

A large number of those composers who have attempted something classical have been content with inventions more properly compared with Jonson's *Sejanus* or Hollywood's *Quo Vadis?* than with the works of Sophocles and Euripides. The operatic tradition of the pastoral lad, the heavenly messenger and the elaborate machines survives vitally and unexpectedly in the work of Wagner, for Siegfried, Waltraute, and the Fafner dragon are but these old Italian conventions in new Germanic guise, and the conventions reappear too in the May King of *Albert Herring*, Mercury of *King Priam*, and the revolving, rising and falling Wheel of Fortune of Covent Garden's *Taverner*. The best of modern opera composers have been faithful not to the actual texts of the Greek and Roman theatre, not to the artifices of earlier fashions in opera production, but to what they discerned of the inner character of a myth.

This is precisely what Strauss managed in the making of his *Daphne* opera with Josef Gregor after Hofmannsthal's death. The opera begins on the eve of the festival of Dionysus. The village girl, Daphne, delicately rejects the offered love of her shepherd suitor, Leukippos, telling him she can only be his sister. She is in love with the sun and the life of the world of nature. She wants only to be at one with the trees and the meadow of flowers. Then she in turn is greeted as a sister by the god Apollo in shepherd's disguise. He promises that she shall never be parted from the sun. As his language shifts from that of brother to lover, Daphne begins to fear him as she feared Leukippos. At the feast of Dionysus she refuses both suitors. Apollo in an angry fit slays Leukippos, but then, repenting, asks forgiveness of Dionysus for the murder of his servant and transforms the grateful Daphne into a laurel tree. In this opera, as in *Ariadne auf Naxos*, Strauss discovers something which has reference to his audience's everyday interest and occupations. The self-questioning of the outsider, the frustration of the civilized human being at being cut off from nature, the necessity of adopting disguises in love, and the dropping of disguises in anger, are themes that the audience can find within the action of the opera; and as they recognize them they may acknowledge Strauss's command of the means by which such subjects are discussed. And as the audience relate these themes to their own lives and ask themselves how the composer obtains such a command, it may be that their attention will be drawn to the meaning the mythic material has for Strauss himself.

Through the discussions in the *Capriccio* salon Strauss had been able to say something about his own assessment of opera. He can make delicate fun of the nineteenth-century conventions in the act of laughing at those of the eighteenth century. This is his old device from *Der Rosenkavalier*. The ironic and anachronistic reconstruction of a long-gone age is used to comment upon recent developments in opera. Rameau and Lully, with their delight in arias that just repeat simple phrases, may stand for the great men of the nineteenth century; while Gluck, blamed for losing the words in the uproar of the orchestra, and Mozart, accused of writing about domestic servants, Strauss nicely presents as his own forerunners. The form of the discussion, which is the form of the opera, becomes in Strauss's design an apology for his practice.

And Strauss presumes that his audience is ready to accept him as the proper heir of Gluck and Mozart and of all other great composers. When Daphne and Ariadne are dismissed as unsuitable subjects for a modern piece, the audience must remember not only Strauss's earlier success with just these subjects, but also the fact that in this he is the successor of Peri and Monteverdi. Strauss thinks of his enterprise as being the proper development of all that has been exciting and generative in the tradition. He finds in the work of the original opera composers an authority for all that is worthwhile in that historical development which leads directly to his own success.

Strauss appears to discover a fragile beauty and a harmonious order through each turn in the myths of Ariadne and Daphne. Desolation and fear become, in his telling of the stories, happiness and exultation. When Strauss was writing his operas about Ariadne and Daphne before the Second World War it was evidently still possible for him to celebrate the kindness of Dionysus and Apollo. Both operas end with the god uniting in love with the human. Not every composer has employed the myths in quite Strauss's way. The myths recur in opera precisely because they are patient of various interpretations. They provide composers with traditional yet original opportunities for the elucidation of themselves and their fellows. There is some difference, for example, between the rousing melodrama of *Ariadne auf Naxos* that Jiri Benda composed in 1775 and Darius Milhaud's *Opera-Minute*, *L'Abandon d'Ariane* of 1928, and other differences between the treatment of the story by Monteverdi and by Strauss. And other composers have felt more at ease with other myths. Lully and Gluck worked wonderful elucidations of their worlds from the yarn of Alcestis. Henze and Britten have shown us our own world through the myth of Dionysus' rout. And Harrison Bertwistle, in presenting in 1978 another version of the Orpheus story, is returning to that myth by which Dvořák, in *The Jacobin*, hinted at the history of the opera composer's art.

In Dvořák's realist, if not *verismo*, opera, Bohus returns to Bohemia from revolutionary France to find himself almost ousted from the affections of the local count, his father. He wins back his father's favour through the effective assistance of the Orpheus figure of the village musician. Like opera itself, the hero starts among the aristocracy, comes to accept the necessity of revolutionary action, is distrusted as a disrupter of convention, proffers a different order for 'reality', and achieves recognition through the vital power of music. The progress of opera from its seventeenth century beginnings and its present claim upon our attention are both properly understood only if this persistent relation to mythic motives is kept in mind.

THE FLORENTINE CAMERATA

Dryden, in the preface to his appallingly bad opera *Albion and Albanius* in 1685, admitted that he had not, in his study of opera, been able 'by any search, to get any light, either of the time when it began, or of the first author'. He had, however, 'probable reasons' for believing that some Italians, having observed the gallantries of the Spanish Moors, 'may possibly have refined upon those Moreque divertisements, and produced this delightful entertainment'. From out of this cloud of tentative clauses there came a bolder statement that the first operas were 'intended for the magnificence of some general time of joy' among the Italian princes.

Other nations remained for some time 'as much provincial to Italy as they were in the time of the Roman Empire'. The first opera in German was performed in 1627, the first in Spanish in 1629, and Dryden's own effort seems to have been designed with some missionary hope of persuading the English to welcome a vernacular opera, while all over Europe Italian troupes were singing their numberless native operas from a repertory whose earliest entertainments dated from a hundred years before Dryden composed his preface.

In 1585 Andrea Gabrieli had attempted to recreate Greek theatrical performance by setting the choruses of *Oedipus Rex* to music, but the history of opera more properly starts from the publication in 1600 by the Florentine poet Ottavio Rinuccini of his librettos for *Dafne* and *Euridice*. Both of these were Grecian shepherd pieces of a sadness surprisingly pleasing to those who were celebrating a princely marriage. It is certainly proper to recognize the claim of the courtly diversions of the Florentine Camerata in the first years of the seventeenth century to be the earliest examples of modern opera. That group of gifted and enthusiastic amateurs of literature and music would not, however, have been much pleased with a reputation for originality and innovation. Their whole endeavour was to recover for their contemporaries the virtues of the ancient Greek theatrical tradition. Those leisured humanists who first set up the conventions of opera wanted to make it plain that they were adopting a classical stance, and from the time of the Camerata onwards it has been from the Greeks that opera composers and librettists have claimed a lineage for their conventions.

Rinuccini wrote a preface for the published version of *Euridice*, and the librettist evidently thought of himself as issuing an artistic manifesto for his contemporaries. He remarks that all cultured persons agree that 'the ancient Greeks and Romans sang their entire tragedies on the stage', and that the only reason why modern plays are not performed in this way is the inferiority of modern music. However, cultured persons can appreciate that the Greek way is yet viable. The examples of *Dafne* and *Euridice* prove that modern men may challenge the ancients. The old conventions may be newly employed.

The patterning of seventeenth-century Italian court entertainment on the plays of the Greek tragedians and the music of the Greek composers was made at once the more and the less difficult by the almost total ignorance obtaining then as now of the conventions and performance of Greek music for the theatre. The Camerata poets were certainly careful in their reading of ancient commentators but they had no examples to confirm their understanding of what these authors meant by their remarks. Even now there is, apart from some pieces of Hellenistic music, only one piece known to modern critics of music for a Greek tragedy. This is a papyrus fragment, first published by Wessely in 1892, of a melody for a few lines of Euripides' *Orestes*. Not much to go on and the Camerata did not even have that much. But, armed with the assurance that the ancient music must have fitted itself to the inflection of the words, the Camerata intuited the nature of that music.

The music Jacopo Peri wrote for Rinuccini's *Dafne*, which was first performed during Florentine court festivities of 1597, has not survived. But the opera was certainly a success. Librettist and composer decided to do more such things. They collaborated with sensational success on *Euridice* for the wedding of Henry IV of France and Maria de Medici in 1600. This opera has survived. It evidences the composer's complete respect for the librettist's text. The music is in places little more than a harmonious background to a lyric intonation of the verses, and when the composer does allow himself a stirring tune or a sad melody he is careful not to impair the clarity of the text. The melodies are wholly lacking in any ornament that would obscure the text. Peri does wonders by varying the length of the sung syllables but he keeps his invention within this lucid limit. His deliberate avoidance of those elaborate devices common in contemporary ecclesiastical music is impressive testimony to his realization that the audience was keen to hear the words and follow the story.

And, at the very beginning of opera, librettist and composer had seized immediately upon that myth which was most powerfully concerned with their own activities. The story of the musician Orpheus and of the power of his singing to charm the creatures of the dark and win his love from death, and of his final frustration just when he thought he had imposed order on the world, was appreciated by Rinuccini and Peri as their own story.

Rinuccini and Peri understood the reference of the Orpheus myth to the relation between art and life, and to the artist's desire to impose order on reality. Orpheus, the greatest musician, is placed in situations which alternately support and question the artist's claim to be a guide through experience. Orpheus can do nothing to prevent the coming of death to Euridice, yet he can by his art make a way into death's kingdom beneath the earth; he can gain his wife's reprieve from that kingdom but he cannot govern his own emotions, losing her by looking back during his ascent to the world of the living. These first brave opera-makers tackled, in their work on this subject, the problem of evaluating art, and the basic truth that the gifts of the artist are not those which enable a man to manage in the crises of human life. The myth seemed eminently about themselves.

And the myth seemed to composers and audiences to be patient of further elucidation. The text that Rinuccini prepared for his Florentine friends was taken up and made into an opera not only by Peri but by Caccini, and in the very same year. The matter was important and worth repeating. At the beginning of opera there are a number of men as daring as Wagner, attempting just as surely as he in *Tannhäuser* or *Die Meistersinger*, to place the artist, find his value and accord him due reverence. And other composers in the generations immediately following worked at other versions of the same myth. Monteverdi in the seventeenth century, and Gluck in the eighteenth, each made of the Orpheus myth a means of renewing the practice of the opera composer's art. The myth enabled them to discover what opera might be and do. And the difference between the working method of Peri and of Monteverdi in dealing with the story is rather greater than that between Monteverdi and Gluck. At the beginning the development of opera proceeded apace.

LA FAVOLA D'ORFEO

The earliest practitioners were agreed that the composer should always take his lead from the librettist. The influential Count Bardi, one of the founder members of the Camerata, told Caccini to make it his chief aim in composing to arrange the verses well and ensure that they could be intelligibly declaimed. And the popular court composer, Cavalieri, in his instructions for those singing in his *La Rappresentazione di anima e di corpo*, stressed particularly that they 'must pronounce the words clearly so that they be understood'. Peri himself had been content to ensure that the meaning of Rinuccini's text came clearly to the audience. His method of plain accompaniment had been perfectly adapted to the taste of that audience. They had wanted to know what Rinuccini was saying. Alessandro Striggio was no less a poet or dramatist than Rinuccini but he could not be sure of such a control of his audience, and certainly he could not be sure of such a control of his composer. Though Striggio gained proper fame for his innovative dramatic verse, which he skilfully subjected to the demands of the action, he could not hope to be the centre of attention when the audience went to the *Orfeo* he wrote for Monteverdi. With this great opera of 1607 the operatic way of presenting love and death, gods and men, was if not quite perfected, rather more than rough-hewn. Monteverdi's contemporaries, rejoicing in his deft combination of such classic conventions as the messenger's account of off-stage events, with tunes of contemporary beauty, recognized a master. Silvia's narrative of the death of Euridice, and the brilliant, trilling song Orfeo in the underworld, were admired not simply because they were elegant in themselves but because they were deftly put together in one work of art. The composer was, for the first time, most evidently in charge. The audience recognized that something new had happened. And their relish for such a novelty was the beginning of the end for the old librettists and their classical conventions.

Orfeo was first performed at the Mantuan court in February 1607, probably in a simple concert version, but after its publication in 1609 the opera was recognized throughout Italy as the chief representative of 'the modern music'. The famous Mantuan singer, Francesco Rasi, who, evidently from the scene with Caronte, could master the most exacting music, was happily astounded by the many novelties of Monteverdi's score. Despite the old-fashioned sound of the eight-part sinfonia and the choral writing, *Orfeo* is a break-through work. Monteverdi's inventive success in this work opened a range of possibilities for opera.

Monteverdi, a great madrigal composer in the fellowship of Cipriano de Rore and Palestrina, was never content to work only according to the old forms. But it is not clear how far he realized that he was altering the balance of opera when he took the librettist's work to be an invitation for him to try out all sorts of new ideas. He seems almost by accident to have discovered the most effective of his musical innovations, the recitative. By this device he made himself the master of the text, able to determine the speed and sound of the verses according to the line of his music. Not that he was at all dismissive of the proper value of the words. Quite the contrary, indeed. There have been few composers who shared his reverence for the text. He attempted to make a musical expression which would parallel the rhetorical declamation of the actor in the contemporary theatre. But, and this is his peculiarity, he does not seem to have felt any obligation to the structures of the sentence or the paragraph. He seems to have set each word singly, and to have looked for the notes precisely fitted to each word in isolation from every other word. This produced an odd disturbance of the audience's expectations. The sense became difficult to follow and the beauty of the voice tempted the listener to neglect the meaning. Words seemed confusing, music harmonious. And the persuasion of music's greater order was increased in Monteverdi's operas by his employment of the *basso continuo*, a supportive accompaniment of continuous harmony beneath the vocal line which was startlingly modern in Monteverdi's time. The movement of the action was thus wholly musical. Everything happened in the music. The most immediately impressive confrontation was not in the drama, between hero and tyrant or hero and heroine, but between the human voice and the orchestral sound.

The regular instrumental procession in the *basso continuo* allowed the human voice an exhilarating freedom, a licence for almost any amount of flourishes beyond the formal pattern of the song. The listener is continually charmed by the elaborate trill and startled by the late entry of the voice, so that he is continually aware of the difference between what is done by the artist and his own expectation of order. The recitative becomes in *Orfeo* an instrument for Monteverdi's announcement of the effectiveness and the limitation of the human will. The voice in the recitative expresses the determination of the human being to express himself in his own way. The *basso continuo* persuades the audience that men can impose their wills on the world only at the risk of being brought into confrontation with the unchangeable character of existence. The audience is left to wonder uncomfortably about how far a man may go against the tendency of the world. It is particularly in the *Orfeo* that the recitative becomes, according to

Monteverdi's design, a perfect expression of the myth. Monteverdi's technique in the recitative was aimed at bringing the audience up short, making them aware of the tension, the dissonance, the fractured character of human experience. The recitative is the signal of the action in his *Orfeo*. And the action is not quite that of the confident Rinuccini.

Monteverdi presents Music as Prologue to the tale of Orfeo. With most conventional-seeming phrases Music is set to speak to the Mantuan court of Orfeo's glories. He is the hero as musician. When his tale is sung no bird should warble, no stream purl, no wind make moan. Nature is to attend on Art. This boasting of Music is continued in the claims made by Orfeo himself in the action of the opera. But Striggio's verses are given an ironic twist by Monteverdi, and the audience is gradually brought to entertain doubts of Music's power.

The great scene in which Orfeo, seeking his lost wife, arrives at the bank of the Styx and applies to Charon for permission to pass to Hades, is managed musically in such a way that an audience may come to question the claims of art. The scene begins with correct and graceful music, setting in ordered fashion the careful *terza rima* that Striggio provided. But when Orfeo has sung this regular verse it is evident that Charon is not to be persuaded by such things. The conventional music of the court will not work in the kingdom of the dead. The artist, therefore, breaks off the formal verse, the metre falls to pieces, and his passion bursts out in fitful tumblings of ungoverned recitative. At least that is how it sounds in performance. Monteverdi has deliberately broken verses which are, in the libretto, as regular as those he had set at the beginning of the scene. This breaking of the verse is followed by Orfeo's acceptance that he can achieve nothing further. And at this point Monteverdi discovers an ironic hint in Striggio's libretto and seizes upon it. Despite what almost every synopsis writer says in opera house programmes, Charon does not yield to the persuasions of formal art, music does not move him, he simply falls asleep. Orfeo claims a famous victory and crosses triumphantly to the other side.

It may be that the audience are still so complacently confident in the conventions of the story as they have learnt it from other sources that few will yet discern the quirks of Monteverdi's version. The scene in Hades which follows must, however, undeceive all who attend the opera. Pluto is persuaded by Proserpina's song celebrating his own great love for her, to allow Orfeo to have his Euridice again. It is wholly through the power of love that her release is secured. Pluto states this plainly. He says it twice. The chorus follows his example. But, when he is brought before the god to hear his judgement, Orfeo, without a word of thanks to Pluto or Proserpina, sings immediately a praise of his art, 'for in the kingdom of Tartarus you have won the victory over every spirit'. He ascribes everything to the music of his lyre. He must seem to the audience now a man who is quite unaware of how things really are. And music must be felt, rather uneasily, to be less than the musician claims.

Monteverdi asserted his control over the structure of the opera right to the end. He insisted that Striggio provide a new ending to the myth. Orfeo returns not to a world in which Dionysiac dancers destroy him and the order his music represents, but to that very grove where Music had so imperiously commanded Nature to be silent at the start of the opera. Now Orfeo appeals to the trees and the streams and the mountains to echo his grief. He admits that 'there is nothing else for me to do than to turn once more to you'. He needs Nature not Art if he is to mourn properly. At this Apollo descends and takes the hero into the heavens where he may contemplate the sun and stars and see in them the beauties of Euridice. This is a wholly new close to the myth and requires some explanation.

It is unlikely that Monteverdi shared Striggio's doubts about the suitability of too tragic an ending for a court entertainment. It is possible that his nerve failed him at the thought of the difficulties of making music for so violent a scene as the Bacchantes tearing Orfeo limb from limb. But, despite his not having discovered the aria as well as the recitative, Monteverdi would have found a way to express anything he wanted to. The close of

Orfeo is shaped so that the audience, as the machinery managed its most marvellous effect in raising Apollo and his poet to the clouds, should consider Monteverdi's meaning: in this world it is not possible to hold life within the confines of art, and artists should not pretend that they can impose order on reality. *Orfeo* reaches its climax not in a celebratory hymn to the artist, nor even in one to Apollo as lord of the arts, but with a chorus to the power eternal who will wipe away all tears. Only in a world of divine harmony can we hope for a resolution of those tensions in experience which Monteverdi brought the recitative to express.

Monteverdi's interpretation of the myth reveals a fine mind of pessimistic culture. In that *Orfeo* represents an important tradition in opera. There is, despite vulgar transmutations, an echo of *Orfeo* in even so unlikely a piece as *Tosca*. Monteverdi's dignified estimate of the artist's limitations has become in the famous aria '*Vissi d'arte*' a maudlin plea for sympathy for those who live for art. But, for once, Puccini does not allow himself to rest with such a statement. As Scarpia sardonically remarks of the opera singer, 'Tosca was never more tragic on the stage': it is all play-acting. Pretence has been made to confront reality. The singer is inadequate. Even when she adopts the ways of the world Tosca proves incompetent. Her lover, whom she supposed, like Orfeo, she had rescued from death, dies indeed and for ever. *Tosca* ends not with a song of eternal life but a sudden rush of melodramatic suicide, but even here Puccini follows Monteverdi, closing in the assurance that only the divine can make a final judgement, '*Avanti a Dio!*' *Tosca*, stiffened by such Monteverdian tradition, is the most effective of Puccini's works. But Monteverdian interpretations of art and life are not for everyone. There are many who require art, and therefore opera, to give them a sense of how to gain a harmonious world. Monteverdi's notions will not do for them. But even these may accept that Monteverdi has offered an interpretation of life and art precisely through his writing of an opera. *Orfeo* represents a musical conquest of the territory of meaning. Staggeringly beautiful in itself, *Orfeo* is a prophecy of what other composers, not Puccini only, may achieve. Monteverdi, by wholly musical means, made the audience attend to his account of the myth and appreciate its significance for him as an insight into the opera composer's situation.

Whatever one's opinion of the ending of *Orfeo*, it is difficult after attending to such a work to think of the history of opera in terms of a progress. Rather it becomes necessary to accept Monteverdi along with a number of later composers as a man who shaped something peculiarly his own and found in the making of an opera a way of putting across his sense of the world. His sense of the world and his expression of that sense differ from those of Mozart or Verdi, but are not in their difference inferior. Certainly his successes amongst his contemporaries were as splendid as those of later composers, and he attracted men of real artistry to the art form he had developed.

DIDO AND POPPAE

In 1608, the year after the Striggio version of the Orpheus myth had been taken up by Monteverdi, the first of those dangerous developments occurred which so often threatened to obscure the mythic character of opera. His sense of the myth of *Orfeo* being about himself persuaded Rinuccini that opera might be more openly human. With Monteverdi he put together an opera which showed their audience the bleak unhappiness of Ariadne on Naxos. This lively piece was performed at the wedding celebrations of Margherita of Savoy and Francesco Gonzaga in Mantua. Of *Arianna* only a few scraps of music and the great lament of the girl deserted by Theseus have survived. It is proper to assume that the happy pair did not identify with the abandoned princess and the caddish prince. The legend would have been for them and their revelling guests simply a fiction about someone else. By their choice of subject Rinuccini and Monteverdi had taken a false step. They had removed from the stage that mythic universality which had been manifested in the *Orfeo*. And, since no member of the audience could long remain content with the way Rinuccini had told him the fiction or with the pale personages who stepped within his libretto, opera moved further from its mythic provenance at the command of those who wanted a livelier narrative and more interesting characters. This was accomplished by the greatly-talented Giovanni Busenello.

Busenello was a rich Venetian lawyer who had no need to make his libretto-making pay. He wrote slowly and carefully, and entrusted his verses to only the most distinguished composers. He wrote five texts. Four for Cavalli, one for Monteverdi.

In all five of his librettos, but especially in the *Didone* for Cavalli, in 1641, and *L'Incoronazione di Poppea* for Monteverdi in 1643, Busenello demonstrated the capacity of opera to present a variety of credible persons. He places all sorts of characters before the audience in short telling phrases. And Busenello's characters move within the real world. In the *Didone* his Carthaginian queen does not really expect the affair with Aeneas to last for ever, and after he sails for Rome she makes do with the suitor who has been on hand since the first act. In his libretto for Monteverdi Poppea may be in love with Nero but she realizes fully the necessity of marrying the emperor if she is to be safe in the political world. In *Giulio Cesare* (1646) Busenello displays in epic manner the history of the whole Roman world from the defeat of Pompey to the assassination of Julius, a history of treachery and corruption and ephemeral display to which the only dignified opposition is that of the stoic. This is a grand work which upturns a good many of the conventions in the very process of employing them. Just as 'prosperity' is shown to be 'unhappy', so the 'happy ending', the *lieto fine* of the conventional opera librettist, is shown to be ambiguous when the tyrant has been magnanimous all through the action. And the audience is continually reminded that this is the world as it has happened and may be happening around them. Busenello's world of epic events was not inhabited by dictators, emperors and courtesans alone. In the *Poppea* the emperor's love-making is plotted in counterpoint with some rough stuff among the servants, and is first presented to the audience through the weary comments of the soldiers who have been set to guard Poppea's room through the night. Similarly in the

Statira of 1655 the grandeur of the Persian spectacle is undercut by the explicit comment in the servant's aria on the miseries that such a war must bring to ordinary folk.

Busenello's skill in presenting the common run of person was exercised within a set of conventions which took their shape from theories of classical art. He had to employ the forms appropriate for an emperor in setting forth a sentry. In doing so successfully he gave each of his operas an epic character which made huge demands upon the composer's skill.

That composers and librettists have never quite let go the hope of making opera an epic art in the manner Busenello suggested is demonstrated in the continuous tradition from Busenello's *Giulio Cesare*, through Metastasio's *Attilio Regolo*, Wagner's *Ring* and Berlioz's *Les Troyens*; in the nomenclature of the reform of opera by Brecht, who laboured for the establishment of 'Epic-opera'; as well as in Prokofiev's *War and Peace*, which, though the composer hoped to write a piece about a few characters shuttled into different contexts, came, under official pressure, to be a grand epic opera of Soviet glory. Such developments in opera do not all, of course, fulfil the demands made by Busenello's contemporary, Dryden, that anyone who would write an epic should obey the authority and example of Homer, and that 'whoever undertakes the writing of an opera is obliged to imitate the design of the Italians'. And there is not much in the work of Italian composers contemporary with Busenello or immediately following his time to suggest that that nation had truly achieved a control of the epic design. Monteverdi was certainly responsive to Busenello's challenge, but Cavalli seems not to have been so happy in either the *Giulio Cesare* or the *Statira*. The great difficulty was to match Busenello's adoption of the heroic conventions with a musical presentation of common folk which would have an inventiveness equal to that of his brilliantly varied verses.

Perhaps Busenello expected too much of Cavalli. His epic vision was not quite within the composer's comprehension. The librettist's appreciation of the kind of experience that the Monteverdi *Orfeo* represented led him to consider other ways of communicating such experience in opera. In his librettos Busenello attempted to open out conventions which had their origins in Greek myth so that they would express common humanity in a common circumstance. The audience should be brought to realize afresh their own capacity for mythic experience. Busenello had done the proper thing. He was certainly making a move towards the future of opera when he shifted the subject of his opera from the hidden impulse to the historical action. But he made it before composers and audiences were ready for such radical reassessments of themselves.

THE FRENCH TRADITION

The immediate effect of the workings of Busenello's intelligence was not a general new discovery of meaning but a repetition of old disputes. Busenello was mostly admired for his skill in the handling of epic material. The *Giulio Cesare* was not thought remarkable for either its author's gently ironic stance or for the subtle delineation of human weakness and nobility, but for its panoramic quality. It seemed to his contemporaries that, in making such a huge matter his subject and carrying it through so magnificently, Busenello not only demonstrated his own poetic and dramatic powers, but opened again the discussion of who ought to be in charge of an opera's structure and meaning. It is most paradoxical that it was within the work of the most autocratic of French composers that Busenello's care for the multitude was most successfully matched.

Monteverdi had no immediate heirs in Italy, merely a gaggle of followers. But in France Lully evidently appreciated the greatness of Monteverdi and determined to do something of equal glory. Lully worked in a wholly French context. The operas of the Italian troupes patronized by Mazarin had, when Lully began his career, been for some time unpopular at the French court. They were foreign, they were expensive, and they were not so much to the liking of the young Louis XIV as the native ballets in which he could himself perform to great applause. If there had to be opera at the court then at least it should not be foreign, and, if expensive, it should at least contribute to the glory of the Sun King. In 1672 Louis granted Lully sole rights in the presentation of opera in France, with the command that his talents should be exercised in the promotion of the royal and French interest. Lully had replaced the librettist Perrin as holder of the royal patent. He did not see the significance of this passing of control; and he made his command seem natural even to those who held to the old notion of opera as chiefly the sphere of the librettist.

Saint-Evremond in his famous letter to the Duke of Buckingham in 1677, in which he described opera as 'a bizarre mixture of poetry and music', insisted that 'the music must be there for the sake of the poetry, not the poetry for the sake of the music', and even put the sentiment in plainer terms: 'the composer must obey the orders of the poet'. But a composer of genius was not expected to conform to the pattern of ordinary musicians' lives. Saint-Evremond allowed that 'Lully should be exempted'. Lully certainly demanded the exemption. Nicholas Boindin in 1719 described the way in which Lully dictated the terms of his collaboration with Quinault. After a committee of the Academy had vetted the libretto, Lully 'examined the poetry they had screened and corrected', he went through it 'word by word', and ruthlessly 'cut out half the lines until he was satisfied'. Poor Quinault had his libretto for *Phaëton* returned twenty times in 1683 until he offered something which pleased the demanding composer. And Lully directed everything to the increase of his own reputation so successfully that Saint-Evremond remarked that 'the audience thinks of Lully a hundred times more often than of Theseus or Cadmus'.

Lully fulfilled the royal command. The king himself was celebrated as the sun god Apollo in the *Cadmus et Hermione* of 1673, the first year of his holding the patent, and this was a theme that the composer was never careless enough to neglect. But at the same time Lully was writing opera for the French. He was not simply hoping to entertain an audience of one. He never managed to present the complex feelings so surely expressed in

Monteverdi's recitatives, he never managed to get his heroes singing freely as in the classic Italian opera, but he certainly managed to do something peculiarly his own with the choral part. Whatever everybody thought and felt in response to a situation, that certainly he could express. Neither Monteverdi before nor Gluck later could have done as well as Lully in the great choral pieces he devised. And equally they could not have managed the grand ballet sequences that Lully offered his audiences. Here, as with his choruses, the composer could create a credible representation of ordinary folk in action. He knew exactly how to register the common humanity of men's responses to the plight of their fellows. Lully presented the participation of the crowd in the heroic story. The famous choral mourning for Alceste in which Admetus, her less than devoted husband, at last joins, is perhaps the best known of the many examples of Lully's sureness in bringing all sorts of persons to the expression of a common emotion.

This was precisely the way to explore the mythic character of opera, and the possibilities of opera as an expression of common human awareness. The shift had still to be made from Greek to modern settings for such elucidations of contemporary consciousness. The mythic Orpheus most appropriately gave way to Poppea, without any loss of immediacy, and Poppea properly gave way to the girl in the crowd. But this was more difficult for audiences to apprehend. Only the most sensitive and noble composers could appreciate the girl in the crowd as they appreciated Orpheus and Poppea.

The Italians who had come to Paris in 1647 to perform Luigi Rossi's *Orfeo* brought a deal of dislike upon themselves by their attitude of despising everything French. Their opera failed to please and a lot of money was lost in the venture by their patron Cardinal Mazarin. Lully eschewed both their myth and their financial failure.

In his opera *Alceste ou Le Triomphe d'Alcide* Lully had made a successful bid to escape the *Orfeo* tradition. For him the great wonder of the story of Orpheus was not the enduring devotion of a magically-gifted husband for his wife, nor the transforming power of the musician, but the emergence of a human being from the grip of death. The Alceste story retained only this one of the *Orfeo* themes. In making it his subject Lully removed the heroic virtue and the artistic power and expressed simply the common human hope of life. Louis XIV might enjoy the sense of his identity with Apollo, but Lully offered more than that single flattery. He made a determined effort to present, through opera, the meaning of the myth for everyone in his audience. He intended to rouse in them, through his music, a sense of the humanity they shared with all who were nervous at the contemplation of death, and hopeful at the thought of an enduring life with those they loved.

By relating myth to the immediacies of life in musical terms, Lully showed a way of shaping opera that was to engage composers as diverse as Gluck, whose *Alceste* is a remarkable celebration of the human, and Egon Wellesz, who in 1924 had considerable success with the *Alkestis* he made from Hofmannsthal's play. The Italians made the myth of Orpheus accessible to musicians. Lully made it accessible to everyone.

Lully could not, however, ignore the primary financial patronage of the monarch. In his famous opera *Cadmus et Hermione* he had ventured to the fringes of the Dionysian cult. He may have wondered about the strange forces which rise in all men, for he was sensitive enough to such human oddities, but he did not make such wonderings into an opera. Cadmus was the father of Semele and, by the grace of Zeus, grandfather of Dionysus. But Lully's circumstance ensures that his design was wholly Apollonian. The monarch rejoiced to see himself again in the sun god, bestowing on his grateful people the gifts of order, beauty and obedience. It remained for a greater composer to make an opera from the possibilities of Semele's story.

Such is the extraordinary snobbery of the ordinary man and woman that audiences grew restive and demanded something grander as the subject of opera. And their demand was not for a return to the hidden wonder of a mythic order, but to a more easily recognizable social order. Opera should not be about themselves but about the grander and stranger persons of popular romance. Everything was to be put at a remove from their own outward action. And therefore at further remove from their own inward experience.

Even sophisticated critics and creative artists shared this evaluation of opera's demesne. Opera, wrote Dryden, might be defined as a 'fiction represented by vocal and instrumental music' whose characters 'are generally supernatural, as gods, and goddesses, and heroes, which at least are descended from them'. The subject, therefore, 'being extended beyond the limits of human nature' allowed the composer and librettist to show 'that sort of marvellous and surprising conduct which is rejected in other plays'. Dryden is here beginning to consider that difficult question of the precise distinction of opera from other arts: from the carnival spectacle, the oratorio and the play. It is significant that he does so by reference to the marvels of operatic plots. This may seem rather thin as an aesthetic distinction, and in its emphasis upon that part of the collaboration which belongs to the librettist is doubtless reflecting Dryden's own delight in his poetic character, but it suggests that unless there were present a recognizably distinguished composer, it was still possible for critics and public to think of opera as a romantic fiction and astounding display.

MECHANICAL HEAVENS

During the course of the seventeenth century opera had become popularly associated with diversions not at all of a kind with Busenello's careful delineation of human variousness, or Monteverdi's generous invention of lovely melodies. Those who paid for opera had demanded rather less civilized delights. They had commissioned librettists and composers to devise operas which would offer opportunities for the grand display of marvellous effects. The engineer came into his own. When in 1632 the Barberini family built a theatre in Rome their architect was instructed to provide a proscenium arch grand enough to hide elaborate machinery from view. The gods must be able to come and go, descend and ascend with marvellous majesty. As the gods came from the prologue and epilogue into the main action, they brought with them a train of heavenly cloud and glory. The pulley and the firework became instruments of operatic orthodoxy. The fanciful librettist, Giulio Rospigliosi, who became Pope Clement IX, was famous for his skill in devising operas which gave room for spectacles of immense grandiosity.

But the Roman spectacle at last overdid itself and the marvels, when imitated in the Venetian public theatres, proved too expensive for commercial managements, and even a trifle boring to the public. By the close of the seventeenth century most of those interested in opera were ready to applaud some hardy reformer. The fourteen members of the Arcadian Academy, founded in Rome in 1692, demanded 'simplicity' of their composers. As in the earliest days of opera 'simplicity' seems to have been associated with a pastoral tone, hardly antique in origin and quite unrelated to the contemporary life. And in Venice a pleasant satire of *Il teatro alla moda*, which mocked the elaborate conventions of the city's operas, was composed in 1720 by Benedetto Marcello, a member of the Council of the Forty, and a moderately skilful composer. He was thus in a fair position, economically, politically, and artistically, to make fun of the professionals. A man who would engage in controversy with composers, librettists, singers, and management, without at least one of Marcello's advantages had better sit on his hands and go to the theatre no more. He was, moreover, endowed with a delightful wit. And, in an age which was pleased to think itself as renewing classical virtues in art, Marcello was distinguished in having read and understood the great classical dramatists. He was not to be bamboozled by the pompous claims that opera-makers made for themselves as the heirs of Aeschylus and Euripides, or even of Seneca.

An opera librettist should indeed, Marcello says, if he wants to be modern, be wholly innocent of Greek and Latin classic authors, 'after all,' as he says, 'the old Greeks and Romans never read the modern writers'. All he need know, Marcello mocks, is a smattering of modern technical terms from mathematics, chemistry, medicine and law, so that he can deck his verses with high-sounding references to these various disciplines and astound the simpler folk in his audience. He should also, as a practical man of the theatre, equip himself with the essential information about how much time the engineer requires for shifting the elaborate sets necessary for any self-respecting operatic spectacle. This would set the length of his verses for each of his arias. And he should find some opportunity to employ the talents of a good bear. Thus armed he should begin writing from line to line never worrying where the story is going. 'The disintegration of the drama as an entity and the intense boredom of the audience are of no importance in connection with all this.' And he should bring the whole to a grand conclusion with a chorus in praise of the sun, the moon, or the impresario. If, as a literary man, he wrote a grand preface to the printed versions of his piece, the librettist should end with a humble disclaimer of responsibility for the success of the piece, allowing all to be the work of the composer and the theatre bear, and for the neglect of classical models, allowing all to be the result of the presumption of the singers and the whim of the bear. If the piece failed he should declare that he was given orders by the bear to cut the best lines and substitute poorer verses.

Marcello took his delight in the trained beast to the lengths of proposing an opera on *The Bear in the Ship*, in which the animal protagonist and the engineer would both have been given appropriate scope.

With and without Marcello's command of satiric wit, those who took opera seriously in the early eighteenth century were demanding a renewal of the forms in which it was then straitened. They were ready for the *opera seria* of what has become known as 'the first Italian reform'.

THE FIRST REFORM

The beginnings of *opera seria* were ordered by the great Apostolo Zeno (1669–1750), who became Caesarean Poet at the Austrian court in 1718. Zeno was almost indifferent to music and convinced that all an opera required in order to be an artistic success was a carefully 'classical' text. He did, certainly, have some sense of what Greek tragedy had been about. He knew at least that it was not primarily a drama of deities descending to set men and women dancing in a ballet. Zeno demanded that opera should concern itself not with the sports of the gods and nymphs but with the emotional entanglements of characters of the highest credibility. He saw to it that each character of his drama engaged the attention and sympathy of the audience by being given the opportunity to express himself in a grand exit-aria. The composer had to provide his best endeavours at those moments in the opera which the librettist had determined to be the appropriate pause in his action. But Zeno certainly knew his business, and composers were prepared to accept his command. His librettos were set again and again well into the nineteenth century.

Zeno established that the emotions of human beings and the twists of action that the free play of these emotions brought about were the true subjects of opera. He was interested in the wide sweep of love and anger, and the sudden rearrangement of men by infatuation and death, and he encouraged his audience to look for some order among the sudden twists by placing his most dramatic reversals at the ends of acts and leaving them to discuss the possibilities of the action during the interval. It is a technique popular among the writers of television serials today. It is a technique more proper in the melodramatist than the poet, and indeed Zeno was not much interested in words. He was succeeded, however, as Caesarean Poet by the most literate and elegant of librettists, the great Metastasio.

The urchin Pietro Trapassi, found in the streets of Rome by Vincenzo Gravina, a member of the Arcadian Academy, was adopted by him, and on his place in society being so wholly altered, was appropriately called by him Metastasio. The boy grew up, squandered a considerable inheritance, fell in love with a singer, La Romanina, and for her wrote *Didone Abbandonata* in 1724. It was a grand success. Success followed success until, in

1729 he was summoned to Vienna. He remained at the Austrian court until his death in 1782.

Metastasio was a master of the spare method. He set about giving artistic dignity to the hasty innovations of the careless Zeno. According to strict rules which he ascribed to Greek method, six or perhaps eight characters, human beings and not gods, engaged in a series of situations throughout three acts, and were in turn each forced to consider the proper emotional response to a situation and to formulate this response in brilliant exit-arias. The line of the action was designed so that aria opportunities for the aristocratic characters sung by the *primo uomo*, a castrato, the *prima donna*, and the *primo tenore*, occurred at carefully spaced moments throughout the length of the opera. The sequence of conflicts of love and reason and honour was brought to an end by the intervention of a generous king or descending god. These formal characteristics make up a paradigm of *opera seria*. With classic neatness Metastasio ruled out all comic scenes, turning away with some distaste from the kind of thing which had rendered human Busenello's grand epic sequences, though sometimes he did allow a less than solemn love story to go on as a sub-plot among the political scenes. Within the frame of the main action Metastasio habitually placed a great and perplexed person who had to examine carefully himself and his situation before taking a decisive step. Metastasio was passionately interested in the workings of the human mind and heart at moments of crisis. *L'Olympiade* is entirely concerned with the convolutions of Licida's mind, and *Attilio Regolo*, his great work which he published from 1740 to 1750, is a study of the great Roman's contemplation of an angry world as he makes his decision to return to Carthage as a prisoner. Metastasio was skilful enough to make this careful interior analysis attractive to the fun-loving public of the fashionable world. He placed the recitative and the aria so carefully that no one could grumble at the contemplative character of his heroes. His success in this matter was based on his happy realization that if there were something exciting going on in the music it was possible to make any audience pay attention to a serious argument. In the contemplative recitative which he gave the composer to set before the aria the situation could be examined and the audience readied for the brilliant expression of the character's emotional response in the aria which completed his scene. The paradox of Metastasio's working method was that he took the acknowledged supremacy of the melody as something which he could use for his librettist's design. The action of a Metastasio opera moves in a musical progression at the bidding of the librettist. At least this is how Metastasio meant the action to move.

Voltaire much admired the way in which Metastasio reformed opera. He seemed 'Greek' in all he did. Voltaire maintains in his preface to *Semiramis* in 1746 that 'the Italian recitative is precisely the melopoeia of the ancients', and that 'the new choruses' in Metastasian opera 'resemble the ancient choruses all the more closely in that their music is different from that of the recitatives, just as the strophe, epode and antistrophe were sung by the Greeks in a manner different from that of the melopoeia of the scenes'. For Voltaire the rationale of opera as a music drama rather than as a spoken one resided in the peculiar Metastasian grandeur. His heroes being men of acknowledged and historical greatness, 'one began to see why feelings so radically different from ours must be expressed in such a different manner'. If Dryden concentrated on the marvellous as distinguishing opera from play, Voltaire concentrated on the intensity of human passion which drove Metastasian characters beyond the limits of speech and into song. The inner force of the situation exploded appropriately as opera.

Voltaire could frame reasons for himself why the words had to be sung. Others were less perceptive and supposed simply that the music was intended to add its peculiar decoration to an exotic entertainment. Such members of an audience were likely to accept a situation in which others besides Metastasio had a say in the presentation of the evening's diversion.

When in full comand of the enterprise, Metastasio was capable of structuring a precise frame within which the rush of human passion could find decent expression. But he could not always be in control. Once the text had been given to a composer all sorts of untoward things might happen. Sometimes he refused to surrender his libretto to a composer he thought inadequate. *Attilio Regolo*, that work of his which he most prized, he kept out of the composers' hands for a decade, considering it far too good for them. And though between 1737 and 1745, when he was in Italy, Gluck had set half a dozen of the Metastasio texts, the librettist never trusted him to do the right thing for his verses. Even in those performances where Metastasio felt that he could make the composer accept his direction, the librettist was conscious of being but seldom in control of the singers. These were ever on the look out for a chance to make the evening an occasion of personal triumph.

Metastasio's command was particularly vulnerable at the very moment when he required it most. His careful psychological drama depended on the composer's appreciation of the recitative. But the composers to whom he gave the texts were often content to set the recitative in a dry manner, lavishing their arts upon the climactic aria at the end of the scene. And the singers were always ready to skip the dry stuff and get on to the show piece. Voltaire, seeking the classic virtue of the Metastasian text he had read in his study, heard in the opera house 'the trills of an effeminate though brilliant voice' whose display was achieved 'at the expense of interest and common sense'.

The brilliant voice was generally that of the leading *castrato* singer who knew himself to be a star attraction for the crowds in the theatre. The *castrati* were generally not interested in the story or the characters of the opera, and their habit of rushing into the great aria displays made it impossible for any in the audience, even if they had so wished, to discover the plan of Metastasio's tight-knit text. So the audience ceased to expect the plot of an opera to make sense and rested content with the astounding displays of the singers. The exit-aria which Metastasio had made the contemplative summary of the action within strict rules of placing, timing, form and imagery, became an embellished and totally undisciplined exhibition of technical mastery.

THE SECOND REFORM

In such a situation a demand arises for someone other than librettist or singer to take charge of the operatic enterprise. The demand for a new reform came in Francesco Algarotti's *Essay on Opera* in 1775. It was taken up by the enterprising young librettist Calzabigi who went off to Gluck with the message that he should return to the wonders of Greece. Gluck himself was not really much interested in classic virtues. Nor did he care for the vitality of Jungian archetypes. Gluck so managed the old mythic subjects that in his telling they became quite demythologized. Though Grimm may have declared on attending his operas that 'I forget that I am in an opera house and think I am hearing a Greek tragedy', Gluck was totally ignorant, as were Winkelmann and Lessing, of the classical civilizations. He certainly responded, however, to the fashionable enthusiasm for decadent Hellenistic culture. He was ready to appropriate any artistic convention which offered him a way of doing what he wanted. The carelessness with which Gluck viewed all theorization may be gauged from his contented return after the reform triumph of *Iphigénie en Tauride* to the older-fashioned stuff of *Écho et Narcisse*. Gluck was prepared to work on any commission as long as he was given total artistic control of the opera.

Algarotti had supposed opera to be capable of anything. All forms of art might be brought within its frame. 'No method more effectual hath been imagined by human invention to afford a delightful entertainment to ingenious minds, than that all-accomplished and harmonious performance, by way of excellence called OPERA.' But Algarotti had felt the need of some over-seeing mastery of so many elements. He looked for someone to provide a purposive ordering of the parts, someone of vigorous and intelligent sensitivity. Gluck was ready to take on such a responsibility whether or no he was conceived to be working as a reform composer. Calzabigi had a number of interesting maxims about 'the simple way' of the ancients, and 'the Greek ideal' of true art, and Gluck was quite prepared to operate with these. He was equally prepared to employ complex, fantastic and truly novel instruments if he saw a use for them in his design. And he was prepared to use old-fashioned devices with whatever minimal transformations as might be necessary to give them the look of being his own latest invention. In the *Alceste* of 1767 Gluck was still using the old form of recitative with *basso continuo*, but placing the Monteverdian device at somewhat surprising moments of the action so that it seemed at such times a recent discovery. In the *Iphigénie en Aulide*, which sounded so much more modern to his first audiences, he had not really given up the dry recitative but he had supplied the *continuo* in the string parts rather than in the harpsichord. This produced a novel sound without in any way requiring him to rethink the conventions within which the vocal part was written. It is well to hold in mind that the famous innovation of syncopated violas at '*Le calme rentre dans mon cœur*' in *Iphigénie en Tauride* of 1778 are not typical of Gluck's imagination.

The only really new device of the reform was the use of the French ballet in a context whose characteristics were otherwise Italianate. The Gluck partnership with Calzabigi began, significantly, with their being introduced to one another by Durazzo, the Director General of Spectacles at the Viennese court. Gluck was always delighted to accept the assistance of such persons. And certainly he never ceased to find the ballet a pleasing diversion in opera. He got better at integrating the ballet in the total design of an opera, but he never got tired of it. The interrupting ballet in *Alceste*, the full dancing climax of the scene in the temple of Eros at the end of *Orfeo*, and the Fury ballet of *Iphigénie en Tauride* which forwards the action and makes its meaning clearer to the audience, are examples of the different things Gluck learnt to do with this element of the French opera tradition, but the differences between the ballet of *Alceste* and the ballet of *Iphigénie en Tauride* are not particularly revelatory of the workings of a reform.

Gluck's realization that the spectacular element of an opera, however delightful he and his audiences found it, must be kept within a formal pattern led him to share Zeno's old enthusiasm for clear-cut plots, strong structural dialogue and impressive key words which would make the audience aware immediately of what was going on in the story. Gluck was never afraid to hammer the simplest idea home. No one in his audience could fail, for example, to notice the repetition of Orfeo's cry '*Euridice!*' at the start of his treatment of the legend, but neither could they fail to be impressed by that repetition. To see Gluck at work is not to be unaffected by his work. The cry both announces exactly where Gluck is starting his version of the story, and emotionally involves the audience at the start of the performance. More carefully concealed, but effective in just the same manner, is the echo of phrases from one scene to another in the *Iphigénie en Tauride*. The phrase in which Oreste declares that calm has come again to his heart is perfectly placed to recall to the audience the scene at the beginning of the opera in which Iphigénie had declared '*Le calme reparait, mais au fond de mon cœur, hélas, l'orage habite encore.*' And if such effects are partly attributable to the ingenuity of the librettist, there can be no doubt that Gluck's anticipation of the Wagnerian delight in recurring snatches of melody from scene to scene is a wholly musical working-out of his consistent understanding of opera structure.

Gluck's inability to be simply a reform composer is to be explained, therefore, in terms of his determination to be master of all that concerned the making of an opera, and not at all by his lack of composing principle. And it was precisely his determination to do things as he wanted that brought about his one recognizable reform of the tradition which he had received. Demanding total control of the opera in order to ensure its being a reflection of his intention, Gluck insisted on the singers surrendering their pretensions to be creative artists. While in the performance of the operas of his predecessors a singer of an elaborated aria might have drawn attention to a character which was wholly out of line with the movement of the narrative which the composer had in mind, and the graceful decoration of a phrase might once have landed a stress on an image or an emotion that the composer had meant to be but lightly touched upon, now the singers were instructed to resist the temptation of any such improper rhetoric. They were not to initiate any modification of the tale or of the phrase. To Wagner this seemed a startling development towards the dominance of the composer. In an essay for *Opera and Drama* in which he was both claiming himself to be the true heir of the Gluck manner of writing opera, and proclaiming himself free of the trammels of all past practice, Wagner declared: 'The so famous revolution of Gluck, which has come to the ears of many ignoramuses as a complete reversal of the views previously current as to opera's essence, in truth consisted merely in this: that the musical composer revolted against the wilfulness of the singers.' 'Henceforth,' and Wagner is suitably cheerful at the prospect, 'the sceptre of opera passes definitely to the composer'. But though the singer was defeated, aria, recitative, and ballet 'stand in the operas of Gluck as they did before him, and as they still stand, with scarcely an exception, today'. Wagner was disappointed in the actuality of the reform whose theory was so widely proclaimed, but Gluck's organizing genius had certainly secured the composer's full control of the structure and effect of an opera.

Wagner might also have acknowledged that Gluck's effective reduction of the old mythic material to the interplay of individual character and circumstance was as important for his work as it was for Verdi's *opera di sentimento*. Gluck's operas, by rendering the public myths personal, opened the way for Wagner to render general, and indeed mythic, the individual stories of persons who were far from Greek. Though Wieland Wagner came to think of Tristan as an Oedipus, the composer had, through Gluck's initial work, escaped the force of such paradigms, and obtained a freer command of all his sources and resources.

It is remarkable that Gluck's command of others should have been equalled by his command of himself. He seems to have come early to the modest conclusion that he lacked the musical resources to shape the recitative in the tense manner of Monteverdi. He learnt, therefore, how the recitative might be relieved of its function in the revelation of character and simply be employed as a contrasting introduction to the aria. Musically this meant that he had to develop the *basso continuo* into a fully orchestrated sound so that it should lead more easily into the aria. The Monteverdian contrast between voice and continuous harmony was sacrificed for the necessary preparations of the declamatory aria. The effect, therefore, is not one of tension or of the sudden rush of a human being's decision to act, as it was in Monteverdi's recitative writing, but of a man coming by a gradual and reasoning process to the conclusion of a steady line of thought. The music is not fractured but progressional. This has its effect upon the dramatic action, and Gluck's realization of this effect is an excellent example of the ways in which Gluck proved again and again that he was a properly dramatic composer, and not a constructor of music for someone else's drama. The operation of the recitative and aria in progressive and coherent style made a character's decision seem not one of whim but of an inevitable will declaring itself.

In Gluck's revolutionary version of the myth Orfeo is a man in control. In the scene in which the Furies bar his way to the land of the dead, Orfeo is not broken by his passion and its frustration as in the comparable scene in Monteverdi's version, but is a man assured of his own capacity to persuade. And he is right to be so assured. It is the passion-swayed Furies who are gradually reduced to silence by his steadfast determination. In this treatment of the story, as in others, it is evident that the figure of Orfeo has become a figure of the composer. The Orfeo represents Gluck's notion of the composer in calm and total command of the situation because of his musical authority. This is an understanding which conditions every dramatic moment in the opera. The return of Euridice is not here a catastrophe for which the hero is unprepared. Orfeo turns back, knowing what is going to happen, and knowing also that there is no other way of convincing her that he does indeed love her. Orfeo accepts the consequences. He wills events. He does not lose command. It is a triumph of dramatic integrity that Gluck and Calzabigi should have found a way of demonstrating his consistency of mind and its disparate effectiveness in the scenes with the Furies and Euridice.

It seemed even to many of their contemporaries a triumph of

idiotic sentimentality that two such gifted men could find no other way than the reunion of husband and wife to bring their piece to a conclusion. Cupid arrives to tell Orfeo that Euridice's second death has simply been a trial set by the gods and that he can now have her back. This comes near to making nonsense of the earlier careful delineation of their clashing tempers and their inability to change either their characters or the situation in which they found themselves. For a hero to be told by Cupid that all his efforts have been made in a fictional situation, that his experience has been a journey into the unreal, seems perversely destructive of all that Gluck has presented of human nobility. While Monteverdi's hero could in his version of the legend properly be taken out of it at the end and received into a more appropriate clime, Gluck knew that his hero and heroine were at home in the world and must, if they were to be happy, rest in the world, and he discovered that no audience would believe the gods' offer of such an earthly solution of the difficulties into which the characters had been driven. The plot seemed at this point to militate against the music which nobly declared the self-knowing and determining Orfeo to be too humanly dignified for such glib treatment. And if audiences in Gluck's day were grudgingly prepared to allow his command of the shape of the legend, audiences are not now at all ready to applaud the way he shaped it. Wieland Wagner was congratulated on his cutting, in his Munich production, of Gluck's happy ending, and his substitution of a formal repetition of the mourning scene with which the opera opens. But it is generally unwise to throw aside the design of an acknowledged master. He is likely to have good reason for his strangenesses. At least it should give one pause to discover that just the same kind of happy ending is contrived for Gluck's masterpieces in the French manner.

ALCESTE AND IPHIGÉNIE

The example of Lully had prepared the way for Gluck to work with tales of less remote characters than Orpheus and the gods.

His own attempt at an *Alceste* opera, made before his arrival in Paris, is famous for its prefatorial remarks about abuses present in most contemporary compositions and performances; the tiresome *ritornelli*, repeats of musical phrases, which repeatedly held up the action, and the singers' cadenza displays. He proclaimed himself the servant of clarity and simplicity, and he declared himself wholly satisfied with the complementary clarity and simplicity of Calzabigi's libretto for *Alceste*. So this is a manifesto opera. And together with a review of matters of musical style Gluck and Calzabigi knew themselves to be conducting a review of conventional plot and characters. The story of Alcestis, who offers to die and go to the underworld in place of her husband, is most movingly told. Alceste's aria announcing her defiance of the gods of the underworld, '*Divinités du Styx*', is a stupendous musical expression of her grief and courage. And almost equally admirable is the declaration of her husband Admetus that he will follow her into death, a declaration which he is, quite against the way in which Euripides told the story, ready to make good by his suicide. After much strongly written music the entrance of Apollo, and his handing back Alceste to her husband is perhaps rather too tamely mechanical. The staged arrival of the god is a little too smooth as a resolution of so much human pain. Gluck himself may have thought the scene required some greater acknowledgement of human nobility. In the Paris version of 1776 Admetus does indeed die and then, with the aid of Hercules, wrests Alceste from the power of death. Apollo's entrance in this version is simply to acknowledge that the love of husband and wife has given them new life. The god is made simply another member of the applauding audience. It is a human triumph. *Alceste* prepares the way for the fully human action of Gluck's French masterpieces.

The first of these operas, *Iphigénie en Aulide*, with a libretto by du Roullet, the attaché at the French embassy in Vienna, seemed to many Frenchmen evidence of there being at last a composer who could hold all the elements of opera together with as firm a grasp as that of Lully. Gluck actually returned to Lullian precedents so far as to set a Quinault libretto for *Armide*. This may have been a conscious move to court popularity in Paris, but it must have been not only his wish to do something in the French manner but his appreciation of Lully's mastery of opera-writing which led him to adopt the great man's techniques in the management of the chorus. There is in the *Iphigénie en Aulide* a glorious moment when the angry Greeks bully Calchas to provide a sacrifice for the gods. The shout rises in vigorous tones: '*Nommez-nous la victime*', and through this shout the catastrophe is brought nearer. In this opera, nicely derived from that play of Racine which Diderot had thought the perfect opera libretto, Gluck presents a situation, parallel to that in the *Orfeo*, in which human happiness is impossible to achieve because the gods have set their decree against it. Iphigénie must be sacrificed before the fleet can sail to Troy. In this grim destiny the desperate efforts of her father Agamemnon and her lover Achilles are swept aside as brutally as is Iphigénie's hope of life. They are all condemned to wretchedness. Gluck's writing for Agamemnon is particularly striking. It has about it a stupendous grandeur. There was in opera no greater moment than the famous refusal, '*Je n'obéirai point a cet ordre inhumain*'. After such dignified tragedy any cheerful resolution must seem wholly vulgar. But, in this hopeless situation, as in the *Orfeo* finale, the gods' decree is reversed and all is presented as ending happily.

The more sombre grandeur of the *Iphigénie en Tauride*, one of the few operas to have no love-interest at all, is equally carefully devised to pit human affection against the inhuman order of the gods. This is an opera in which every incident of the action as it is presented in the song, the dance and the machinery contributes to the total movement of the drama. There is, within a generally impressive command of structure, a remarkable musical subtlety in Gluck's portrayal of the lonely Iphigénie, caught at first between her duty to the temple worshippers and her but half-apprehended sympathy for the Greek youths, and then discovering the horror of having to further the will of the gods and sacrifice her own brother on the altar. The opera's action reaches unremittingly towards a massacre of all the characters, and this is only prevented by the sudden intervention of the goddess Diana. Again the divinely organized situation of human unhappiness is shattered by an intrusive clemency.

Iphigénie en Tauride established that the proper subject for a composer of opera was one in which human beings are shown, after a heroic resolution of their problems, to exercise a decisive will. Iphigénie is presented as being in a turmoil of indecision from which she has to emerge fully determined to follow her own mind through any terror. She is the first really wilful character in opera. The first of a great company. Brünnhilde wills a catastrophe for the world rather than surrender the ring Siegfried has given her, Rodrigo is willing to sacrifice his credibility, his friendship with Don Carlos, his honours from the King, and his life in his desperate effort to win freedom for the Netherlanders, Owen Wingrave resists to the death the ghosts of social and familial convention which gather to demand his obedience. This is the stuff of opera.

In his presentation of Agamemnon in the first and Iphigénie in the second of the Euripidean operas, Gluck achieved that truly faithful renewal of Greek tragedy which opera librettists, composers, and above all critics, had so long sought. *Iphigénie en Tauride* is an achievement that may properly be compared with the work of the ancient dramatists. Why then the strangely perverse endings? Why the sudden descents of the divine among men?

Though in Euripides' *Iphigeneia in Aulis* there had been no happy ending, Athena had appeared to put things right at the end of *Iphigeneia in Tauris*, and it may be that Gluck saw nothing odd in employing the machinery of descent and ascent in any 'Greek' action. Or it may have been simply that he thought the public liked happy endings and gave them several. But then the response of quite a number of his contemporaries would have shown him that this was not always the case. Or it may have been that Gluck himself liked happy endings and enjoyed his own stories in a wholly romantic fashion. But then he would not have shaped his operas so that the happy ending strikes so oddly upon the movement of the action. Or it may have been that he considered all human life intolerable, his observation being that everyone was condemned to a life in which the will to love was ever frustrated by the very course of things, and that the very nature of the world prevented people from being happy. Happiness is rare, rage and despair unworthy of a noble mind, and only divine intervention can offer the first or prevent the second. Only through divine mercy and grace may a man live in peace with others, for the world is naturally, according, that is, to its normal workings, against him. For most men there is only a small hope that, if they bear as best they may the frustrations of their lives, they may be rescued by a divine power. Gluck, in *Orfeo* and his succeeding operas, looks forward to the 'rescue-opera' tradition, only, whereas in that tradition the rescue is habitually given a political colour, Gluck does not put hope in any human talent or exertion, rather conceiving rescue in divine terms.

The distinction of Gluck's mind is evident in the challenge which he gives to the *lieto fine* tradition precisely at the moment when he is employing its conventions. The distinction of Gluck's humane sensitivity is evident equally at such a moment, for then he is translating what he has appreciated in the myth to the particular historical circumstance of his character and, eventually, of his audience. The myth of Orpheus took in his mind the shape of a farce in order that it should be a mystery. The Iphigeneia operas are rendered farcical because the myth has shown that nothing human can be taken seriously, nothing human can be expected to exert a causative effect upon the state of things. The gods descend, if they care to do so, in order to re-arrange reality. Happiness, if given, is not merited. This may not be a pleasant translation of the myth's significance but Gluck achieved that connective elucidation of the Orpheus myth and his artistic experience for which earlier opera librettists and composers had worked.

Gluck's working of this myth certainly had an effect on the structuring of a number of opera conventions. The influence of *Orfeo* is to be discerned in the most disparate situations. There is something expressive of Gluck's view of things in the structure of *Idomeneo*. Mozart leads the audience to a sense of the wonder of the young princess whose love would bring the prince back from the clutch of death, but he does not allow the human voice to be decisive. The execution is not stayed. Only when the god intervenes and alters the situation which the god's own will has made is there a possibility of human happiness. Again, the influence of *Orfeo* may be discerned at several moments in the 'rescue-opera' tradition, and in the greatest opera of that tradition. But Beethoven had a more generous notion of human possibility and so structured *Fidelio* that it became a celebration of the harmonious working of human and divine sympathy. A more direct acknowledgement of Gluck's judgement is to be found in the work of a later composer.

A measure of Gluck's achievement may be deduced from the admiring parody of Jacques Offenbach's *Orphée aux Enfers*. Though the myth is in this delightful piece given a series of irreverent twists, and though the lament Gluck wrote for Orpheus is subjected to a deal of ribbing, Offenbach quite clearly has accepted Gluck's interpretation of the myth. The artist, like every human being, is quite unable to control his experience. The dramatic reversal which occurs at the arrival of Cupid in the penultimate moment of Gluck's opera is echoed precisely in the jolt given at the same point in Offenbach's telling of the myth by Jupiter's sudden thunderbolt. The Can-Can at the end of the opera is a dance celebratory of the fact that divine intervention has quite unexpectedly and even irresponsibly prevented the ordinary ways of the world cramping every human happiness.

Offenbach easily accepted the machinery by which Gluck had suggested the workings of divinity. It was, after all, what was traditional in opera. The old Greek deities who had graced the marriage of Francesco Gonzago and had been descending from the clouds upon almost any excuse throughout the course of seventeenth- and eighteenth-century opera, had at Gluck's bidding become as Rinuccini and Striggio, Monteverdi and Cavalli hoped they might, the immediate symbols of real powers. The Greek stories, heroes and gods and all, were for Gluck and, at his persuasion, for his contemporaries, acceptable ways of talking about the modern world and their experience of it.

But Gluck had achieved rather more than Offenbach had space to recognize in his sprightly pieces. Gluck made it possible for his successors to write operas of mythic import, operas which said something of the hidden springs of human action, without feeling constrained to employ the machinery of gods and heroes. Gluck made it possible for Mozart and Wagner and Britten to move easily between the worlds of gods and of men, for them to confront Poseidon and Wotan and Dionysus with Idomeneo and Siegfried and Aschenbach. But, more importantly, he made it possible for these composers, and for Verdi, to make their universal meanings within wholly human contexts.

His transference of meaning from Orfeo to Agamemnon and Iphigeneia effected a situation adequate for anything Mozart might wish to say about our ordinary loves. But Mozart did not surrender anything of myth in his enjoyment of the human. That easy relation between worlds which Gluck affected is most openly exhibited by Mozart in the structure of *The Magic Flute*. In this opera the tale of Orpheus is split in two. The heroic princely figure of Tamino, who charms animals with his flute and vows to rescue his bride by braving the kingdom of the dark Sarastro, is evidently an Orpheus image in mythic mode. But then there occurs a strange transference. The love duet is sung not by Tamino and Pamina but by the heroine and the bird-catcher after he has saved her from the dark villain with his magic music. From then on while Tamino maintains the mythic language, the demythologization of the tale is carried through in the adventures of the most human Papageno.

Verdi admired the 'powerful dramatic sense' Gluck exhibited in the construction of his operas. Wagner admired the command Gluck exercised over all the elements of their performance. Both benefited from Gluck's establishing the composer as responsible for the opera, its structure, its grace, and its meaning. Both took advantage of the situation Gluck had effected and did something quite their own. Gluck's influence on French grand opera, which reaches at least to Meyerbeer, and probably to Berlioz, may be yet more precisely noted. France has not yet produced a composer whose operas exhibit as masterly and individual a tone as that evident in the works of Verdi and Wagner. The tradition of Gluck is, therefore, the more easily discerned in operas performed in nineteenth-century Paris houses.

Cherubini, in choosing *Medea* for his subject, was certainly making a bow to Gluck who had rendered such mythic material tractable. Spontini's antique invention for *La Vestale* is a more interesting and more influential acknowledgement of the exemplary character of Gluck's humanizing achievement. With this opera Spontini established himself as the composer most fit to shape Parisian taste. The work of this Italian, who worked first in Paris and then in Berlin, was much admired by Berlioz and, for a while, by Wagner. He was imitated and in some inessential ways surpassed by Meyerbeer. Spontini, deploying with some relish the command Gluck had obtained for the composer, set out to employ every means he had in, as Wagner said, 'enthusiasm for a lofty purpose'. He made a great deal of orchestral noise, he compelled singers towards ever more brilliant song, and demanded unparalleled effects from the engineers. The sound was tremendous, the action overwrought, the spectacle stunning. Meyerbeer noted all this and made several attempts to overtop Spontini. But Meyerbeer, though he exploited the possibilities of a religious interest according to the example of *La Vestale*, had not Spontini's sympathy with the human being caught in an intolerable situation. Spontini's operas abound in moments when the composer, through his management of dramatic recitative and splendid aria, forces the audience to attend to the dignity of an individual. In this he is the true inheritor of Gluck's humanism.

THE MYTHS AGAIN?

There is a danger that as Meyerbeer's unhappy desire for greater and greater effects was a perversion of his perception that opera most properly deals with great ideas, so that power to express passionate interest in the condition of the single human being which Spontini derived from Gluck's practice may be debased, by meaner men, into a concentration upon the particular trivialities of an individual life. The masters of later opera have been those who knew well enough to eschew the pettier forms of realism while employing the instruments of humane interest that Gluck had demonstrated. Though some, Mozart, Spontini and Verdi, have been eager to take advantage of his demythologization of opera, others have looked back to the myths and have discovered as the old composers did, that they provided a means of articulating their deepest concerns. And for encouragement in this enterprise they have not looked to Monteverdi and Gluck and their employment of the Orpheus myth, but, perhaps surprisingly, to another composer, not less distinguished but certainly less successful in his choice of myth for the figuring-forth of the artist and his audience.

Handel, appointed Kapellmeister of the Duke of Hanover in 1706 on his return from years of studying Italian opera, was for thirty years the composer of Italian operas for the London stage. It would not have been at all surprising had Handel alone, by the sheer glory of his tuneful music and the craftsmanship of his structured plots, effected a reform of opera. But those who were interested in the renewal of opera in the late eighteenth century, as at later times even until now, seem to have paused at his development of a set of conventions, the *aria da capo* with its endless reflection of seemingly random phrases, for example, or the sequence of solo scenes unrelieved by ensemble or chorus, and not to have appreciated properly his peculiar operatic gift of placing an aria at just the moment when it would forward the action. Handel's arias are not the halting concert pieces that their demanding performance suggests. They occur at crisis points in the action. Handel, as much as any composer after him, appreciated that the music must be the action of the opera. Everything happens in the aria. Of course some stories, those with quick changes of temper and fortune, were more suited to this sudden kind of writing than others. The variety of mood within the mad scene of *Orlando* must convince every hearer of Handel's perfect command of dramatic tensions within a close compass. The shifts from stirring heroic numbers to wistful love songs, and to such a piece as the famous 'Art thou troubled?' in the course of *Rodelinda* show the variety of musical line that was easily within Handel's range. But perhaps he was most magnificently in command in the shaping of the *Giulio Cesare* of 1724. The swift alterations of the first scene, in which first clemency and revenge are juxtaposed, then the virtuous middle was stated by Caesar and then, in a reverse pairing, anger and lamentation are exhibited, make this immediately recognizable as the perfect story for Handel. The structural scheme of the arias in this scene prefigures the structural scheme of the whole work. Fury and kindness alternate in the minds of all those who stand at the side of the just and contemplative Caesar, until the penultimate scene in which Cleopatra's unhappiness is turned to joy on her release from her enemies and a happy song by Pompey's widow celebrates the death of Ptolemy. After this there is nothing to be sung in the world but praise of Caesar. All the action is in the balance of opposites that Handel has presented in his music.

In *Giulio Cesare* the centre was occupied by the sustained power of a benign and humane justice. It may be that Handel saw his own artistic enterprise as the establishment of such a balance. The *aria da capo* certainly, if played out to its full length, convinces a listener of the composer's command of musical symmetry. But Handel also, it appears, had a sense of the irruptive character of art, and, however greatly he disliked revealing this knowledge, felt himself in one opera forced to concede the violence that lay hidden beneath his balanced sequence of arias. Taking up in 1744 a libretto which Congreve had written in 1706 for the English composer John Eccles, Handel discovered a design whose dangerous theme so fascinated him after the Hebrew solidities of *Messiah* and *Samson* that he shaped what I am certain is his best opera. Human kind cannot bear very much reality. *Semele* was not a popular success. Neither oratorio nor Italian opera, neither new nor old fashioned, it fitted no one's liking and was, alone among all Handel's English works, not revived after the year of its first performance. The story was thought unsuitable for the Lenten fare of mid-eighteenth-century entertainment, but Handel never did anything better than the layered richness and variety of his music for this disturbing tale. Semele, princess of Thebes and mistress for the moment of Jupiter himself, brings about her own destruction when, at the clever prompting of Juno, she asks her lover to come before her in all his divine splendour. The god reveals himself and Semele dies in the fire of his too-powerful presence.

The sequence of arias in this opera moves at a more sedate pace than it did in *Giulio Cesare* or any other. The most effective songs in the piece are all of a dignified kind, including a famous aria in which passion has become a walk in the garden of paradise, and another in which the god of sleep demands to be allowed his slumber; the very epiphany of the lord of heaven is effected by 'a mournful symphony'. The opera begins with a processional dance of some solemnity which opens suddenly upon a total change in the music. Apollo announces the coming of Dionysus and the people are immediately caught up in a sprightly chorus. Beneath the solemnity Handel has revealed hints of the orgy.

The composer knew exactly how he might, within the limits of contemporary performance, suggest what strangeness lay beneath the manners of his time, what violence beneath the elegance of love. The god Jupiter figures forth the strange powers that lurk in every man. The scene in which Semele is forced to recognize the naked energy that Jupiter had disguised on his visits to her suggests the ferocity of animal nature that is restrained by the social conventions of human civilization. Congreve and Handel, like T. S. Eliot and Mr Johnny Dankworth, made their audiences admit that 'Any man might do a girl in.' No aspect of love and its expression is left unchallenged in Handel's opera. While Pope's splendid verse and Handel's melody made 'Where e'er you walk' one of the most beautiful of love songs it is well to remember that the song is designed to further the success of a lascivious Jupiter. And there is a similar disjointure in the scene in which Juno successfully disturbs the god Somnus by offering him a physical realization of his romantic dream of the girl he desires. The world of *Semele* is replete with such opposing notions of love. And the composer commands them all. He has the resource for expressing each one of them. Handel's musical invention perfectly reflects the ambiguities of his subject. The dry recitative suddenly irrupts in tiny arias, and at one moment even finds itself becoming a full-swelling duet. And throughout the opera there are sudden and disturbing changes of time. Winton Dean in *Handel's Dramatic Oratorios and Masques* has counted twenty-three different terms for the *tempi* Handel uses in this work. Nine of them occur only here among all Handel's English dramatic works. If not everything, then a good deal is at sixes and sevens. And at the end a sudden space is cleared for the irruption of Dionysus. The dangerous passion of Jupiter, which has destroyed the impertinent Semele, is now fully incarnate as a young god free to wander through the world and effect the ruin of the human race.

Dionysus, having used violent means to persuade his mother's relations to honour her as the beloved of Zeus, set out across the sea in search of his own adventures. He came first to Circe and then, not at all content with the kind of relationship she offered, sailed in his boat towards Naxos. That, at least, is the sequence which Strauss selected for the events leading up to the beginning of his opera. There is some evidence for an identification of Semele and Ariadne, but for the opera within an opera of *Ariadne auf Naxos* Strauss simply followed the popular Dionysus myth and brought the god to wed the girl abandoned by Theseus on the island. Romain Rolland was not happy with the romantic close of this interlude. He told Strauss that if he was not going to offer an ironic comment on the situation, he should at least have ended with a Dionysiac frenzy, 'chorus and full orchestra'. Strauss himself, in his *Recollections and Reflections*, admitted that on the entry of Bacchus, for the god here has his Roman name, he was suddenly unsure of his ability to render, with an orchestra as small as he had been content to have up until that moment in the opera, the 'dionysiac urges' which rose in him. Hofmannsthal persuaded him to forgo the wild sound that might have been managed by one of his massive bands, and to present the innocent youth of the god in the delicate music of a chamber orchestra. The opera ends not in a riot but in a romance. Though Strauss and Hofmannsthal were right to keep within the pleasant confines of this myth, for the Greeks held Ariadne in peculiar esteem as the only girl who could claim Dionysus as her husband, the frenzied element of the god's character has seemed rather more attractive to other modern composers of opera. Gradually it has become apparent how such frenzied forces as Dionysus represents may be most convincingly presented to a modern audience.

Significant steps in this progress were taken by Karol Szymanowski in his second opera, *King Roger*, first performed in Warsaw in 1926. This opera is concerned with another incident in Dionysus' triumphal journey through the Mediterranean world. As the god's cult spread from Asia Minor through Greece to the Greek colonies, Szymanowski has warrant enough for placing the action of his opera in Sicily. He had been made aware, during a holiday tour of the island, of the conflict between West and East, Christian and pagan, in its culture, and he saw in the myth of Cadmus' house a way of presenting such oppositions. The action of the myth was translated to twelfth-century Sicily in order that he might voice the peculiar contrasts of that society. But Szymanowski was unable to work out the relation of his theme to his action. The myth became a fiction, and, indeed, rather a muddled fiction.

King Roger begins magnificently with a confrontation between the clergy and the shepherd, who is Dionysus in disguise. They engage in a tussle for the King's allegiance. Gradually the court turns to the shepherd. There is a stunning wordless hymn in his honour sung by the Queen. And this stirs in the King a sense of the stranger's menace and fascination. But the action does not get anywhere. In the third act the Queen explains to the King that the god is all around them and he need have no fear of him, but then she leaves him alone just as he had feared. *King Roger*, as it falls apart, makes plain that a composer must have the dramatic and musical resource to communicate his contemplation of a myth or he will make himself ridiculous in the attempt. A fiction most men can appreciate when told in another's halting speech, but a myth is as much the audience's as the composer's story and must be told properly if it is not to seem an impertinence.

The celebration of the coexistence of Apollonian and Dionysiac forces within us is allowed in Szymanowski's opera to evaporate into some charming incidental music. That the story has not been operatically shaped is manifest in the ease with which Pawel Kochanski made a wholly acceptable transcription for violin and piano of the best song in the work. Szymanowski would have done better to have sought his theme and action elsewhere. That he felt the myth to be the proper mode of communication suggests how closely related in the tradition myth and opera seemed to him.

After the Second World War the myth of Cadmus' family was taken up again, though not, as might have been expected at such a time, to express figuratively the composer's revulsion at the rise of irrational violence in the recent history of Europe. Hans Werner Henze's reconsideration of the myth in 1966 seemed rather to lead him to conclusions of quite another kind.

Henze in *The Bassarids* takes up the tale of Semele just where Handel put it down in 1774. At the close of *Semele* the shining Apollo proclaims that from the ashes of the girl there shall rise a new god, Dionysus, who will prove 'more mighty than love'.

Henze's opera begins with the arrival at Thebes of Dionysus, disguised as a shepherd-priest, and tells the story of his gradual destruction of all who refuse to acknowledge his dangerous reality. At the end the king is dismembered, the royal family exiled, and the palace burnt down as Dionysus ascends to his place in heaven, raising his mother to a place at his side. The opera, despite its grisly incidents, leads to an epiphany of wonder. All is harmonious at the end. And while Handel's music had expressed the violent changes of experience, Henze has written music of a carefully directed kind which reaches an inexorable and proper climax at the final revelation of Dionysus.

Whatever Auden felt in his collaboration with Kallman on the libretto for that opera, it is rumoured that he agreed to work on *The Bassarids* only if Henze would 'make his peace with Wagner'. Certainly this is an opera which concentrates attention on that world beyond reason which Wagner had made his stamping ground. And it is, too, an opera characterized by a Wagnerian delight in variations upon a group of related musical inventions. Henze asked his librettists to provide him with the movements of a continuous and symphonic piece. This gave him opportunities to write kinds of song which his previous more Italianate and traditional opera structures had not afforded. He and his librettists opened the structure of the legend wide enough to include an anti-masque which, in its jarring presentation of alien modes, does manage to give a sense of that unruliness which the Greek dramatist had hoped to express in the *Bacchae*.

In his going to modern writers for a libretto, Henze was most evidently operating on the assumption that the legend had a continuing vitality independent of any ancient treatment. He did not wish to suggest to his audience that he was simply setting Euripides to music. The struggle between Pentheus, the king who has repressed whatever is within him by the power of a reasonable will, and Dionysus, the licensed god, is evidently paradigmatic of a struggle within each one of us. And the opera shows that the discipline under which Pentheus placed himself has, far from bestowing honour upon him, prevented his achieving a worthy integrity. He is led on to madness. Dressed as a woman he creeps into the mysterious grove to gaze upon the rituals of the god. Discovered by the excited votaries, his own mother among them, he is torn to pieces. Pentheus has not accepted his own humanity, he has attempted too single a life, and the clashing forces within him, unreconciled, have destroyed him. Henze's picture of Pentheus' disintegration puts an end to the making of operas with heroes like Ernani. The man of single purpose has been brought low. The irrational forces have not simply deprived him of external honour and victory, they have deprived him of his interior harmony, revealing him to himself as mad. This opera represents a rejection not only of Verdi's ethic, but, as was to be expected, of the conventions worked out for the expression of that ethic. There is in the opera an interlude designed to exhibit the diseased nature of the king's imagination. It is conducted wholly in the old terms of recitative, aria with cabaletta, round, trio and quartet. The steadfast hero and the controlled ensemble are dismissed together. Henze has produced a visual antithesis of the final scene of Monteverdi's *Orfeo*. The gods' positions are reversed. The Semele story has been employed not only to act as an image of a world entirely different from that Monteverdi knew, but as a manifesto of a view of art and life wholly opposed to that which the earlier composer entertained. Though Henze agreed with Monteverdi that harmony is not to be discovered in this world, he has rejected Monteverdi's hope of another world. Henze does not want the triumph of Monteverdi's Apollo. He wants Dionysus to reign now.

There may well be some in the audience who remain unconvinced by such loud announcements of the Dionysian wonder. These may admit that Nietzsche was exploring a real aspect of being human when he considered the inward relation of Apollonian and Dionysian elements. But to allow Nietzsche's rightness in recognizing the lures of ordered beauty and of irruptive violence is not to applaud the triumph of exotic sensuality. Henze's opera may seem to such members of the audience to be rather too simple in its presentation of complex matters. They would feel that something more satisfactory was being attempted in Benjamin Britten's opera *Death in Venice*. Though they might not be much encouraged by the conclusion at which Britten arrived, what he says must be given proper attention as the culminating expression of a composer who was much concerned with the inward state of man.

A SERIES OF ATTEMPTS: BENJAMIN BRITTEN

That no one can deal knowledgeably with another was expressed once and with great beauty by Debussy. But such beauty may seem unlike the reality of loneliness. It was the continuing design of Benjamin Britten to make immediate the starkest sense of human isolation, though he but slowly schooled his own command of alluring sound. Neither the wondrous melodic line of Peter Grimes's appeal to the Pleiades, nor the haunting wail of 'Alone' is, for example, enough to bring each member of the audience to a sympathy with Grimes for more than an instant. Britten did not in this opera manage to scotch the worry that the borough gossips may perhaps be right after all and his hero a dangerous madman who had killed two young boys. It is commonly agreed that some of Britten's finest music is to be heard in the score of *Peter Grimes*, so whatever failure there is in the endeavour of the composer to convince his audience that his meaning is acceptable is of peculiar interest to those who would discover how a successful opera works. The musical competence of Britten at the time he was writing *Peter Grimes* is indisputable. So the reluctance of the audience to accept his suggestion that our sympathy should be given to the isolated individual must be attributed to the composer's incapacity at that time to carry his meaning in ways appropriate to the peculiarities of opera. It may be significant that the most popular and highly praised music of the opera consists of sea-scape interludes which are eminently transferable to the concert hall. The music is not yet the drama, nor the drama the music. Yet the composer had had a properly operatic concern. He had in mind a theme that he well knew could be presented through opera.

I heard a German critic recently discussing *Death in Venice*, and lamenting that 'Britten always writes the same opera.' He was objecting to the recurrence throughout Britten's works of the theme of the lonely outsider. But repetition, if that is what it is, need not be all bad. In a world where authoritarian regimes are becoming stronger, where blue jeans are worn by almost everyone under twenty-five, and by a good number of persons over that age, and where advertisements are identical on the hoardings of Colchester and Cairo, it may be of great value to say again and again that the singular man is important.

In the operas which followed *Peter Grimes*, right up to the recent *Owen Wingrave* and *Death in Venice*, Britten set out to consider the chances of a man surviving alone. And it is encouraging that he was most successful in giving this concern musical expression in his last opera, *Death in Venice*. Britten's achievement in this opera is perfectly in accord with what the earlier composers of opera had been doing. Beethoven had hoped to persuade his audience that if they put their energies into the establishment of a just society they would be blessed. Mozart does not seem in his operatic work to have put trust in the workings of such a divine Providence. Rather he suggested to his audience that within the disjointure of their lives they could, if only they would learn to love, share with other ordinary human beings a worthy life. Verdi could not believe that ordinary men would be able to do anything to alleviate the terrors of life. Nor would great men. They could only suffer with dignity and die with honour. 'Nothing will come of nothing.' But he says this again and again because he is certain that men will close their minds to the meaning he presents to them. Wagner recognized that despite their extraordinary differences of content, these great composers, and all others worth noting, held in common the view that opera is declaratory of mind to mind. The composer declares himself to his audience. It was for this that the others had worked, and for this that he valued the opportunity of opera. He made opera the immediate instrument of self-expression. And there will always be a great many who realize that in talking of himself Wagner talks of them. Wagner's communication of the mythic reality which all men have within them was done under the control of intelligence. He talked of the orchestra as manifesting the creative urge towards the infinite which was within him, and of the voice manifesting the clear appreciation of the value of such stirrings. The orchestra and the voice together expressed the reality which he wanted the audience to know. Not the orchestra alone. Writing home from Bayreuth in 1891, Mark Twain expressed the wish that he could attend a performance which would 'leave out the vocal part' and be 'done in pantomime', but on this he was, unusually for so delicate a critic, mistaken. The character makes it apparent that what is being communicated from composer to audience can only be communicated in a human way. Wagner's consciousness was ever seeking self-understanding, he was ever questioning himself, ever debating within himself. And so the figurative presentation of his mind was properly made in the dialogue. His operas are carried through by relay pairs of singers. This is particularly true of *Siegfried* but it underlies all his work. But another composer, while recognizing the necessity for the human to be presented visibly upon the stage so that the character of the music may be observed, and the composer's mind known, may not feel that the debate within himself requires to be translated into a dialogue. A composer might be satisfied that the humanity of his controlling mind is more truly represented by one single figure on the stage, or at least by one character set among figures who provide the changing impulses of his inward moods. This certainly is what happens in Britten's operas. Gradually he came to the point of being able to express through one voice all that he meant.

It is not the Orpheus myth which had revealed for earlier composers something of the relation of the artist to his lover, and to all other members of his society, but the Apollo and Dionysus myth of oppositions which the modern composer hopes may show his inward struggle.

Thomas Mann's novella *Death in Venice*, at some slight remove from autobiography, is the story of a famous writer who, holidaying in Venice, falls in love with a graceful boy. He never reveals his love. Never speaks with the boy. In the lazy heat the scurrying phantasms of his mind make something rabid and parasitic of his love. It destroys him. He lingers in the plague-infested city until, watching the boy at play on the last day of his stay, the writer dies in a deck-chair on the beach. The servant of Apollo has been destroyed by the ravages of Dionysus.

The communicative modernity of Mann's version of this myth, and his use of it to speak appropriately of the artist provoked Britten's best and last work for the opera house.

Mann had been most artful in his delicate suggestions of a Grecian guise for the events of his novella. Aschenbach's first sight of Tadzio, 'beautiful as a tender young god' rising from the waves, was enough to conjure mythologies. 'It was like a primeval legend, handed down from the beginning of time, of the birth of form of the origin of the gods.' And as Aschenbach watches he sees in the precision of the boy's form an image of all that he had striven to liberate from 'the marble mass of language'. The intensity of Tadzio's beauty is an image of the artist's achievement. But gradually the writer finds himself unable to live within the bounds of aesthetic delight. As he sits in his tent he imagines Socrates beguiling the youthful Phaedrus with his subtle phrases. Thought becomes feeling. And feeling becomes uncontrollable. The precise lines are broken and desire brings chaos. Again the Grecian language stirs. But it is the language of a darker Greece.

Aschenbach has a fearful dream, 'if dream be the right word for a mental and physical experience which did indeed befall him in deep sleep'. The theatre of the dream seemed to be his own soul, and its action the coming of 'the stranger god'. A Bacchanalian troupe of shrieking women and hairy males, of garlanded youths and goats, all joining in a wild shout of long-drawn sound. And the dreamer became one of them. He took part in an orgy of the god. Waking, he is a Bassarid still. Painted and perfumed he makes a frantic effort to keep within the dance of younger blood. The beauty of the golden god eludes him, the power of the dark god destroys him. The artist dies as the pale and lovely summoner smiles and beckons amid the shallow waters.

Mann's novella is shaped as a warning against the tugs of two great forces. It is a warning to all artists. Beauty and the desire for beauty may between them destroy a man. This tale was used by Britten for his most impressive opera.

Strauss's correspondence with Hofmannsthal has often the appearance of a public document, as if the two great men had been aware of a future reader. It is possible through their letters to observe the process of creativity which led to the final operatic version of their intentions. The letters present in vital sequence the lively interaction of word-maker and music-maker. More public still are the stages in the process from Thomas Mann's novella through Myfanwy Piper's libretto to Benjamin Britten's *Death in Venice*. More public, but less lively. Mann cannot in this instance react to the suggestions of the collaborators. Nor can he have any new ideas. Librettist and composer, in the making of the opera, initiate each adaptation, each change of emphasis, each addition. The novella is not, of course, patient of every translation. Each work of art has its own way of protecting itself against impertinences. The librettist and composer have to take note of the character of the writing if they are not to show themselves as rash intruders on the novella. A comparison of novella, libretto and opera at significant moments in the development of the action reveals librettist and composer as perfectly sensitive to the risks of their attempt. And they have realized their ambition to create not a verbal or musical reproduction of Mann's work, not a libretto or tone-poem version, but an opera. Taken by themselves Mrs Piper's words rarely offer the reader a sense of Mann's novella. Her words, when read, seem dull and unimaginative. They are not a play. But they are a libretto. Dull and unimaginative, and seemingly at such a distance from the allusive vitality of Mann's prose, they prove in the event inspiring. Benjamin Britten has been enabled to make from them something true to Mann's original and as fine. The opera is not a reproduction of the novella but in a wholly different art form a new creation of like intent and effect. In so many ways the genius of the novella is, at the prompting of the libretto, bodied in music. Mann's evocation of the Venetian lagoon is not turned into verse and set to music, but is beautifully translated into the moment when the manager of the hotel opens the window of Aschenbach's room with the common phrase of his trade: 'and look, Signore, the view!' This becomes at Britten's imaginative command an instant of revelation. The music sweeps for a moment into a splendid panorama of the sea. Again, at the equally decisive crisis of the action, when Aschenbach sees the boy Tadzio for the first time, Mrs Piper has curtailed Mann's account of the man's reaction and the artist's 'treacherous proneness to side with beauty', and has by this curtailing cleared a space for the music to perform its properly suggestive function on the ear. It is at the sounding of this music that we are made aware that we are not going to attend to the singing of a play. The action is in the transmutation of events and words into music. The librettist has not simply accepted but has delighted in the composer's capacity to make a world of music, and has prompted him to exercise this capacity to the full. The music moves between the dancing boy and the elderly writer, and is their only element. They have nothing else that they may share. They cannot speak to each other. The music communicates all that may be communicated between them. And the music itself makes it clear that not much can be communicated. The orchestration of Tadzio's dance is done in alien percussion sounds. His music is wholly self-contained. It remains so. While Aschenbach's music is burdened and contorted into strange forms at the irruption of his uncontrollable and disintegrating emotion, Tadzio's music remains as untouched as the tantalizing boy himself. At the end of the opera the vibraphone rattles out his familiar and unfeeling theme against the long-drawn melody of the orchestra which signals Aschenbach's death. And around these two musically separated characters the ordinary folk, the young men on the boat, the strawberry seller, the strolling players, even the mysterious stranger who leads Aschenbach to his destruction, are given conventional tunes of the operatic world. In this the opera fulfils in a most perfect way, more perfect than the original tale itself, the demands of the action.

Mann had in his narration to use words to communicate to his readers that words finally fail to communicate. Britten has perfectly understood that a composer may, quite deliberately, make an audience conscious of the difference between speech and song in order to suggest that through song they enter a different world from that in which speech is adequate. He may suggest a song within the mind. In the novel the silent soliloquies of Aschenbach are, most paradoxically, and often unhelpfully, the speeches of a lord of language, forming an exquisitely public explanation of what he feels. In the opera they have become wholly interior song. They are there, as Mann's sentences could never quite be, the voicing of 'mental experiences which are at once more intense and less articulate' than that sense of outward things which a man may hope to express in good set terms. And having, through the song, been made inhabitants of the mental world of such experiences, an audience will know what stance to take among the dancing images of the boy and his family, the demonic transformations of the temper, the dream appearances of Apollo and Dionysus. The music makes us native to this new mind. For a time, while the music sounds, we know what it is to be Aschenbach. And afterwards we may admit that we have come through his music to know that there is something of Aschenbach in ourselves. His experience has been made our own and cannot be denied. Britten's powerful sound has its way as surely as Wagner's ever does. The comparison is not, in this matter, an awkward one. Britten has renewed the nineteenth-century master's exploration of the mind.

Certainly he has made a great effort to give his audience a clear apprehension of those tugs of Apollo and Dionysus that Szymanowski had fudged and Henze had rendered so unequal. At a crisis in the opera Aschenbach admits the attraction he feels for 'the charming Tadzio' as a hint of the beautiful god: 'Here I will stay, here dedicate my days to the sun and Apollo himself.' And as he dreams in his deck-chair Apollo's voice sounds first, and then his very image is seen: Tadzio comes down the beach as the chorus sings 'No boy, but Phoebus of the golden hair.' As the image dances the voice upon the air proclaims 'Beauty is the Mirror of spirit', and Aschenbach realizes at last 'I – love you.' It is a ridiculous statement, he admits, but sacred too and no, not dishonourable even in these circumstances. The music has done all that needs to be done for this to be a moving declaration. And in the music's progress the audience is brought by Aschenbach's journey through the horrid passages where disease threatens, to the doorpost where the man leans and calls the boy not Apollo but Ganymede, the object of desire, and to the moment when the artist can question 'what is reason, moral sense, what is art itself, compared to the rewards of chaos?' The gods come in answer to this question. Dionysus and Apollo propose to him in a dream the mysteries of nature and the perfection of form. The Bacchanal begins around him, cries of wild beasts are heard, and on the climax of their dance, Aschenbach himself joins in the cry. In this moment Britten has shown his audience how it is that Aschenbach fails to preserve the values of Apollo, but he has not suggested that Dionysus must always be the more powerful force in ourselves. Britten had made an opera from the myth which, while the music and the meaning work together in a controlled fashion quite beyond Szymanowski's powers, did not require that distortion of the match of forces that Henze had felt necessary.

Aschenbach, the central character of the opera, is presented through a soliloquial method, the setting of his diary entries being distinguished from the rest of his music by being in unmeasured prose recitative in which the singer is allowed to make his own way deciding upon note and length and tone by his own instinctive musicianship. It is not simply that Peter Pears was asked what he thought would work as the composer put his opera together, or that the part was designed for the particular character of his voice. Such considerations by composer and singer would not be new. What was new in the composer's demand, and in the confidence he showed in the singer, was that he should be in control of the song, and should exercise his judgement each evening as to how the composer's intention should at that moment be expressed. Perhaps it is the more remarkable that not to Peter Pears only, but to every singer of the part, such a demand is made and such trust shown. It is certainly a startling revelation of the opera composer's sense of the singer as the responsible agent of his meaning. Each night, evidently, the part may be sung and heard a little differently from all other nights. And, in an opera when the subtleties of expression are of immense importance, Britten is trusting a great deal to the singer standing alone on the stage, even though he shows him the way by the fixed notes upon the piano in spasmodic accompaniment. The soliloquy form, the individual self-direction of the singer, the silence of the orchestra at important moments in the score, the emptying sound of the piano, are eloquent musical signs of that isolation with which Britten means to confront his audience. Opera is again realized as the communication of the composer's mind to his audience.

Such respect as Britten shows in this opera for the musicianship of his singer directs attention to the actual performance, to the contributions made to the evening's success not only by the singer but by the producer and conductor.

Five

How is it done?

There is, at the settling on to a balcony bench or into an orchestral stall, at the arrival of the band, and the dimming of the lights about the house, a sense of excitement. Opera is not customarily experienced as an irrational and expensive entertainment but as an interpretation of our common existence. The audience expects the composer to share with them something of that understanding of the world's meaning which his heightened sensitivity must surely give him. The curtain's opening suggests that some hint is about to be given of the hidden structure of experience. Before the curtain opens, however, if the composer's sense of the world is to be communicated to his audience, a host of persons must put in a great deal of effort. All those who in one effort with the man at the box-office and the Chairman of the Board, do their work at typewriters and sewing-machines and rehearsal pianos are necessary for the putting on of the show, but of this multifarious company the man who raises the money, the producer, the singer, and the conductor, require some special attention to their work.

MONEY MATTERS

The financing of an opera house is now, and usually has been so in the past, as complicated a matter for those responsible as the preparation and performance of the house's artistic enterprise, but its character may be quite shortly stated. Opera always costs more than those who would attend its performance can afford. Some rich patron, a duke or a banker or an arts council, must always be sought if an opera is to take place. In the beginning the wedding festivities of some courtly family provided money enough for performances of some splendour. Rinuccini's *Arianna* for the marriage of Margherita of Savoy was doubtless presented with 'no expense spared'. And in the middle and later years of the seventeenth century there were enough families like the Barberini in Rome rich and ready to build private theatres and pay for private performances of highly elaborate entertainments, and enough merchants in Venice to sustain a season of equally expensive shows at several public theatres. But by the start of the eighteenth century there were fewer rich men willing to spend their money on such spectacles. And when those who paid demanded a different tune the Italian entertainers obliged them with a 'reform' opera which did not require the marvellous machinery of the earlier pieces and cost much less to put on. A similarly close look at the books of the Italian troupes in Paris was in part responsible for their expulsion and Louis XIV's establishment of a national opera company. Everything depended on the singular taste of the one man who constituted the paying audience. A change in the patterns of spending of a cardinal, merchant, or king, led immediately to a change in the pattern of performance. And what delighted these men was not necessarily the talent of the composer. They might prefer all kinds of operatic elements to the music. And so might the general audiences of the public theatre. Benedetto Marcello's 1720 account of Venetian opera and the conditions of its performance is perhaps most diverting when he recommends a librettist who seeks commercial success to read over to the impresario only those scenes of his opera containing the poison, the divan and the bear. And if these delights are not enough to get him to sign a contract Marcello recommends that further popular conventions should be shoved into the text. It is noteworthy that of all the devices recommended to the librettist who would please the impresario none was likely to prove expensive except, perhaps, the bear. And that animal, like the more famous beast of *The Winter's Tale*, might well be borrowed from the neighbouring bear-pit or pavement musician. Evidently the Venetian theatre manager was by the middle of the eighteenth century looking very carefully at his account books. And composers began to take serious note of the new financial conditions of opera-making.

It was not simply his own individual greediness that Leopold Mozart was expressing when he wrote to his son in 1778 that 'if one can but win applause and get well paid the deuce take the rest'. Mozart wrote back from Paris that year of his determination to write 'a grand opera', for then 'I shall be better paid, I shall be doing work I rejoice in, and I shall have more hope of a success'. The economics of opera were of proper importance to the greatest of composers as to the least, and had for Mozart their peculiar difficulty. He was determined in his writing for the commercial theatre, as in everything else he did, to 'come through it a whole man'. Mozart's appreciation of his own integrity prevented his adopting the shifts lesser composers allowed themselves in the quest for popularity. However urgent his need for money he could not publish works that, though they would content all others, did not satisfy the critical demands of his own genius. He had to manage without the bear, but he had, as his father advised him, to write 'for the unmusical as well as the musical public'. The operas of Mozart's maturity exhibit both his astoundingly inventive musical talent and his exact appreciation of what would delight his fashionable audience. His works could be received by managers in the assurance of box-office success. Their customary rapaciousness prevented Mozart's enjoyment of his share of the proceeds he had earned them. Schickaneder even managed to defraud the composer in the subsequent matter of publishing the score of *The Magic Flute*. All Mozart's care did not, therefore, procure him enough to keep his family in modest comfort. But he had certainly understood that the public and the managers who sought only to relieve them of their monies had necessarily to be pleased if any of his operas were to be performed. The theatre was evidently as subject to economic pressure as any other institution. This was a lesson that most later composers learnt. And quite a number of the most distinguished composers learnt too, from Mozart's burial in a pauper's grave, that they must look out very carefully for the progress of their own finances.

In 1847, Verdi, close on that age at which Mozart died, had achieved some financial success and a deal of business competence.

He was in the financial position to suggest to his publisher, Giovanni Ricordi, that they share the expense of putting his forthcoming *La Battaglia di Legnano* on the market 'so that you will not have to suffer the entire loss if the outcome is not a happy one'; and in the artistic position to demand an exorbitant fee from Benjamin Lumley, the London impresario, when he suggested that Verdi become the Musical Director of Her Majesty's Theatre. But Verdi remained very careful of money matters. Ricordi came under severe attack when the composer found that his foreign earnings were being calculated at a poor rate of exchange from francs to lire. And he was quite aware of those artistic sacrifices an impresario must make if he is to remain in business. He knew that the best performances are given in a repertory theatre where the members of the company learn to work together, 'but I don't think it could be achieved'. Audiences in Italy 'would not be contented with a *prima donna* who cost only eighteen or twenty thousand florins a year, as in Germany'. They would demand 'the *prima donnas* who go to Cairo, St Petersburg, Lisbon, London, etc., for twenty-five or thirty thousand francs a month'. No repertory theatre would be able to pay them. And even if a management were rash enough to attempt to run a repertory with the great singers appearing night after night the public would get bored even of these and stay away. Verdi remembered an old impresario's story of La Scala's selling, on an evening when the best and once the most popular singer of his time was appearing yet again, only six tickets. Verdi had no intention of ruining himself by insisting on theatrical presentations which would lessen box-office receipts. Not that his operas exhibit signs of commercial cobbling. Like Mozart in this, at any rate, Verdi could please his indiscriminate public without sacrificing anything of his own critical integrity.

Mozart and Verdi took pains to earn their money. Wagner was rather more resentful of the connection between composition and cash. At one time he wrote to Liszt that 'the spreading of my operas is entirely a matter of business to me; this is the only real point; all the rest is, and remains, fictitious'. At another he abandoned this self-deceptive cynicism and announced that he was fit to do only 'what is strictly my business', and demanded that he be given enough money to get on with the making of operas: 'it is not my business to earn money, but it is the business of my admirers to give me as much money as I want, to do my work in a cheerful mood'. Wagner required, evidently, a continuous subsidy for himself and his operas. The large works he offered managements could not be produced without enormous expense and enormous risk. His answer to the problem was the hugely self-confident foundation of Bayreuth where his operas could be performed in proper splendour and the money would somehow be found.

Wagner's compulsive blandishments and bullyings achieved wonders. Bayreuth was built and the operas presented in lavish manner. But opera houses today which lack his demonic management have to think carefully about putting Wagner's works on their stages. They have, indeed, to think carefully about every production they put on. The high cost of opera in every country makes it necessary for managements to rely on public and private gifts while they are quite unable to conduct their affairs in ways which would make sense to efficient businessmen. The directors of Covent Garden have recently explained that their financial difficulties are not to be solved by following any of the most popular recommendations about employing less international stars, performing only old and favourite operas, ceasing to stage new productions, or doing things more simply. But such explanations do nothing to temper the harshness of the present economic conditions of opera. Troubles conspire against almost every management.

Lord Morley wrote of the business in Gladstone's day:

To manage an opera-house is usually supposed to tax human powers more urgently than any position save that of a general in the very heat and stress of battle. The orchestra, the chorus, the subscribers, the first tenor, a pair of rival prima donnas, the newspapers, the box-agents in Bond Street, the army of hangers-on in the flies – all combine to demand such gifts of tact, resolution, patience, foresight, tenacity, flexibility, as are only expected from the great ruler or the great soldier.

To that list should be added those matters which now tax the talents of a modern manager. We live in times when *The Bassarids* comes to a sudden halt in London as the scene-shifters go on strike for more money, their rates being not nearly so bad as those of the chorus singers and the orchestra players. When a Milanese journalist thinks it merely an annual ceremony when Signor Grassi, the *sovrintendente* of La Scala, 'knocks on the doors of all the banks, he begs, and in the end he borrows enough money to keep going'. And when the Metropolitan, New York, asks its staff to take a ten per cent cut in pay, and the St Paul Opera Association has after over forty years to cancel its season for lack of funds. These things affect every aspect of opera. The English National Opera has cancelled its production of Frankel's *Marching Song*, Covent Garden had to postpone its recent *Siegfried*, and composers have gloomily put aside opera projects in favour of string trios which have a chance of being heard.

Singers, too, are quickly affected. Signor Nicolai Gedda has several times lately complained of the added pressures upon the singers resulting from the financial difficulties of opera houses, not only in the smaller Italian towns, but in the great international houses like the Paris Opéra. A huge budget is no protection against huger demands. Each item of expenditure has to be looked at with rather too much care. Things are done rather too cheaply. And something, therefore, goes wrong every day. A tension is created in the house which is wholly inimical to good singing. Signor Gedda is already thinking of retirement from the hassles of normal opera house existence.

The general intendants and managers of modern houses are not, evidently, confronting an experience new in the history of opera. No one, not even a Renaissance cardinal, has ever liked to spend more money than was necessary for his pleasure. Those financing and managing opera have generally, therefore, been ready to listen to those who promise them better entertainment for money, or the same entertainment for less money. Those responsible for the marvellous spectacle, the trilling high note, and the pace of the music have at various times and places persuaded managements to accept them as the leading spirits of the performance. These are the participants in the opera enterprise who yet may claim to attract most of the attention. It is their work which is commonly discussed at the interval and on the journey home.

Certainly, these artists, however splendidly they contribute to the success of the performance, cannot attract ticket-buyers enough, or subscribers on the mailing-list, for the cost of the performance to be covered by the ordinary takings, yet unless they fulfil the demands of the audience in a notable and boastworthy manner, no one else, no government agency or philanthropic fund, will be persuaded to supply the vast sum required to keep the opera house open. Those who are concerned with the economics of opera must, therefore, on this, if on no other score, realize the importance of the work of producer, singer and conductor.

THE PRODUCER

Perhaps Marcello's talk of the bear and the ship is an indirect reference to what is now accepted as the vastly important work of the producer in the opera house, but his general silence about any man other than the librettist, the engineer and the impresario having a charge of what happens on the stage witnesses to a practical revolution in the opera house. It is not now possible to converse of opera for more than a minute or two before coming to talk of the productions of widely famous directors as easily as of the sound of favourite singers. It is the mark of a good producer that he devises action which fulfils the direction of the music. There is a real difficulty, however, in establishing any rules about how he is to achieve this desirable fulfilment. What may seem to a highly intelligent and sensitive producer the inner meaning of an opera's composer may seem to many in the audience who have not his gifts, nor his time for considering these matters, a mere indulgence of his own fancy. Sometimes they may be wrong, sometimes they may be right, but either way the result will be the same rejection of what the producer is offering. Producers have, therefore, to be careful to get right not only what the composer intends but what the audience may be persuaded to accept as the proper presentation of his intention. A producer who wants simply to play funny games with an opera may find that the composer has his own way of signalling to an audience just what is going wrong. The appalling vulgarity of the current Frankfurt *Così fan Tutte*, in which the elegant girls and their beaux are sent clambering among the rumpled sheets of an on-stage bed, merely displays the mean imagination of the producer. Mozart prevents such things by making his own meaning clear in the music. And those several producers who hope to enliven the dull scene of Cherubino's singing to the Countess in *Figaro* with a little love-play have found that the music unaccountably defeats them. Mozart simply has not left a space for such vulgarities between bars. And the audience senses how hurriedly such business has to be shoved into the scene and refuses to applaud the unnecessary distraction from Mozart's music. Wilfulness is its own undoing. Wagner, too, can defend himself. He can fight back. The Frankfurt *Götterdämmerung* collapsed on its first night and, beneath the derisory shouts of the audience, the management and producer muttered threats of lawsuits. Wagner was not at all disturbed. His music remained inviolate.

Such sorry examples should not prejudice those interested in opera against either the Frankfurt house, which currently presents one of the finest repertories in the world, or the growing power of the producer in every house. Certainly that power is growing. Even in Britain where, unlike the great houses of Europe, producers have never had much say in what happens in the opera house, it is beginning to be accepted that production matters, that the presentation of the dramatic structure of an opera is an important element in the transmission of the composer's meaning. That producers of intelligence and ingenuity, like Mr Peter Hall and Dr Jonathan Miller, are successfully at work with opera companies in this country is a new departure. And the journalism of opera is now as concerned with producers as with singers.

There are a number of admirers of opera who maintain against all persuasion that the opera in their ear while the gramophone or the tape is playing from the four corners of their private room, is a more just rendering of the composer's intention than anything a producer could do in the theatre. They think, perhaps, of the older productions where a couple of singers, weighing two hundred pounds apiece, declared their first-sight love, or four equally fat folk thumped out an ensemble along the footlights. Or they think of the newer productions where some lean and sinuous lady sprawls on her tummy shrieking her passion amongst the flashing lights of a science fiction set. But these are, happily, kinds of rarity.

FROM CONVENTION TO CONVENTION

The bringing together of audience and composer which is the essential purpose of the producer is a rather more complex enterprise than it used to be. From the earliest times of opera until almost the end of the nineteenth century there seems usually to have been quite enough musical talent, and just enough financial backing, available for the theatres customarily to present works by contemporary composers rather than, as is now the general case, revivals of operas from previous generations. Composers, therefore, since they shared the conventions of their audiences, wrote within an immediately recognizable social, moral, and epistemological frame. This enabled them to indicate by quite small signs their distinct and individual attitudes. A modern audience does not enjoy the possibility of this immediate appreciation of what is going on. It is not, for example, at once apparent to most of us as the action of *Così fan Tutte* develops when Despina is being properly helpful and when she is being improperly impertinent to her two young mistresses. Mozart's audience would mostly have, without having to take thought, made nice distinctions that we, if we are even aware of our lack of social sensitivity, must work to understand and can never accept as ordinary. Similarly, though these are examples of matters less central to the operas, few of us jump at the political implications of Lully's *Phaëton*, or are unsurprised by the number of telegrams sent during *Intermezzo*. We can, however, since these are the worlds we recognize from newspapers and television, move easily among the ghetto tensions of *Porgy and Bess*, the awkward moments at the dinner table in *Owen Wingrave*, and the group-therapy games of *The Knot Garden*. As it is with these enclosing social conventions so it is with the theatrical conventions of a generation. Later generations cannot find the *lieto fine*, the exit-aria, or the Wagnerian monologue as immediately communicative as they once were. But we have no difficulty at all in accepting, in undisturbing harmony with our knowledge of group-therapy, our theatrical convention that madmen have shaven heads and sing with painfully exquisite exactitude melodies of delicate beauty. The conventional structure of opera, therefore, makes it easier for a composer to communicate with his contemporaries and very much harder for later audiences to appreciate what he is doing.

Such a situation is evidently not confined to opera alone. Similar difficulties confront us when we attempt the proper response to the allegorical delights of *The Faerie Queene*, the simple elegance of a Georgian terrace, or the wan stiffness of Goya's portraits. But we may read a poem again, consulting footnotes as we go, and there may be time to walk up and down Bath until we have a sense of the design, or we may take up various stances before a pale Duke. An opera makes its effect instantaneously. Or not at all. We cannot stop the performance while we think a little, or ask to have some part played over again. At least most of us cannot – King Ludwig, who enjoyed private performances, might do so. But even then the composer has not designed his work to proceed in such a way. Wagner walked out in fury when the King, having been granted a repeat of the *Parsifal* prelude, suggested that the *Lohengrin* prelude might then be played for purposes of comparison. So we have to take in as much of the alien conventions as possible at once. It is the task of the producer to facilitate this strenuous business. He has so to interpret the work of a past time that it becomes available to a modern audience.

In this enterprise the producer may adopt any one of a sequence of devices between two extremes. He may, if he feels immensely confident of his own knowledge and talents and of the composer's forcefulness, trust wholly to a reproduction of the original form of presentation persuading a modern audience to react in just the way the composer's first audience reacted. He may hope to produce a total environment within which a modern man will react in an appropriately antique manner. Such a thing has now and again been attempted for early opera, and there was some hope that Bayreuth, for the centenary performances of *The Ring*, would provide Fricka with real goats to pull her chariot. In the event the production conventions of early opera were found to be too remote for an audience to feel themselves part of that world, and Fricka just walked on like any ordinary person. It sometimes seems to an equally confident producer that the composer needs a great deal of help in making himself clear to an audience. The composer must be made into a modern man in order to impress us. Generally, however, producers elect some course between reproduction and invention. They hope to interpret.

A producer has to become fluent in the conventional languages of the composer and the audience. He has to give the composer a modern opportunity. And in arranging this meeting he has to exercise a nice judgement in a multitude of matters. Producers have commonly employed the technical resources of the contemporary stage in realizing the epiphany of Apollo. They have commonly not used their electric instruments to present Fricka's goats. The producer who is working on an original language production must make a series of decisions between gestures which hint sufficiently at the meaning of a verse and those which so simplify things as to suggest that the composer is a crude oaf. The producer who has to deal with a translated libretto must consider carefully how far the gestures appropriate to the original context can be retained with due loyalty to the original impression. Should Verdi's lovers rub noses when they perform before Eskimoes? How is the changed significance of the handshake to be conveyed from German to an English rendering of the opening of Tal's *Temptation*? These are difficulties which may seem merely incidental but which, if not successfully resolved, may distract members of an audience from the opera. They are, certainly, not matters upon whose quiet solution a producer may expect to make much of a name for himself.

The producer who would make himself as well-loved as the singer or the conductor has to do more than get the details right. He has to convince an audience that it is through his eyes that they best see the action. And to achieve such an esteem a producer must work from the known to the unknown; from the accepted conventions of our society and theatre to a composer's enduring discernment of what it always means to be human. To an audience it may seem, as they applaud the producer's endeavour, that he has shown that the composer was more modern, less 'convention-ridden', than they supposed. The producer will know, if he is the right sort of person, that he has made apparent the atemporal community of those who speak in different conventions. For this he is employed.

Managements who have noted that it is modern to write opera as an exploration of the mind, have noted also that it is expensive to produce. So many of their regular patrons are not, it seems, particularly anxious to find out what is happening within the composer or themselves if this entails, as it so often does, listening to some very odd sounds. Managements have, therefore, encouraged producers to look again at the old favourites. And producers of intelligence have found that the older composers were quite competent in these modern interests. The psychological interests of modern opera-goers have lately been assumed to be large enough to warrant all kinds of re-interpretations of past operas. The modern convention that psychology tells all has been invoked to give the composer new dignity in our society. Donizetti's *Lucia di Lammermoor* at Hanover, Wagner's *The Flying Dutchman* at San Francisco, and Debussy's *Pelléas et Mélisande* at Munich have each been treated as the thoughts or dreams of one of the characters. In M. Maurice Bejart's Brussels production *Traviata* is conceived as an action within the heroine's mind. Her imaginings give character to the dummies around her. And M.

Bejart suggests that Verdi wished to communicate such a power of dreaming to his audience. 'Opera is not there just to tell a story,' he wrote in a programme note, 'but to make us dream.' Through our dreaming we may 'live it ourselves'.

Such an interpretation of the main tradition of opera certainly has very little to do with Puccini's notion of *verismo*. It would be a silly producer who would hope to persuade an audience to see *Bohème* as Mimi's delirium as she is dying, *Tosca* as the thoughts passing through the secretary's mind as he waits to give evidence at the inquiry into Scarpia's assassination, or *Turandot* as Liu's imaginary justification for the prince not loving her. Interpretations of this kind can be provoked only by composers who have taken seriously the powers of mind and will in men, and who have constructed their operas in the hope of expressing something of human importance. Only such composers will have given the necessary attention to the forces which impel the characters in their operas, intending that through their contemplation of such a spectacle those in the audience should discern something about themselves. There is no such intention in Puccini's opera-making: he was interested in only his own dreams. And it may be doubted whether Donizetti was always capable of following so serious a purpose. Nor is it quite evident that Verdi was ambitious for something of just this kind. But Wagner certainly was.

Wagner has become the producer's composer in our generation. His opera of the mind has been seized upon by the most inventive and intelligent men working in the opera house and made into the accepted announcement of how we now think we are. And there is some essential propriety in the producers' discovery of Wagner as their composer. He is the one composer, after all, not simply to say in the manner of Gluck that his music was designed only to further the meaning of the text, but to insist at actual performances on the stage action being recognized by the conductor as of greater importance than what was going on in the orchestra. This was what he intended by his championing of 'drama' as opposed to 'opera'. And since it is in productions of Wagnerian opera that the characteristic attitudes of the producer in the modern opera house are to be seen most plainly, and since it is from the contemporary experiments with Wagner's works that producers have learnt to make such interesting discoveries as M. Ponnelle's *Idomeneo* at Cologne, or Wieland Wagner's *Aida* in Berlin, a limited discussion of the producer's work is, I think, most suitably conducted through some Wagnerian examples.

VERSIONS OF WAGNER

Wagner devoted a deal of his attention to details of stage direction and scenery description, building up in his imagination the ideal performance. Actual performances were not up to his concept. He became convinced that while the conventional theatre of his time was all he had at his disposal he would never be able to present his meaning to his audience. The founding of Bayreuth, and the first production there of the *Ring* in 1876, showed what he had in mind. Everything in Bayreuth was designed by Wagner to enforce attention upon the action of his music drama. For the first time the theatre was conceived as containing an audience whose single purpose was to hear and watch the opera. They had come from a distance especially to be at the opera. They had, like medieval pilgrims in Compostella or Jerusalem, taken over the inns of the town. And now at the opera they kept silence. The house lights were extinguished, the orchestra and conductor hidden from view in a sunken pit, and the hard seats, discouraging anything but erect attention, were raked in an arc concentrated upon the stage action. Only under the conditions he established at Bayreuth did he suppose that his music would make its proper sense.

Wagner's care for his own work was intelligent. He had indeed worked out just how it could be performed to greatest effect. At least he had worked it out so far as he himself could understand his own work. Every one of his directions for the station and movement of the singers, the operation of the machinery, or the transformation of the scene, counted towards the realization of a magnificent single stage picture. And that picture was so in harmony with the music that its glory convinced Wagner that things were at their best when the producer was also the conductor of the opera. Then all would be one, and the audience would enjoy that one experience which he had when he wrote his 'universal art-work'. Such care from such a man compels respect. It has to be taken into account by every later producer. While Wagner had sometimes been frustrated by the inability of the theatrical machinery of his time to produce just the effects he had imagined, the modern producer can expect the designer, manufacturer, and lighter of his set to do anything he demands. It is now a possibility for the Rhine maidens to swim and the Valkyries to fly at the producer's word. And there have been suggestions recently that Wagner's stage directions for these and other wonders should be faithfully applied, at least at Bayreuth. But, ungratefully, most opera-goers have now no relish for such spectacles. And producers have anyway little relish for simply reproducing someone else's imaginings, not even the old magician's. And this not because they want simply to make a new name for themselves. The producer who most respects Wagner may yet be the one who finds in his music something that is not expressed in the composer's own theatrical directions; something, perhaps, that the composer himself did not realize might be articulated in a different form of production. Reasons of obedient art may direct a producer to do things that Wagner never understood he had ordered.

It has been Wieland Wagner, as director of the Bayreuth festival after its re-opening in 1951, who has found some of the most effective ways of interpreting his grandfather's work. Bayreuth having been turned into 'Hitler's court theatre', as Thomas Mann expressed it, by Wagner's English daughter-in-law, Wieland Wagner rethought the whole question of Wagnerian production. What Wieland Wagner aimed at achieving and the effect he had on the opera audience may do as exemplars of the producer's part in the making of an opera performance.

Wieland Wagner began from a great reverence for his grandfather's genius and a belief that the Bayreuth institutionalization of Wagner production had, while it claimed the composer's authorization, confined the great works within the artistic limits of lesser men. He determined to liberate the splendour of the operas.

I remember how strange and at first disappointing were Wieland Wagner's productions in the first post-war seasons. They were the first productions of any part of the *Ring* cycle that I had ever attended and I had hoped to see Fricka come with her goat-drawn chariot, and Brünnhilde leap with her horse upon the *Götterdämmerung* pyre; nothing of this sort occurred, and though there was a sort of dragon, even that was disappointingly symbolic. Wagner once remarked, in his essay *On Opera Libretti*, that a composer should when considering whether a subject would do for an opera, place the central character 'in a dimly lighted place, where he can just see the gleaming of its eyes'; if its brightness comes across in such a circumstance he will know what can be done. His grandson seemed often to have taken that prescription for his production and left the audience to catch the gleam. But gradually this production made sense. Wieland Wagner saw the world at the beginning as a great platter held together by Wotan's will. Gradually, through the progress of the *Ring*, as Wotan's hold on the world was loosed, the platter began to heave and split apart, until Wotan surrendered his power amid a broken landscape. This was an immediate visual explication of what was going on in the music and it is typical of Wieland Wagner's method. At all times he endeavoured to express what was going on in the composer's mind so far as this could be known from the music. He was an obedient director. But, of course, so finely-minded a producer could not remain content with any particular rendering of the composer's intention when the composer was as evidently complex a man as Wagner; as several of his artistic colleagues noted, Wieland Wagner's insatiable curiosity and speculative temper led him into divers forms of obedience. His development as a director has been analysed in several ways but it seems most simply described as a growing recognition of the subtlety of his grandfather's self-reflective work. Wieland Wagner began his career by taking it to be his business to see that what was going on in the music should be faithfully reproduced in the stage action. While he never wanted real goats, for these were not in the music, he worked hard to ensure that the singers' movements corresponded to movements in the music. Gradually, through his experience in producing the operas in a number of the finest German houses, he began to employ the stage picture not as an illustration of the musical action but as an independent commentary upon it. The movement of the singers suggested how far the psychological forces expressed in the music could control the events of the narrative, and how far the characters understood themselves and their motives. Wieland Wagner was thus, in the final phase of his career, able to suggest at once two levels of experience to the audience. Not only at moments of one character deceiving another, or of Wagner's explicit reminder in the *leitmotiv* of some other element of the action, but at all moments the audience was required to recognize more than one kind of event. It was according to his first concept that the *Tristan und Isolde* of the 1952 Bayreuth Festival became, as Wagner had himself hoped, 'the most beautiful of all dreams'; the action was at one with the sound in erotic and almost total darkness. It was according to Wieland Wagner's later concept that the musical action of his 1962 *Tristan und Isolde* was intensified by his telling the singers that Tristan was not the nephew but the son of King Marke whose bride he stole, and by his showing the audience that the prow of Tristan's ship was a great phallic symbol; and, in parallel with this intensification of the psychological forces of the musical action, and its effect in making the experience of the lovers seem the more powerful, the outward force of the society against which they had to assert their passion was intensified by the stepping of King Marke and his knights on board Tristan's ship as the lovers gazed at each other oblivious of their actual circumstance. What was asserted as supreme in the music was shown on the stage to be dangerously vulnerable. And for the audience *Tristan und Isolde* became a much more complex and interesting commentary upon their own experience of the clash of will and circumstance.

Though in this example he had gone against Wagner's explicit stage directions, in his general progress as a producer Wieland

Wagner took his grandfather's talk of the 'universal art-work' more and more seriously. He came in his last productions to concentrate attention not upon the music but upon 'the theatrical idea' which music, text, and staging reflect. 'Music,' he wrote, 'can and should serve only to illuminate the mind or state of mind of the stage character, to reveal the psychological background.' There was something more to Wagner's achievement than music. And that something came gradually to assume, as was to be expected by any who knew anything of opera's tradition, a classic shape.

Nietzsche had for a while heralded Wagner as the man who could renew in German culture the glory of Greek art. In 1958 Wieland Wagner had discovered a Greek dramaturgy in *Lohengrin*, and he had brought this out by standing the chorus round the action as commentators and rarely participators. By 1962 he had come to see Tristan as Oedipus, and in that year too he was ready to say that for him the *Ring* was not primarily a Germanic tale but 'a revival of Greek tragedy'. He now described the platform upon which the action took place as the equivalent of the buskin, the platform-shoe, by which the Greek tragedian raised himself to be the better seen by his audience. Wieland Wagner's mode of production was a recognition of the classic character and status of his grandfather's work. And Wieland Wagner accepted, as his predecessors at Bayreuth had not, that, being classic, Wagner's operas were patient of a great variety of interpretation. He never thought of his productions as definitive interpretations either for others or for himself. In a 1962 BBC programme he remarked: 'Wagner's work is inexhaustible and there are always new aspects to be revealed. For that reason I think my method of production is capable of further development.' But he was not to live to make this further development. And for a while it seemed as if no other producer would do so. Wieland Wagner's method was imitated in opera houses up and down Europe. Every theatre built its platter. And for each of Wagner's operas. *Rienzi* might not be done much, but the grand operas, *Tannhäuser* and *Lohengrin*, began to be treated everywhere as if they were the same kind of work as *Tristan und Isolde*. It was even a refreshment to attend an old-fashioned production like the Wiesbaden *Lohengrin* where, as large ladies scowled with wickedness and simpered with innocence, the chorus singers made uniformly bored gestures, and every scene seemed made of hessian and cardboard. It was a refreshment of another kind to attend the late nineteenth-century *Ring* Joachim Herz put on at Leipzig, in which Fricka's scenes with Wotan had evidently been written by Ibsen, or the more up-dated *Ring* of Ulrich Melchior at Cassel, which featured Siegfried as a beaded hippie and gave a final glimpse of a decrepit Wotan ruling the ruins of the world from a wheelchair.

These were good escapes, better at any rate than the half-hearted science fiction that the English National Opera has been toying with to the detriment of some fine singers, and very much better than the dullish modifications of Wieland Wagner's early style that have recently been staged at the Metropolitan Opera, New York, and the Nationaltheater, Munich. There are now signs, however, that some producers have been able to look at Wieland Wagner as a helpful predecessor and to develop for themselves that further understanding of Wagnerian production for which he looked. At Bayreuth his brother, Wolfgang Wagner, who now directs the festival, produced a 1975 *Parsifal* which, for the first time in my experience of the opera, was neither boring nor absurd. Wolfgang Wagner had seen how he might, with modern stage machinery and lighting techniques, realize his grandfather's musical changes of scene, and how he might, by such a careful and informed reading of the text as his brother had practised, discern the significant gestures of the action. The hero he presented was not the fey creature of nineteenth-century Arthurian fancy but a young man growing in impatience with the trammels of outworn ideas and freeing others through his own mature enjoyment of freedom. This Parsifal moved in a stirring world where the Grail Knights were not emasculated monks, as in the production at Munich I saw in the same week, but rough barons anxious for action and ready to slay their king if he would not lead. Altogether he made this opera manifest as the appropriate climax of Wagner's mounting hatred of the world as it is and hope for what it might be. And he accomplished this by making something of his own from Wagner's directions and Wieland Wagner's explorations. Wolfgang Wagner has not however yet managed to make such a stirring revelation of the *Ring*. Indeed for the Bayreuth centenary celebration of 1976 it was announced that the new *Ring* would be produced by a young Frenchman who gained a deal of publicity, most of it good, all of it doubtless helpful in his career, from the rumour that he had never seen the *Ring*, and could not read German.

Though M. Chéreau, in his rough way with the *Ring*, was backed by M. Boulez, and loyally seconded by a team of willing singers, Wagner defeated him. His bright ideas were time and again revealed by the music to be mere gimmicks. Those who liked the production found significant reasons for some of these. Mr William Mann, discerning more of a design in this production than most of the audience, remarked in *The Times* that the sight of a lounge-suited Hagen hunting with an early medieval spear had a 'ludicrous' effect, but went on nicely to suggest that 'Chéreau must have intended' this effect as a criticism of any interpretation of the *Ring* which depends upon 'the timelessness of mythical subject matter'. I did not find the bald juxtaposition of properties and costumes and manners from everywhere and everywhen either ludicrous or challenging. I thought the production merely silly. Criticism of the mythic understanding of Wagner's work is not to be presented so glibly. M. Chéreau did not persuade me that here was a way for me into the music of the *Ring*. I thought of the vast expense of time and energy and money and hope which I and so many others had borne to attend this *Ring*. And I was angry.

It seems to me that he who radically questions the contemporary interest of an opera should resist the temptation to produce it. It is not often that the virtues of an *enfant terrible* are required in an opera house, and it is rather Götz Friedrich's work on the *Ring* at Covent Garden that represents the greater hope for Wagnerian progress.

Like Wolfgang Wagner at Bayreuth, Götz Friedrich has noted Wagner's frustration at the inadequacies of his contemporary back-stage machines and his prophecy that 'the ideal theatre conceived by me would one day exist'. And Götz Friedrich has understood how Wagner came to place such importance upon the staging of his operas. At Covent Garden the world is a revolving, heaving, rising and sinking platform, Wotan is thrust vertiginously above the audience, the rainbow bridge stretches to Valhalla, the forge breaks with a mighty clash as Siegfried strikes out with his famous sword, but, in the midst of all these tricks, this producer thinks that anyone who reads the score will, as he writes in his introductory pamphlet, 'naturally omit Fricka's goat and the horse Grane'. I am not, even after all these years, quite happy to give up my adolescent vision of the goat and the horse. And the dragon was rather more of a disappointment in 1975 than in 1951 because uniquely at this point Götz Friedrich has gone back to the earlier version of Wieland Wagner's method and made the stage action merely illustrative of the whole. It was a wasteful and distracting duplication of the musical effect of the return of the Fafner tune at the death of the dragon to show us the giant within the carapace. But it is evident that Götz Friedrich has worked out for himself a way of reading text and score which makes clear the necessary distinction of the essential from the accidental. He has accepted it as his brief 'to open up the drama of the *Ring*, not to encapsulate it; not to encircle its ideas, but rather to offer them up as questions'. The audience is to be shown that Wagner's questions about politics and love and civilization and nature are their questions. They are to enter into Wagner's mind and discover themselves. The barriers between composer and audience are to be broken down by the producer. So at Covent Garden the curtain is already raised when the audience comes into the auditorium. The traditional frontier is obliterated. And at the start of the opera audience and singers share the single darkness. They come, as the production moves forward, to share more than darkness. They share in a direct questioning of the action presented on the stage. To Götz Friedrich it is clear, from his reading of the score, that Wagner meant the audience to be included in the *Ring*'s action not as if it were a representation of what was done, but as if it were happening in the present: 'The music makes it possible and necessary for our production to use the front, the stage and outer part of the platform for remarks and questions by the stage characters who address the audience directly.' In his notes Friedrich says with total truth, 'By involving the audience musically, we seek to make them intellectually involved.' So the outsider Loge leans against the gilt procenium arch of the Royal Opera and points to the meanness and weakness of the gods, Wotan sends the ring of fire round Brünnhilde and challenges each of us in the audience to be the hero who will break his power, pointing the spear of his laws at us, and Alberich stares out into the auditorium, watching us as well as the forest lair of Fafner, and directly stating his intention to rule us. And, if we are of their time, are they not of our time? The outlaw Loge, the head of state Wotan, the industrialist Alberich? And, perhaps, the technicians of Cape Canaveral Fasolt and Fafner, the proletariat Nibelungs, the politician Gunther? Something of these. Nietzsche had it right when he remarked that the *Ring* was concerned with 'very modern problems, problems which are at home in big cities'. But he did not have it wholly right. The *Ring* is about the dimmer times of the heroes and the modern times of the factory-workers, but it is more importantly about the dimmer workings of our minds and the plainer struggles of our conscious actions as they are present to us in the theatre. Wagner has made something which in each age since his own has in performance been contemporary with his audience. The *Ring* is neither a memory nor a commentary but an experience for those who attend to the music. As Götz Friedrich says, 'The "once" and "now" is the "time of action" for a *Ring* performance.'

Götz Friedrich's success is in his getting his audience to attend to what Wagner is doing. And to ask themselves if they are quite happy with it. Those who would ally themselves with 'law and order' are shown gods who are effete and spiteful oppressors, and to whatever traces of honest feeling remain in Loge are to be attributed his refusal to climb the stair into Valhalla with such divinities. These gods, greedy for youth and wealth and power, stealing, cheating, bullying and blustering, are a worthless crew. These are the representatives of the rulers of Europe who inspired Wagner with 'the most bloody hatred of our whole civilization', and 'a contempt of all that springs from it'. These are commonly our gods. We should be dismayed at the new hero, Siegfried, who ignorantly will smash all which opposes him until civilization is brought down in chaos. As Shaw remarked in *The Perfect Wagnerite* 'godhead means to Wagner infirmity and compromise, and manhood strength and integrity'. Those who watch Götz Friedrich's production must realize that Wagner has placed them between the oppressive will of the past and the destructive will of the future. They may not like either Wagner's account of men or the producer's presentation, but, as this frightfulness confronts them, they must acknowledge that Götz Friedrich has served both Wagner and his audience with proper faithfulness.

The attention that producers like Wieland Wagner and Götz Friedrich so evidently pay to the wishes of the composer as they are discoverable from the score has its effect on members of the audience not only when they confront the operas of Wagner, but whenever they go to the opera house. What is learnt at one performance is not unlearned for another.

A REVIVAL OF FRENCH OPERA

That Wagner himself was content to convert Meyerbeer's grand opera conventions to his purpose may suggest that modes which have proved helpful in the modern presentation of Wagner's work might be converted in their turn to the service of the French nineteenth century repertory.

It is evident that something must be done. Most recent productions of such operas have been very sad affairs. It is not simply that foreigners lack the appropriate sympathy with French opera in the grand tradition. There has been no success lately in French, or even in Parisian, attempts to stage Meyerbeer. And no one could have lavished more affection on the music of Berlioz than Colin Davis in the recent muddled revival of *Benvenuto Cellini* at Covent Garden, no one unless it be Miss Sarah Caldwell producing and conducting a spectacular *Les Troyens* in Boston to small effect. It is, however, likely according to the norms of art that if audiences persist in attending performances of French opera, and not only Parisian audiences, there must eventually appear a producer of a genius akin to that of Wieland Wagner who will discover for them a new way of presenting these French pieces. Such a way will have to be precisely attentive to the peculiarities of French opera. Despite the 'Meyerbeer triplet' it is not by concentrating on common denominators that peculiar difficulties will be resolved. But at least the success of some recent interpretations of Wagner's work, in making the strangenesses of his heroic and religious themes available to modern audiences, should give hope to those who would communicate the sense of composers in this tradition.

Not a few producers have found ways of dealing with the works of those composers of French opera in the second part of the nineteenth century who were concerned with the intimacies of domestic action. The English National Opera's 1977 staging of Massenet's *Werther* worked rather better than that of the Metropolitan Opera a decade earlier mainly because the producer had suggested, with swings in the trees, children in the garden, and writing-desks galore in the study, the small scale of life within which the lovers' passion is contained. But a delicate sense of the interior quality of some episodes in the operas is not ordinarily enough to guarantee success in the communication of the composers' intentions. William Sterndale Bennett once remarked that his not having composed an opera was 'Not for the want of trying', it was simply that he had always been offered librettos which began with students or soldiers drinking. The fustian heartiness this suggests is characteristic of what is done too often with the chorus scenes of revivals of French opera. *Faust* has become almost impossible to hear because of it. Once the great 'Golden Calf' scene had been muddled into fussiness in the recent Covent Garden revival of this opera, it was of little import that such later private moments in the action as the poor girl's terror beneath the menacing baroque saints were well managed. The larger scenes must exhibit a producer's confidence in their musical and dramatic viability. A Frenchman at a performance of that *Faust* remarked, in most unchauvinist tones, 'They'd have a better chance of reviving something not quite so dead as this,' adding with recovered patriotism, 'What about Meyerbeer?' He may be mollified by Covent Garden's plans for *L'Africaine*.

The difficulty for the producer who attempts the operas of the earliest part of the century – the operas designed for imperial celebrations or for the smaller triumphs of later French governments – is to find, in harmony with the full sound of the music, some visual excitement equivalent to that which first impressed the Paris audiences. What is there now, for instance, within even the most lavishly financed producer's command that could achieve an effect comparable with that of the electric light sun which shone at the close of Act I of *Le Prophète* in 1849?

Perhaps something equivalent to Wieland Wagner's 'breadboard' revolution may yet be managed for such operas.

It was managed quite literally by M. Jean-Pierre Ponnelle for his Munich production of *Pelléas et Mélisande*. This is the most apt production of an opera I have yet attended. Every element reflected Debussy's intensification for his own purpose of that inward action he had discerned in Wagner's later work. Slowly the disc of the acting-area revolved as the composer turned the story in his mind. As in a dream, events were foreknown, dissolved, and present in perplexing instantaneity. The high axle shape, now tree, now castle, beneath whose branches Pelléas was, at the start, already dead, and at whose window Mélisande sat, turned and there again she was, tossing on her bed in Allemonde, and at the same time standing to stare at her younger self meeting Golaud in the wood. The opera turned in our minds.

M. Ponnelle was careful of the demands of Debussy. But, evidently, this delicate mode is not suitable for other operas. Something more general must be devised.

Mr John Dexter at the Metropolitan Opera has both talent and economic resource for such an enterprise. His production of *Aida*, the first of his new partnership with Mr James Levine as Musical

Director, showed both that he had taken the point of Wieland Wagner's dark Egyptian setting, and that he could do new things with it. His production placed Amneris and her father as members of a decadent culture, expressing emotion in absurd and grandiose gestures, delighting in the public games of victory, cringing beneath the statues of unfeeling gods. Mr Dexter's appreciation of the largeness of Verdi's design suggests that he may be the man to make it possible for Meyerbeer to be taken seriously by modern audiences. The production exhibited Dexter's comprehension of the social forms which rouse men to patriotic fervour and religious zeal, a comprehension which is essential for anyone who would work in the French grand opera milieu. It exhibited, too, his command of the conventional instruments of that tradition. His is the first production of *Aida* that I have attended – and it will be recalled that I have been to a great many – which made the ballet sequences an integral part of the exposition. The triumphal dance of the Egyptian gladiator over the unfairly beaten Ethiop champion told the audience a great deal about the society within which the action was played out. Something in this useful manner might have been expected, therefore, when Dexter tackled the religious fable of the Anabaptist revolt in Meyerbeer's *Le Prophète* and came to the moment when the skating ballet occupies the stage. Mr Dexter's production of that opera was not, however, a total success. He seemed to hesitate before the full demands of the work.

There were signs in his placing of the intimate scenes of *Le Prophète* on a wagon-cart to the fore of the great New York stage that Dexter wished to produce for Meyerbeer an equivalent effect to that concentration of light upon a pair of figures at the centre of a darkened stage by which Wieland Wagner had directed the audience's attention. Both devices achieved the effect of a movie close-up. The device failed in New York, however, because Dexter did not have sufficient confidence in his own idea. For the most important intimate scene of the opera the cart was simply shoved to one side of the stage because the next incident was going to occupy the whole of the acting area. The production here actually obscured the sense of the story, suggesting that the final collapse of the castle was of greater interest than the final recognition of truth by the prophet, his betrothed and his mother. Dexter was more observant of overall design and more skilful in his dealings with problems of staging in his next production of a French work.

He who had contented himself with some frightful muddles in *Le Prophète*, achieved clarity that same 1976–7 season with the equally melodramatic *Les Dialogues des Carmélites*. And made the opera at once recognizably a member of the French tradition, and universally modern. Poulenc's 1957 opera is dedicated to Debussy, Monteverdi, Verdi and Mussorgsky. Dexter has accepted the inward character of the action but he has rendered it public. The tightly organized music, held together by several recurring phrases in the orchestra, and on the stage presented almost wholly by female voices, was reflected in the simple permanent set which, by its sharply-outlined white cruciform platform, upon which the entire action was presented, figured the single motivation of the plot. Dexter's intelligence as a producer was plainly evidenced in the changing patterns of the rarely-singing dark-robed chorus. The nuns' movements created that closed community of order with which the heroine's uncertain life was ever in dialogue. Poulenc's solos and duets were given a dramatic context. What is, in the customary design of an opera score, done by choral singing, was here supplied by choral movement. The silent Carmelites' mimic action following the music shut the audience out of their lives. And shut out any character who did not at any moment share their religious life. This made the effect of the death of the delirious prioress doubly remote and lonely. The nuns moved away from the acting area, the action was concentrated around her simple bed, and as she lay blaspheming, the close-up achieved an alienating effect. The prioress was understood as belonging neither to the world of the community nor to our own. But so powerfully did Dexter establish the image of community as it worked in the young girl's mind that when, at the end, in a long line from the footlights to the depths of the stage the nuns moved up the cross to darkness and guillotine, the tug of such a community might be felt not only by the novice but by each member of the audience. Dexter, on a platform obscurely derived, I suppose, from the Bayreuth board, had made Poulenc's belief in the Carmelite life and the way of the cross as credible to his sceptic audience as Wieland Wagner had made his grandfather's belief in the romance of Tristan and the way of love in death. The wagon-cart remains as an indication that he may yet manage to do something similar for other composers.

John Dexter's production of *Les Dialogues des Carmélites* works so precisely because he has listened carefully to the music and made his singers listen with him. This is always his approach. It is the approach of all good producers of opera: of Filippo Sanjust with *Rigoletto* at Frankfurt, who made the whole plot race excitingly from the opening distrust of the Mantuan courtiers for their prince; of John Cox with *Der Rosenkavalier* at Houston, who began with the evident male-domination assumed by Octavian wrapped in the Feldmarschall's military cloak and worked his way to a final gesture from Sophie's father indicating that he had chosen this second suitor for her; and of András Miko with *I Lombardi* at Budapest, faithful to Verdi's discrete scene-making in his treatment of each incident as a separate entity. Such care by a producer makes unusual demands upon the sensitivity of his singers.

Once the lights have dimmed and the overture has begun the producer has to withdraw from the scene, leaving the singers – with whatever energy they may command in the midst of the exhausting effort to make a good enough and loud enough noise – to present his interpretation of the action. There is a nice tale of Cosima Wagner rebuking a singer who had advanced his opinion on some aspect of the part he was taking: 'My dear friend, in Bayreuth we have no opinions. Phrase it according to the sense. Take care to pronounce each word with due attention to the rhythm set down. You are not asked to do anything more than that.' If singers do indeed do that much an audience may fairly be satisfied. But producers now ask much more of them.

They do not always ask the proper thing. And there are on the present opera stage singers whose intelligent appreciation of their art has brought them to a nicer understanding of a composer's intention than those who would direct them. At the 1976 Bayreuth *Ring* the best moments occurred when an intelligent singer – Gwyneth Jones, Yvonne Minton, or Duncan McIntyre – stepped out of the stuff that, at the producer's bidding, littered the stage, and simply sang Wagner's music. These were the singers who gained their audience's gratitude and applause. Similarly in Munich the year before, when a foolhardy producer displayed Rossini's *Il Barbiere di Siviglia* (*The Barber of Seville*) before an enormous female torso, complete with pubic hair for the amorous count to climb amongst, and window in the breast at which the the charming Rosina might appear, the audience clapped enthusiastically when Hermann Prey gave the set a sardonic look. This certainly was not what they wanted in a revived French opera production. Audience and singers on these occasions entered into a conspiracy with the composer to resist the nonsense of the producer.

Mostly, however, the producer may now rely upon a cast endeavouring to represent his understanding of the opera. At least at the start of the run. Towards the end a muddle of jerks and waves may supply the place of the meaningful gestures he invented for the music, and the artist have lapsed into being simply the singer.

THE SINGER

Paradoxically a producer is often far better off in one of the smaller opera houses of Germany or Italy than he is in a great international house like Munich or La Scala. The man working for Kent Opera may be in greater control of the enterprise than the resident producer at Covent Garden. At least in his command of the singers. The advent of the jet age singer who can manage in a few weeks, or even a few days, to be singing in Buenos Aires, Paris, New York and Vienna, has made it imperative for the producer at a great house to acquire strange new skills. He has to be able to put together something which can be assimilated by a visiting singer in a few hours. The quick explanation of a producer's ideas in the taxi between the airport and the opera house is not likely to make much difference to a singer's performance of a part whose conventional performance he has learnt in other houses. Nor can a sensible producer expect it to do so. The singer has a difficult enough task without trying to do it for a few nights in a quite different way.

It would seem a remedy to engage the singers for several weeks of rehearsal and to make this as profitable for them as singing in performances elsewhere. But even if the money was available the singers might not be. Sir Rudolf Bing's memoirs include several stories of artists arriving in New York long after their contracted dates. The row about *Bohème* with di Stefano is famous. Other intendants and producers have similar tales about other singers. And if money and singers can come together once it should not be assumed that they will come together when the opera has been re-rehearsed after cast changes.

When people complain of the dull productions of the New York Metropolitan, or the sadly dusty walk-throughs of old Covent Garden pieces, they should bear in mind that in the large international houses, which must, if they are to pay their way, open each night of the week for a longish season, the resident producer's chief business is to facilitate the entry of new singers of distinct and personal fame into other men's productions which were long ago designed for quite other singers. And it must be remembered that singers quite often have a suspicion that the producer is simply inventing something new for himself without much care for anyone else. Though audiences applauded the inventions of Felsenstein at the East Berlin opera, the singers were not so enthusiastic about being made to sing out at the tops of their voices for most of the rehearsals of the previous three months. And the man who made the young Frankfurt singers lie flat on their stomachs for some of the most difficult passages of *Così fan Tutte* cannot have earned their affections. Young singers may have to take whatever direction is given them. The great ones of the international circuit may be better able to defend themselves from such demands. And, of course, better able to resist a producer's reading of an opera's meaning. They may resist at rehearsal and divert the audience in the performance.

Given the physical fact of the singer's facing the audience from a lighted stage, while the composer is in his darkened box, or darker tomb, and the conductor has his back to everyone, it is not surprising that a good number in the audience should be persuaded of the singer's especial importance in performance. Wagner, for example, listening to Ludwig Schnorr as Tannhäuser, 'gained a glimpse into my own creation', and felt that the singer had given him 'new insights into my own work'. But generally singers have not the reputation for such helpful artistry. They have rather been thought wilful, extravagant and irresponsible. The term *prima donna* is now used easily of anyone, female or not, who throws a tantrum. And even if it is often the leading male singer, *primo uomo*, who causes all the fuss on the night, insisting that some poor black-tied manager face the audience at the start with a sorry statement about 'indisposition', 'gallantly carrying on', and 'asks your indulgence', there are enough stories about sopranos to give some colour to their image. Melba, for example, was known as 'Miss Sweet and Low' because 'her voice was sweet but her language was low' as one who sang with her declared.

It is not, however, by tales of Grisi, Pasta, Melba and Callas that the singer's influence upon the structures of opera may be assessed. It is evident that opera depends upon some human beings possessing the power to make a loud vocal sound and the talent to make that sound pleasant to hear. The composer has, in his planning, to take the power and the talent into consideration and write within the limits these impose. Of course every composer writes notes or series of notes which are more than usually demanding of the singer, and singers often enough complain, transpose and omit such notes, but opera can happen only if the customary thing is for the composer to stretch the singer up to the limit of endurance and for the audience to appreciate the precise artistry which enables the singer to endure so much.

The singer works in conditions of extreme physical discomfort. The dressing rooms at Covent Garden, for example, are squalid, and in the new house at Sydney the singers have to clamber up on to the stage in unwieldy costumes, and everywhere they have to face the extraordinary experience of another human being making the loudest sound at the closest range. They need every help they can get. Kirsten Flagstad, asked by a young soprano if there were some secret to her singing of the great Wagnerian roles, replied, 'Yes, there is. Always wear comfortable shoes.' It would have been foolish for a designer to complain of her ruining his effect. The sound of such a singer is evidently the result of the singer working hard and long to achieve the mastery of the note in accord with the composer's will. And designers, like composers, have, amid their general complaints of singers' flaring tempers or habitual lateness, to recognize their dependence upon the singers's art.

One of the earliest references to the soprano, in Jacopo Peri's 1600 preface to *Euridice*, is most complimentary. Peri thanks Signora Vittoria Archilei who:

> has always made my compositions worthy of her art by adorning them not only with those turns and long trills of voice, both single and double, which by the liveliness of her talent she constantly invents . . . but also with those charms and graces which cannot be put into notation and, if put into notation, cannot be deciphered.

Such praises are as uncommon among Italians in the seventeenth century as among other nations in later times. And their rarity is a commentary upon the importance of other elements in the practical business of putting on a show. Few singers were brilliant enough to enter into competition with other diversions the impresario provided, with flying machines and descending cupids, with wind machines and rising Neptunes, with coasts of Bohemia and prowling bears. In the Venetian theatre Benedetto Marcello knew in the early eighteenth century few in the audience were much bothered about the singer's part in the story. All they demanded was a good bear to roam the stage, a mechanical nightingale to serenade the heroine, and genuine-looking lightning-bolts to harry the villain. From the singer nothing but a strong noise was required. Even when the excessive costs of the spectacle forced managements to publicize their star singers rather than their amazing machines, and when audiences were ready to turn from the repetitive circlings of so many cupids and so many sea-horses, hardly anyone expected the singers to perform their trills with any sensitivity of intelligence.

Marcello himself suggested with a gallant smile that the librettist should pay frequent social calls on the *prima donna*, 'since the success of the opera generally depends on her', and hinted at her view of the librettist with his mock-suggestion that he should change his plot and verse 'as her artistic genius may order him to do', making at her command cuts in everyone else's part, even that of the bear. A lady might well resign herself to being up-staged or even off-staged by a bear, especially if, not having read the story, she came upon the beast unexpectedly. But tenors, baritones, and other sopranos might present a different sort of danger. 'What would you cut from *La Traviata?*' Maria Callas was asked on her asserting in Chicago that most operas were too long. 'Most certainly the baritone aria in Act II,' she replied without hesitation. Madame Callas was speaking as the latest in a great procession of popular singers who have known very well that the public was prepared to pay a manager a great deal of money for the excitement of hearing them sing.

In 1725 Giuseppe Riva, the Modenese ambassador in London, wrote home to the historian Muratori a description of the London theatre and its requirements, which were that any librettist must for the next three years at least so arrange things that Francesca Cuzzoni and Faustina Bordoni, two popular Italian sopranos, would have equal parts, and that Senesino, the *castrato* singer, would have a good chance with a heroic leading part. Gradually during the eighteenth century the singers persuaded audiences and those working with them in the theatres that upon their voices the whole opera enterprise should be structured. The editor of the *Encyclopédie*, Diderot, was quite aware of the importance of the singer. And after the tinsel and the candles and the bear, he suggested that the planning of an opera should begin by taking into account what singer there was available to take the parts. He had the favourite project of making Racine's *Iphigénie* into an opera. Gluck may be said to have taken up this idea, but he did not follow Diderot's specific advice and employ a certain little lady. Diderot says, 'Let these lines be sung by Mademoiselle Dumesuil and, unless I am greatly mistaken, she will render the confusion in Clytemnestra's mind, the feelings which succeed each other in her soul. Her genius will provide her with the proper clues.' In accord with this praise Diderot allowed himself the dangerous suggestion: 'It is with her declamation in mind that the composer ought to approach his task.' Diderot seems to have been much less interested in the tenor, baritone or bass in the company. This is a common aspect of opera criticism. The tenor may be the most interesting of all voices but it is not accompanied by those precious hints of delight that the soprano trails along. Indeed of all the male voices that which has attracted most critical interest has been that which comes nearest to the soprano range. The *castrato* voice dominated opera right up to the arrival of Gluck in Paris, and it did not die away at all quickly: a fine *castrato* sound could be heard even in the twentieth century. And it is rather of this male sound that tales of egotistical domination of performances should be told. The flurries of *castrato* jealousies were great fun for audiences and a great source of worry for managers all through the seventeenth and eighteenth centuries. At the beginning critics had taken the male singer to be but another species of servant, but once the *castrati* had discovered what could be done with the Metastasio exit-aria there was no holding them. They grabbed the moment and with a profusion of trills and grace notes commanded the ecstatic applause of the audience for their own technique regardless of the proper demands of plot and character. The *castrati* were themselves reason enough for the famous reform.

It was evident to Gluck and Calzabigi that if they were to dominate the structure and effect of an opera they would have to defeat the *castrati*. In his rather wild dedicatory letter to Grand-Duke Leopold of Tuscany accompanying the *Alceste* in 1769,

Gluck speaks first of his determination to rid his opera of those abuses introduced by 'the inappropriate vanity of the singers' which have long disgraced Italian opera and which 'have transformed the most stately and most beautiful of all spectacles into the most foolish and boring one'. He would have none of the fashionable dwelling on a single vowel in order that some singer should have an opportunity of displaying his fine vocal technique, and he boasted that he had

> refused to let the singers glide rapidly over the second part of an aria, which may be the most passionate and important one, to have them repeat four times the words of the first part, or to end an aria when its full meaning has perhaps not yet been conveyed, in order to give the singer a chance to show how capriciously he can vary a passage in divers manners.

And in the 1770 dedication of *Paride ed Elena* to the Duc de Bragance he explained that 'a note more or less sustained, a change of tempo or rhythm in the vocal part, an untimely *appoggiatura*, a trill, a coloratura can ruin an entire scene in an opera'. Gluck is famous for restraining the power of the *castrati*. And yet if Gluck really broke the power of the singer how is it that so many of those who know a little of opera suppose the singers to be just such trilling creatures as he describes? It is evident that there have been many composers who, if they have not wished the singer to warble freely, have themselves written arias which would fit Gluck's account. Stendhal, for example, complained in his *Life of Rossini* (1824), of the doggerel produced by composers inserting a 'multiplicity of repeats' among the librettists' phrases. How did this come about?

It often seems that the answer to such a question must be the obvious one: that the luxurious vocal parts associated with opera were composed for just the reason one might expect. The 'canary fanciers' in the audience exerted an economic pressure that the singers knew well how to exploit.

Audiences grew bored at least as easily with the classic heroes of the reform opera as they had with the old flying machines. They came to such performances only because of the new singers.

Grétry, who spent seven years in Italy from 1759, remarked that the audience came only to hear a particular singer and, having applauded his aria, returned to the back of their boxes to play cards and eat ices. And managements, who had now to please a public rather than a patron if they were to pay their way, commissioned singers' operas from composers.

And composers seem to have complied without much grumbling. In the singers' opera the librettist was required only to arrange a melodramatic situation which would provide an excuse for a fine aria, and the composer was required only to discover what a singer could do well and provide the necessary opportunity for his display. Not every critic was, however, so easy to please as the opera audience. Voltaire complained of the new proliferation of ariettas, and in Italy certain cultivated persons were amazed that a composer should sacrifice the balance of the opera to provide a great singer with some extra display pieces for a minor role. In both France and Italy critics noted the increasing irrationality of opera actions. The scenes were no longer, it seemed, designed with any other end in mind than the climactic song. Plot, character, and meaning were supplanted by sound.

If it were only composers of an untried or second-rate talent who took such notice of the singers and their popularity then it would now be possible to dismiss the eighteenth-century opera practice as simply a decadent aberration. But, of course, the most famous and distinguished of composers was quite ready to engage in the business of the singers' opera. Mozart's letters to his father witness to his appreciation of both the singers' capacity to draw in the audiences, and the need to adapt his musical invention to the peculiar character of the individual singer's voice. There is a nice note on the first Osmin in *Seraglio* in 1782. Mozart had stood up to the Archbishop of Salzburg in the matter of Herr Fischer's bass voice, and had gone on, 'since he has the whole Viennese public on his side', to write a couple of extra arias for this minor part which would exhibit 'Fischer's beautiful deep notes' to the confusion of the Archbishop. Another aria Mozart sacrificed a little 'to the flexible throat of Mademoiselle Cavalieri'. And, if proof were needed that Mozart did not feel improperly constricted by his having to take such account of individual singers' capabilities, it is remarkable that the tenor aria '*O wie ängstlich, o wie feurig*', which was written as Mozart said 'expressly to suit Adamberger's voice', was Mozart's own favourite in the opera. The singer's voice had spurred Mozart's musical invention in a way which completely satisfied him as a composer.

No one would suggest that Mozart, simply because he wrote some of the most brilliantly difficult music and thereby supplied some famous singers with opportunities for their greatest successes, was a cheap seeker after easy popularity. His operas are evidently expressive of his greatness. Those, however, who readily allow him this status should as readily acknowledge that it is precisely through the accurate singing of his beautiful songs that most men have learnt of his greatness. It is when the role of Fiordiligi is sung supremely well and the audience is roaring its approval, that Mozart himself is being acknowledged and the desire to know him better is most likely to be formed in the opera-goer's mind. Of course Mozart can make himself heard in the most adverse circumstance. The first *Così fan Tutte* I ever heard was in a cold Durham village hall with half-a-dozen valiantly inadequate singers singing against a not-too-secure piano accompaniment. And despite this, I realized that something of value was going on in his opera. But Mozart himself, in taking so much care to fit his song to the voices of the available singers, was evidently aware of the importance of the voices sounding as if the music were made for them. If the singers could encompass the song provided then the audience would have a better chance of seeing clearly just what Mozart was offering them.

And he was not offering them a meaning which could be separated from the music. Whatever value there is in Mozart's operas for the shaping of a worthwhile human existence is acknowledgeable only so far as he is understood to have achieved his musical ambition. The beauty of his music rightly persuades his listeners that he knows something about the ordering of the chaotic elements of their experience. And generally the listener recognizes that he shares in Mozart's order, in his aesthetic which is an indication of his cosmology, through sharing in the composer's happiness at the sound of the beautiful human voice. Mozart wrote wonderful parts calculated to display all kinds of voices because he could hear the beauty in each of them. He rejoiced in the sounds they made. The human voice, extended to the limits of its possibility, delighted him and he communicates this delight to his audience in the songs he writes for his singers.

It is, fundamentally, because the beauty of the human voice, when controlled by a singer of real ability as a musician, is so splendid that composers have been pleased to accede to the demands of audiences for brilliant arias and ensembles. Composers have shared audiences' enthusiasms. And their common pleasure has its natural effect upon the box-office and the livelihood of the composer as well as everyone else employed by the management of the opera house. Since it had to be acknowledged that a show-stopper or two would keep the company in a good financial condition, many composers after Mozart willingly supplied their managements with what was demanded. Rossini was complacent enough under such a regime, at least for most of the time. Donizetti obliged the company soprano in *Lucrezia Borgia* with a final cabaletta, a fast and ornamented aria to sing after the mass murder of her guests. Bellini, having been commanded by the San Carlo management in Naples to write parts suitable for Adelaide Tosi, Giovanni David, and Luigi Lablache in his *Bianca e Gernando*, was suddenly told to rewrite everything since the first two principals were unable to sing at the première and Meric-Lalande and Rubini were to take their places. In 1831, when he was beginning work on *Norma*, Bellini received a letter from Donzelli, the *primo tenore serio* of La Scala, giving a precise account of what his voice could do, chest tones from bass D to upper G and from there up to falsetto, and always better descending than ascending. The composer was not at all offended by these implied directions. On the contrary, he replied saying these were just the things he needed to know, and was certainly content in 'having to compose my opera for a celebrated artist like you'. And he took Rubini off with him to the country so that every phrase of his part in his next opera, *Il Pirata*, might be exactly suited to his voice.

Among so many undistinguished and indistinguishable Italian opera composers of the early nineteenth century Bellini stands out as a careful craftsman who knew what he could do in opera, and knew, too, how to persuade others to let him do it.

The commercial considerations of the managers of the dozens of little opera houses clamouring for a new piece each season, and his actual success in putting together peculiarly effective operas for house singers, had been arguments enough to convince Bellini's paymasters of his value. The composer rejoiced in the opportunity the managers gave him to communicate something of his own assessment of the world to his audiences. Though he has become famous as the servant of great singers, his arias were not designed to give them a simple chance to stop the show but to forward the action he had in mind. The famous scene of Amina's sleepwalk in *La Sonnambula* is certainly one to make a singer's career if she manages to get through it with proper brilliance, but it is not just a singer's prize song. Verdi noted in Bellini's operas 'long, long, long melodies, such as no one before him produced'. These melodies are expressive in purely musical terms of Bellini's hope that his jumbled experience, lacking the easy reassurance of repetition, or the comfort of ensemble relations with others, was yet held together by some controlling power. And Bellini knew that these long melodies were immensely demanding on a singer's technical skill and immensely rewarding both in terms of the singer's private satisfaction at having successfully found the way through them, and in terms of the public cheers from the audience. In his writing of such parts as Amina or Norma he was entering into an engagement with the soprano. Bellini needed a great soprano to manage the long melodic scenes he wrote. If there were no singer capable of showing an audience the progressive yet controlled structure of his melodic writing then whatever he had to say would never be heard. The cheers at the close of the scene would, he thought, indicate not only that she was acknowledged as a great singer but that something of his sense of the universe had come across. Bellini was not reviving the old eighteenth-century situation in which the composer simply gave the lady a chance to astound the hearer with her shrieks, he was establishing an aesthetic alliance through which composer, singer and audience would come to know each other and themselves the better.

There is as direct a relation between his view of the world and the forms of his music as there is in any other composer. It is not accidental that Bellini's most famous opera, *Norma*, should lead, after the intricate weavings of a revenge plot, into a finale of forgiveness, fidelity, and self-sacrifice. Bellini's brilliant, intricate, and extended melodies, cruelly demanding on the voice, lead commonly to the cheering resolution of a clear high note.

Singers became enamoured of the Bellini style, they much enjoyed holding the audience for the length of his melody, and startling them into applause upon his high note. Verdi, inheriting this opera tradition, and indeed inheriting some of those who had sung in Bellini's operas, complained of the singers' delight in such things. He knew that his fine ensemble at the end of *Rigoletto* was commonly ruined by the soprano taking her part up an octave, and that, equally commonly, the tenor gave scope to his ambition by finishing '*La Donna è mobile*' on a high B. But Verdi, as much as Bellini, recognized his dependence upon the right singers to make his operas work. Verdi did not go in for long, long melodies and startling high-note trills, he did not go in, either, for operas in which charity finally resolved the plot, but he knew that in performance he could only put across what the singers could manage. The more inventive and skilful the composer in devising ways of making known his sympathies through the sound of soprano, tenor, contralto and bass, the more urgent must be his search for singers to realize his music. And if the singers he requires for one design do not appear then he must give it up and create another. Verdi might have written his *Re Lear* for the Teatro La Fenice in 1843 if the Venetian management could have found him a good enough bass or baritone. He might have written it in 1846 for Lablache to sing at Her Majesty's Theatre if the singer had not been ill for most of the season. He might have written it for him in 1847 if the London management had not just signed up Jenny Lind and demanded an opera for her. He wrote *I Masnadieri* instead. His dream of *Re Lear*, though it was with him until his death, remained unfulfilled. Perhaps he should have made the effort and trusted that the singer would appear. It is a sign of Verdi's realization of his dependence on the singers available to him that he did not. In this Verdi is representative of the middle opera tradition.

They managed things in just the same way in France. Gounod composed the trills of the 'Jewel Song' in *Faust*, which is rather out of the character's compass, for Marguerite, at the behest of the creatrix of the part in Paris, and the romantic lyric praise that exactly declares the character of her brother, Valentin, for Santley, the first singer of the part in London. And for the first *Faust* the composer obligingly inserted a stupendously long and elaborate trill whose evident difficulty ensured the greatest applause for the singer who managed it. But then Gounod's Marguerite, Miolan-Carvalho, changed her voice in order that she might more perfectly fit the part, and his Faust, Barbot, almost at the end of his career, was so ready to learn at rehearsals that he was reckoned by the critics to have sung better than at any other time in his career. Such singers helped the composer restore the intimacy of design that Meyerbeerian opera had eschewed. Gounod is peculiarly dependent not on his singers' technical skill or dramatic strength, but on their intuitive sympathy with the delicacies of his endeavour. They must be in sensitive command of the natural weight and nuance of his French phrases. Some things in the text that Barbier and Carre made from Goethe are as 'babyish' as Aaron Copland once admitted the libretto for *The Tender Land* to be, and yet Gounod treated everything with care. He startled his singers at a rehearsal for *Faust* by shouting from the pit, 'I know the tune, I wrote it, give me the the words.' That was how he made his opera work. From the first sound of the world-weary *rien* as, in the prologue, Faust greets his last day, the audience must sense that the piece is about their own frustration; and, as Mephistopheles provides the hero with a vision of Marguerite, from the precise inflexion of '*O merveille!*' the audience must sense that the opera is about their own capacity for wonder. Gounod can do much. Orchestra and text serve his purpose. The vision is accompanied by a hint of the later love duet, and that love is itself shown to be at risk as the scene ends with the ominous cry '*à moi les plaisirs*'. But he cannot do everything. Singers must interpret his purpose. His *rien* must not sound like Verdi's *nulla*. It requires a peculiar French timbre. If this is achieved, the opera is customarily a success. Men have responded gratefully to what singers have shown Gounod to be offering. In 1934 the Paris Opéra gave its two thousandth performance of *Faust*. The opera was performed at Covent Garden every year from its first appearance in 1863 until 1924, except for 1912 and the war years when no operas were performed. The necessary singers are rarer now than they used to be. That Frenchman at the recent Covent Garden revival could not appreciate Gounod's design. I was as mystified as he was. But my father used to talk enthusiastically of Campaniolla and Marcel Journet at the close of the first decade of this century, and of Laurence Tippett and Vezzani at the close of third, who in splendid voice made audiences aware of the subtleties of Gounod's intention. The tone of the opera, he also remarked, was determined from performance to performance, as one or other character was taken by the more mellifluous singer. But evidently there was once a successful conspiracy of composer and singers to impress audiences with the meaning of the opera. If we do not have such a conspiracy to forward Gounod's intention in the modern theatre, we have other instances of the necessary alliance of composer and singers.

After the idle triumph of singers who hoped to dominate the composers, and the exchange of confidence of composers and singers who saw how they might help each other to accomplish grand designs, there came composers who, imagining new things, created a demand for new singers. And new singers came. Oddly, Tchaikovsky seems to have been one of the first composers to envisage singers of a kind he had never known. Considering *Eugene Onegin* he wondered if he might not abandon all the old Russian opera stars who knew well how to succeed again and again in the safe structures of the imperial opera, and give his work to new, young, vigorous singers who would not tame his opera until it conformed to established norms. He was afraid of those confident singers who might claim, as Madame Callas is reported to have done at a Chicago Verdi conference, that 'the singer knows better than the composer' what will work in performance. The situation of the Composer in *Ariadne auf Naxos* as each member of the theatrical company instructs him in his business is evidently not entire fiction. But that the composers have conjured for themselves singers who can attempt things outside conventional norms is clearly audible in performance of modern opera. The trouble that Tchaikovsky had, or even the uproar when Strauss told his ladies what they could do, seems strange now that composers have created for themselves so many singers of artistry ready for anything.

In the modern opera house, though some are still content with the old-fashioned methods of the *répétiteur* to get them from one end of the role to the other, there are a great many singers who have the skills and sensitivity of extremely competent musicians. The sounds demanded by Janáček or Tippett or Henze are not to be made by chance. Composers may rely now on singers shaping their voices to whatever demand is made upon them. But for the composer, as for the producer, there comes the moment when he must retire from the direction of the enterprise. He cannot always be listening to the opera in his head. There must be an end to his reconstructing of the music and his re-imagining of the singers. That opera may take place in the theatre he must hand over the score to the conductor and allow him to exercise an authority in performance.

THE CONDUCTOR

Our modern interest in what has been done by producers and singers in the theatres of the past may in some measure be satisfied. There are a number of quite informative accounts of the ways in which opera has been presented during the past two hundred and fifty years.

There are records, descriptions and drawings and, more recently, photographs of the ways in which producers have responded to the challenges presented by composers of opera. And there are, to enliven this study of records, a vast number of more anecdotal reminiscences which convey other aspects of their productions. The reading of the accounts of those engines that Giacomo Torelli produced for French court operas in the seventeenth century, the Verdi notes for the staging of *Falstaff*, or Alfred Roller's production book for the first performance of *Der Rosenkavalier*, may be neglected by the student in favour of some smaller matters. We may wonder again at the horses of the sun who pranced from the waves at the first performance of Caccini's *Il Rapimento di Cefalo* in 1600, or smile at the 'gorgeous scenery, charming ballets and dresses as pleasing as they were happily contrasted' produced for Gluck's *Écho et Narcisse* in 1779, and cringe in sympathy at the breakdown of the revolving stage for the Zefferelli production of Samuel Barber's *Antony and Cleopatra* at the opening of the Metropolitan at Lincoln Center in 1965. Producers and their efforts, though they be dead and dust both, can be conjured from such accounts and anecdotes.

And we may be satisfied if we wish to have some sense of how the old singers sounded. There are aids to appreciation. We may not be able to hear most of the singers of the past at all, and none of them with any liveliness of sound, but we may gather something of how they were. We may read Peri's praise of Signora Vittoria Archilei in his *Euridice*, Bellini's admiring account of Giuditta Pasta, who made him 'shed many tears' at his own *Norma*, and Puccini's remark that the Brescia performer of the Consul in *Butterfly* was 'a little sausagey', and have thus a notion of the effect these singers made. And, from those who lived in the age of recording engineers, we may glean something more. Especially if we know how to listen. Caruso, singing on a Milanese cylinder recording, may have made himself a world-known performer seventy years ago, but a playing of the cylinder today does nothing to enhance his legend for most of us. However, those with ears may always hear. Richard Tauber was fond of recalling the hours he had spent playing Caruso's 1904 Red Seal records. These had been for him 'the finest lessons any young singer could have'. Patti was over sixty years old when, as the greatest singer of her time and living in her Welsh castle, she received the technicians. She was luckier than caruso. Skills and techniques had improved in the ten-year interval between their recordings. Something of her artistry comes across at the playing of her records now. But of that great era, sixty years ago, only Chaliapin's rich tone and rushing rhythms reach us with convincing vigour. These we can all hear with wonder. But if Chaliapin is in this as, reportedly, in so much else, exceptional, for all the old singers of repute we have a bundle of press notices which tell us a great deal of the singer's voice.

Notices of the singer's sound, like accounts of the producer's staging, have survived in plenty from the quite early times of opera. There is far less information about the achievements of the conductors of the past. This in itself demonstrates the slow process of public interest in the conductor's contribution to the evening's success. Marcello, for example, says little about the man in charge of the orchestra. Perhaps he did not think it worth while to comment upon a function so often performed by the composer himself. There was no such thing as a distinct profession of conducting. Even in 1829 Bellini sat at the cembalo and steered *Zaira* through its first performances. And this tradition of the composer being responsible at least for the first few performances was carried on by Benjamin Britten until illness prevented his conducting the first performance of *Owen Wingrave*.

Britten's practice was not, however, one universally adopted in modern opera. Sir Michael Tippett is well known to have remarked of Colin Davis that 'I prefer him to myself in my own works'. And Hans Werner Henze, though he is a most exciting conductor, chose rather to produce the first performance of *We come to the river*, and left the conducting to David Atherton, not because it was quite easily done, but precisely because it required immense and special musical skills. Modern composers who rely in this way upon the artistry of a conductor are working according to a pattern of things established only in the latter part of the nineteenth century. Though Verdi was in 1871 anxious to have Mariani conduct *Aida* in Cairo, he did not then make much fuss about distinguishing between the rest of contemporary conductors; 'you will find,' he wrote to Draneht Bey, 'quite the same good and bad things in all of them'. By 1893, however, he was writing to Mascheroni, who conducted his opera's first performance at La Scala, as 'the third author of *Falstaff*' with Boito and himself. The changing conditions of opera performance had brought him to give greater attention to the chief musician in the pit. And in this he was in agreement with the greater number of his contemporaries in the opera house.

As greater attention was given to the conductor, it must have seemed to many who frequented a particular house, or who were responsible for the continuity of its style in performance and the security of its finances, that their sole hope lay in the stability of the conductor. While producers became quite used to their free-lance condition, and singers began to appreciate the joys of travel, conductors seemed for a time the only ones to commit themselves to a certain house and see it through a season, and even season upon season. Busch used to stay eight months of the year with the Dresden opera, and this was not thought exceptional. And though now conductors have joined in the game of speeding by aeroplane from city to city, and have learnt to play it as well as singers, it remains true that the stability of the evening's performance is still dependent upon the conductor's work.

The producer may have flown off to work on a different opera in another part of the world, the singers may have flown in from divers parts of the world that afternoon, but the conductor, as he threads his way among the violinists and acknowledges the audience's encouraging clap, assumes command of the evening. Though he himself may not be a resident member of the house company, though he may be much occupied with problems of his own distant company, though he may be leading orchestra and singers through a score prepared by some other conductor, the audience looks to him to keep things going according to the intention of the composer. He is to muster the talents of the performers for the realization of the opera there and then. The audience looks to him, and generally he is visible. At least from the shoulders upwards.

I remember sitting in the front row of the stalls at a performance of *Les Troyens* by the Boston Opera Company and finding that whatever was not obscured by the ranged harpists was concealed by Miss Caldwell's back. That gave me some idea of the conditions of the old pitless performances. I did not care much for it. Nor did I really want to see so much of orchestra and conductor as Herbert von Karajan's arrangements for the New York *Die Walküre* allowed. Raising the pit level was in this case quite contrary to the composer's intentions. Wagner, having achieved total control at Bayreuth, lowered the orchestra into a deep pit and further concealed players and conductor and their necessary lights by erecting a wooden henge whose great curving rim hid all. This was a disposition which much appealed to Verdi, who was similarly disturbed that the visibility of orchestra and conductor should present so intrusive and what would now be termed 'alienating' an element between the audience and the opera. Verdi wrote to Ricordi in July 1871 outlining various notions he had of making attendance at opera a more forceful experience, among the chief of which was making the orchestra and conductor invisible. Sensitive as he always was to critics' charges of plagiarizing the German master's ideas, Verdi was quick to acknowledge that 'this idea is not mine, but Wagner's, and it's a very good one'. He went on with some indignation to declare that 'It's incredible nowadays that we should tolerate seeing horrid white ties and tails, for example, between us and the costumes of Egyptians, Assyrians, or Druids etc. etc. and, in addition, see the whole of the orchestra which should be part of a fictitious world, almost in the middle of the stalls among the crowd as it hisses or applauds.' And Verdi linked with this absurdity the ludicrously annoying sight of 'the flailing arms of the conductor waving about in the air'.

It would seem to be the opinion of these two great composers that conductors should be unseen and unheard. Not every member of the audience will agree with them, at least not at once. There is for many a fascination in seeing someone else at work that is not in the slightest lessened by his being Herbert von Karajan rather than a hard-hat on a building site. However these composers' distaste for the obviousness of the orchestra and conductor indicates that the works of Wagner and Verdi are, in the imagination of the composers, better done in such conditions. Those who have sat in the darkened arc of Bayreuth seats have usually felt themselves more nearly appreciative of what Wagner was attempting than on those occasions when the lighted orchestra pit has gaped between the darkness of the auditorium and the darkness of the stage. And perhaps Verdi's operas would make their effect more clearly in similar conditions. But it would be odd to expect that any arrangement would suit equally the work of every composer. What Wagner demanded and Verdi desired is not immediately recognizable as appropriate for Mozart or Strauss or Berg, who have in different ways exploited the theatrical conventions of alienation, including that of the lighted pit. Nor is it always better that the conductor should remain unheard in the theatre. Most of those who have sat in the front of the Covent Garden stalls while Mr Davis was making his rhythmic and atonal sounds to the orchestra have surely been content to hear the great controller of the evening drive the orchestra forward.

Visible or invisible, audible or inaudible, the conductor has to hold the performance together. And that activity is indescribable except in either extensive detailed talk of 'the nuances of dynamic expression' and 'the omission of the second flute from the fourth bar', as Wagner does in his writings on *The Art of Performance*, or in the quick impressionistic talk of 'a commanding grasp' and 'notably free of fussy detail' and 'feeling for the architecture of the music' with which the newspaper correspondent has to content himself. If criticism done in the first manner is really concerned with the composer's score and not much with the actual performance, the second does not commonly do more than to distinguish a pleasing from a dull evening in the theatre. It is perhaps marginally better to say simply that the conductor is above all concerned with setting the pace of the performance.

Certainly pace is at least as important in the shaping of a performance of an opera as of a symphony. In his writings about the conductor's job at the performance, Wagner declared that for a conductor the question must always be 'Has he given throughout the proper tempo?' Only if the orchestra receives this basic guidance satisfactorily can anything further be achieved at the performance. And Wagner thought that the giving of this proper tempo was hugely demanding upon the musical talent of the conductor. If the orchestra's being encouraged to give the correct rendering of the music depends upon their being led at the correct tempo it is also true that 'only through a knowledge of the correct rendering throughout can that proper tempo itself be found'. The conductor must school himself for the work before he can appreciate what time is needed for each part of the performance. What seems merely elementary to those who listen is only achieved by the most sophisticated and disciplined interpreters. So Wagner thought it a self-respecting composer's duty to provide correct guidance for his conductor. Earlier composers, Mozart for instance, had been confident enough of the musicianship of the conductor to publish their scores with simple directions like *allegro* and *andante*; Wagner began by giving careful directions at all places in the score and fixing them by stating the pace with reference to the metronome. But performances of *Tannhäuser* sounded so unlike his design, and yet were so exactly in accord with his statements, that he learnt to distrust the value of mathematics in music. He came to content himself with a general direction at the start and detailed remarks about modifications of the set time. But even this careful method, he noted, could not prevent some conductors dragging *Rheingold* out to over three hours and others scurrying through in not much more than two. Such experiences in the theatre convinced Wagner that the appreciation of the composer's markings of modifications was 'the point where the conductor has to show himself worth his salt', and 'the attentive reader will understand that we here are handling a positive life principle of all our music'. Not a witty playing with the music – though even this he allowed with *La Figlia del Reggimento* and *Martha* – but a serious obedience to the song of the music.

The length of the *Ring*, even when taken at a galloping pace, makes it a famous test of conductors. But the conductor has other kinds of crisis to manage, even in the Wagnerian corpus. He who tackles *Tristan und Isolde*, for example, must have the stamina to keep a hold on every moment of the opera, otherwise chaos will come again. That stupendous effect of the 1952 Bayreuth *Tristan und Isolde* was in large measure due to the compelling mastery of Herbert von Karajan's conducting which kept in perfect balance the grand orchestral sound and the clear-voiced singing of Ramon Vinay and Martha Mödl. These things must be done together. No amount of lovely singing or lively acting will take the place of the necessary orchestral tension. Though it seems to me perverse to play, as Wagner permitted and arranged, parts of this opera as an orchestral concert piece, it is certainly the case that a great deal of the action of the opera takes place in the orchestra. All would fall apart if anything happened like the incident at a *Traviata* I attended in New York. The conductor lost his place several times but because the orchestra could muddle along in the accompaniment recovery was achievable in a matter of bars. A momentary disconcertment of the band and the singer was all that had occurred.

It will not do, of course, to generalize from these examples and suggest that while Wagner's works take some managing a novice might properly start with operas of Verdi's maturity. But it is true that a young man may make less of a mess of a Verdi performance than a Wagner one if he has by intuitive and trained musicianship a sense of the world within which Verdi's action moves. And such a sense is not necessarily achieved with age. The scenes in a Verdi opera are customarily short and divided by curtain calls and intervals. For such a style of composing to hold together at all in the theatre the audience must feel at the moment of re-assembly that something has been resumed in a firm manner. Verdi, in most of his operas, like Mozart in *Don Giovanni*, may have been content to show the chopped-up character of human experience, but he required that an audience should realize that it was experience he was presenting and not just a set of grand scenes and splendid songs. Some most experienced conductors when faced with one of the great Verdi operas, with *Aida*, say, put themselves to the matter with great verve in each successive part but are wholly unable to hold the opera together. And some can recall attention after a half-hour interval as Signor Muti demonstrated again and again at a recent much-gapped production of that opera at the Teatro Communale in Florence. To his sustained care for Verdi the singers and the orchestra, of course, responded. The sound seemed precisely that which, if one had had the imaginative power, one would have made for oneself from reading Verdi's score. The effect was fine in each section and culmulatively tremendous, so that by the last act the conductor had brought those on the stage, in the orchestra pit and in the auditorium to realize something which seemed precisely what Verdi had intended. Those who had collected their raincoats in the final interval, and those who had asked each other whether they ought not to leave before Amneris's great scene, stayed to cheer long after the finish at one in the morning.

That performance of *Aida* was one of those which, precisely because the singers and the producer are heard and seen at the beginning to have done their work perfunctorily, demonstrate the encompassing scope of the conductor's responsibility in the presentation of the composer's work. Such a performance justifies the modern custom of allotting the conductor the final solo bow at the conclusion of the opera. If anyone in the theatre represents the composer it is the conductor. The great story of a conductor's representation of the absent composer's interests is that of the young Toscanini laying down his baton at the first performance of *Turandot* on 25 April 1926, after the scene of Liu's death, and turning to the audience to say 'At this point Giacomo Puccini broke off his work. Death on this occasion was stronger than art.' And only on the second night did he conduct the opera to the end that Franco Alfano had provided.

Though not every conductor is faced with a score left unfinished by the composer, every one is faced with deciding just how the score is to be interpreted into a performance. In his writings on conducting Wagner seems to be suggesting that there is only one 'correct' pace for each moment of the opera. This is natural in a composer. He has worked hard to realize exactly the invention of his own mind, and knows how he hears the music in his inward ear. But it is possible, without entering upon an amateurish psychological discussion of the relation of composer to composition, to suggest that others may discern in an opera a perfectly proper 'modulation' of the piece which the composer himself had not appreciated. It seems to me, and to a number of other listeners that, as Desmond Shawe-Taylor remarked, the 'dramatic power and thrust' of Stravinsky's *Oedipus Rex* is so much more evident in Colin Davis's 1962 performance than in the oratorio-like version the composer himself produced. At Sadler's Wells the work pressed forward with an urgency and immediacy which no other conductor has managed. Even with the composer's own rendering on the record-player, Colin Davis's seems an eminently possible way of doing the work.

Certain conductors have discovered within themselves talents more appropriately used in the service of one composer than another, but any opera conductor who wishes to earn enough to pay his rent must be ready to tackle a largish range of works even if one may baulk at Peri and another at Berg and a great many more at Wagner. And a conductor who takes his service of some admired composer with due seriousness may well be offended at what is going on the stage. Hans Knappertsbusch was never happy with Wieland Wagner's unrealistic production of *Parsifal* and quickly decided to give up his association with the Bayreuth festival, though he relented on the sudden death of the conductor who replaced him and seems not to have worried much more about Klingsor not having his spear. Colin Davis is said to have disapproved of the Covent Garden production of Berlioz's *Les Troyens*, and his conducting of the opera lacked his customary musicianly elegance; on the other hand this conductor's rumoured delight in Peter Hall's realization of Tippett's *The Knot Garden* in 1970 seemed to be wholly confirmed by the splendid integrity of the performance. The composer himself remarked, 'I know that Colin has an instinctive understanding of what I want.' He is a conductor who suggests rather more persuasively than any other that Berlioz and Tippett are not simply good to hear but have something interesting to communicate.

Such a sympathy of conductor with composer will not be characterized by the conductor's losing himself in the composer's world. In setting the pace the conductor expresses his own response to what he has truly discerned in the music. So in Wagner's own example of the conductors who took his work at greatly differing paces, it may be that a conductor who does things differently from Wagner's own pacing of *Rheingold* will persuade in performance that his reading is also a possible way of undertaking the score. And there may be a goodish number of such possible ways. It is not necessarily because one conductor is himself so much faster a person than another, but that one supposes Wagner's work to go at as driving a pace as the relentless action he presents on the stage, while another supposes that the work demands a long-held attention to the slow-growing complexity of Wagner's musical form. Each may rightly claim to be obedient to his understanding of the will within the opera.

It is one of the livelinesses of opera that Wagner's will as expressed in the opera itself, and that of every major composer, is large enough to encompass more than one pace of the action. Bayreuth has kept meticulous records of how long each act of Wagner's operas took when played under the direction of each of the long line of those distinguished conductors who have been engaged there. There is a considerable variation even in these solemnizings of Wagner's own festival. Some in the audience will prefer one pace and grumble or even stay away when some differently-minded conductor is in charge. And critics will like to dispute about such matters. Bernard Shaw thought Siegfried Wagner as good a conductor of his father's music as Hans Richter, but Debussy was not at all impressed, judging the son to be merely 'mediocre'. It is patent that, given the necessary sensitivity in a conductor to the intention of the composer, the conductor will, in presenting the composer's music communicate his own appreciation of how things are. The making of the music allows him to speak to the listener himself. 'Above all,' Colin Davis once remarked, 'in our music-making we must present our real self or it all means nothing.'

The conductor's responsibility for the pace and coherence of the performance has as its complement the conductor's total control of the evening's enterprise. At the raising of the baton and the giving of the decisive beat to the orchestra there is no one but the conductor who has any hope of shaping the audience's experience. And there is no one but the conductor to keep the performance going from moment to moment. The conductor has to know everything that has been designed to happen in the pit and the stage, and he has to hold it all together from bar to bar. This requires a talent that is rather more out of the ordinary than audiences usually acknowledge. It should command more admiration generally. While there are enough to applaud a conductor on the emergence of a fine dramatic sweep in the performance, there are certainly not enough to recognize those moments of craftsmanship when he has rescued it from absolute disaster by heaving the orchestra and quite a number of the chorus forward by eleven bars when a solo singer has skipped a bit. On the wielding of such command the success of an evening may wholly depend.

No one else has such an immediate command in the opera house. All those who have worked to put the performance together in the days of planning and rehearsal, even the masterful producer, are on the night of the performance wholly dependent upon him. If, for example, the conductor loses his grip on the various forces that are deployed in the first five minutes of *Rigoletto*, the orchestra, the chorus, the soloists, the off-stage band right playing one air and the off-stage band left playing another, nothing that anyone else can do will get the opera safely to Gilda's death and the hunchback's collapse beneath the curse of Monterone. This is ever the case in the opera house. It proves sometimes most irksome for producers who have a lingering sense of themselves as creators of a meaningful action, and who suspect that the conductor is rather more interested in getting the sound right.

It was with such feelings that Wagner had so ordered the proceedings in the orchestra at his festival that the activities of the conductor and the players should complement those of the producer. The 'Bayreuth style', as it was begun by Wagner and perpetuated by his fearsome widow, consisted chiefly in the subordinating of everything in the orchestra pit to what was happening on the stage. The conductor was to keep the orchestral noise down and allow the singing actors to command the audience's whole attention. Felix Mottl, one of the most favoured of Bayreuth conductors, protested in 1880 that he 'thought of nothing but the stage' when he was conducting. Such attitudes are not universal. There are a good many conductors who sympathize with that angry man at the *Khovanshchina* rehearsal who complained as he left the podium that the chorus was failing to sing with the orchestra because there was far too much acting going on. The conductor has to think first of the composer's intention as it is manifested in the music if the opera is to make its way to the audience's appreciative understanding.

It sometimes seemed to Wagner that things could only work out well if producer and conductor were one and the same man. But even he left the 1876 Bayreuth performance of the *Ring* to the conducting of Hans Richter. Few later men have possessed in Wagner's measure the necessary duality of talent to bring off a success all by themselves. Herbert von Karajan has in recent years at Salzburg tried his hand at producing as well as conducting, but whatever success he has had with *Don Carlos* and *Lohengrin* has not protected him from charges of being too ambitious.

Most of those concerned in the making of a performance have a suspicion that they could very well do someone else's job. Chaliapin was hated by the other singers at the Imperial Theatre because he so often suggested ways in which they might better convey the characters they were singing. In his autobiography he recalled with pleasure that his interference in the St Petersburg production of Mussorgsky's *Khovanshchina* turned an evening of boredom into one of exciting success. It did not matter much to him how many folk he alienated. Lately rather more modest singers, like Regina Resnik or Sir Geraint Evans, have tried their hands at producing operas in which they have already achieved some success as singers under others' direction. And both Placido Domingo and Dietrich Fischer-Dieskau have with some grace taken up the conductor's baton in the recording studio and the concert hall. Conducting in the opera house, however, is recognizably a more demanding business. Few singers have attempted it. The intrepid Chaliapin did indeed once ask himself whether he ought not to step down from the stage and take over the conducting of an opera, but, foreseeing 'another Chaliapin scandal', he wisely decided to let the opportunity pass him by. Whatever Wagner's aesthetic hopes or other men's selfish ambitions, the best results in opera are not to be obtained by the single efforts of one star performer. Opera achieves its excitement from the coming together of distinct and talented persons in a cooperative mood. And under the leadership not of producer or singer, but of conductor.

A producer and a singer can at moments of rare sympathy manage to do things they might never have dreamt themselves capable of alone. Wieland Wagner's 1962 production of *Salome* at Stuttgart was given vital energy by his relationship with Anja Silja. An understanding of this kind is not rare between conductor and singers or singer. Such a sympathy has customarily been the structural element in the making of a strong ensemble company in the opera house. Beecham knew well how to bring his customary singers to unexpected triumphs. Herbert von Karajan's best work recently has been accomplished with a relatively small family of favoured Salzburg singers. Such a sympathy may also have a brilliant individual effect. Riccardo Muti, lamenting that now too many conductors walk into the orchestra pit 'without really *knowing* about the voice and how to bring the best out of a singer', pointed enthusiastically to the way in which Tullio Serafin had cherished and developed the talents of Maria Callas. Kiri Te

Kanawa, in another interview published in *The Times*, spoke of Colin Davis as a conductor who 'makes you work and work to achieve what seems impossible', and of him and others who 'take all the time and trouble in the world' to get what they know the singer can accomplish.

And most famous of all modern examples of such artistic sympathy is the inter-dependent work of Richard Bonynge and his wife, Joan Sutherland. They have brought one another along tremendously. Bonynge's enthusiasm as a conductor for the work of Bellini and Donizetti enabled him to discern in Joan Sutherland a great dramatic coloratura soprano ready to sing the heroines created by these composers. She found in him a conductor with whom she could realize the unknown wonders of her own voice. One of the nicest anecdotes of modern singing is that which relates how Bonynge, knowing his wife did not have perfect pitch, tricked her into registers that she would not have believed to be within her compass, until at last she heard herself singing an F sharp at full voice. And she, knowing how carefully he controls the orchestral sound so that her proper effect is obtained, has brought him as her conductor to the great opera houses of the world. Others may grumble, but the success of their partnership is maintained only because audiences have heard in the freer sound she makes when he conducts a singing nearer to the intention of Bellini or Donizetti than at any other time.

Success comes in obedience to a composer. In opera it is only when the conductor, trusted and obeyed by singers and players, has, not in his own name but in the name of the composer, taken control, that he will find his proper way to the audience's approval.

Six

Who goes there?

Voltaire remarked in a letter of 1732 that 'the opera is only a public meeting-place, where one gets together on certain days without knowing quite why'. Certainly one does not go with any serious purpose. His opinion was backed, thirty years later, when Rousseau framed a graceful definition of opera for the *Dictionnaire de Musique* in 1764: '*Opera*: a dramatic and lyrical spectacle in which one endeavours to combine all the graces of the fine arts in the representation of a passionate action, with the intention of arousing interest and creating illusion by means of a pleasant sensation.' Rousseau had seen the sense of *opera*, a combination of works, a coming-together of various skills, but he had, from the example of contemporary operas, no thought of all this effort producing more than a pleasing fiction, a passionate sensation, in the theatre. And not everyone was greatly pleased or immensely stimulated.

It is a recurring complaint of French critics, made by Saint-Evremond in 1677, Grétry in 1789, and Beaumarchais later, that, as this last critic said, 'even the most enthusiastic opera-lovers, even I myself, are always bored at the Opéra'. Yet Saint-Evremond could not stop talking about the funny things that happened to him at the opera, even paying the compliment of satire in his book *Les Opéras*; Grétry persuaded Voltaire to provide him with a couple of librettos; and Beaumarchais's *Le Barbier de Séville* was first designed as a comic opera libretto. The comic evidently attracted such men more than the grand.

The social acceptability of the comic form seems to represent a willingness among audiences to approve any attempt to preserve the delights of opera while relieving them of the burden of the composers' indulgence in the extravagance of dull solemnity. In the consideration of this, as of every other stage in opera history, account must be taken of the audience's appreciation of the potential of opera for present reference to the action of their lives clashing with their dissatisfaction at the distancing effect of the stuff offered in the stage action of a decadent theatre. Such was the occasion of *opera buffa*.

SPEAKING AND SINGING

There is a tradition, begun in Italian *opera buffa*, and continuing in German *singspiel* and French *opéra-comique*, of combining lively songs with spoken dialogue. While the modern fashion for everything in musicals to be sung represents a leaning towards the recitative and aria forms of *opera seria*, the effect of *opera buffa* was rather like that of the old musical comedy. This has at times seemed to its audiences to be at once real and amusing.

Unkind gossips have suggested that the form began with cheap provincial satires of small musical quality. The eighteenth-century Neapolitan *opera buffa*, however lively, was not simply a bright and cheerful romp through musical comedy situations. In the famous *La Serva Padrona*, for example, which began as an intermezzo for one of Pergolesi's *opere serie*, the writing for the young maid Serpina is beautifully tender as well as brilliantly funny. And when in the middle of the century Galuppi and Piccinni were writing for *opera buffa* singers who were not too well-voiced they turned this want to advantage and paid full attention as composers to characterization within the music and the acting of the incident. Algaroth admired the 'expression', Gray delighted in 'the variety of gesture' of such Italian singers in London and the *opere buffe* of the Italians at the Académie Royale in Paris were so good that chauvinism was anticipated in the *guerre des bouffons*. In 1752 an Italian company had arrived in Paris and, much to the disgruntlement of the more nationalist critics, had become the fashionable rage after their performance of *La Serva Padrona*. Rousseau himself had in 1752 composed an *opera buffa*, *Le Devin du village*, which had much pleased the king, and even Diderot, the editor of the *Encyclopédie*, got as far as sketching an *opera buffa* libretto, remarking as he did so that after *opera seria* 'we need something more forceful, less mannered and truer to life'. 'Truer to life' is not quite the same as 'greater realism'. Diderot and his friends could have no idea of what Mozart, Wagner, and Verdi, would make of the form. They simply had a sense that something was very wrong with the kind of thing they witnessed in the contemporary opera house. These great men had grown tired of the harmonious Rameau and his uniformly delicate court entertainments. Rousseau noted that no one could endure the 'drawling music' of French opera after the *opera buffa* liveliness.

But, however attractive the *opera buffa*, it was not quite French. The nationalists set about chasing the Italians out of Paris. At the end of the *guerre des bouffons* in 1754, *opere buffe* having been driven out, the way was clear for *opéra-comique* to take up the devices of the expelled Italian troupe, and to find new ways of using old French devices. The first step was taken by the translating of *La Serva Padrona* into French and the introduction of French spoken dialogue where the Italian original had recitative. The arrival from Rome in 1767 of André Grétry, an energetic and talented composer, signalled the start of fashionable delight in *opéra-comique*. Grétry in the service of a demanding public managed to produce over seventy operas none of which is now performed, though in Tchaikovsky's *The Queen of Spades* the aged Countess sings softly to herself an air from Grétry's *Richard Cœur de Lion* as a reminder of a gracious past.

Other composers have recognized that the conventions of opera, since they are designed to persuade those in the audience to identify with the character and to learn from that experience, militate against the telling of unconsidered trifles and yarns of no import at all, and have seized upon *opéra-comique* as a way to tell such tales. Of these the greatest is Bizet, and the triumph he managed in *Carmen* was effected precisely because he could keep the audience out of the action as simple spectators and listeners to the tale. Bizet knew exactly what he was doing even though the experts were not aware of the nature of the conventions he intended to employ. When Leuven, the administrator of the

Opéra Comique, was told of Bizet's plan for an opera based on Merimée's *Carmen*, he was horrified, 'You'll frighten our audience away', he blustered in his apprehension of what would happen to their hopes of making a nice profit that year. Bizet retained some of the popular *ópera-comique* elements, like the grand entrance of the toreadors and Michaela's touching song in the third act, but he stiffened the last scene despite Leuven's plea: 'Death at the Opéra-Comique. That's never happened before, do you hear, never. Don't let her die, I implore you.'

Leuven feared that *Carmen* would prove unsuitable for his family audiences, and the wedding parties who filled his boxes. Such a degrading tale could not, if told in a realistic manner, do anything but offend. The Paris critics thought *Carmen* a startling and provocative work designed to break through the carefully controlled conventions of operatic art and social morality. *Le Gaulois* suggested that if it went one step further the police would have to be called in. While the critic of another paper preserved decent normalities by declaring the character of the heroine to be in a pathological condition 'likely to inspire the solicitude of physicians'. Everything about the opera seemed to be very real to the professionals of the theatre. There was certainly an aspect of realism to the Toulouse production when the bullfighters came straight from the local arena to swell the last act procession. But neither the death of Carmen, nor the life she led, shocked the members of Leuven's audience. Not even those in the wedding-party boxes. They all knew full well that this was happening to someone else. The way in which the story is told by Bizet deliberately prevents it being understood as a story about ourselves. So anything may happen and you and I, who are free of such things, may watch untouched. This is recognizably fiction. *Carmen* is the one full-length *verismo* opera whose popularity is unquestioned and whose artistic merits are not inconsiderable.

Nietzsche in *The Case of Wagner* in 1888, announcing his full recovery from Wagner who was 'merely one of my sicknesses', was delighted to advertise the Provençal cordial of Bizet's opera.

Celebrating the twentieth time he had gone to Bizet's *Carmen*, he exclaimed: 'Have more painful tragic accents ever been heard on the stage? How are they achieved? Without grimaces. Without counterfeit. Without the *lie* of the great style.' Nietzsche at least evidences how monstrous are the feelings of those who slough off their enthusiasm for Wagner's work. Debussy was a little like this, too. But it is obvious that it is not simply anti-Wagnerism which persuades Nietzsche that Bizet's opera is wholly real.

'No Senta-mentality', he punned on the name of Wagner's heroine in *The Flying Dutchman*, but love as it really is, 'the deadly hatred of the sexes', that is what Bizet offered. *Carmen* was the perfect example to persuade men of 'the necessity to Mediterraneanize music'. Bizet's discovery of 'the south in music' made Wagner seem ridiculous. It is ironic that, at its catastrophic first performance in 1875, *Carmen* was generally thought to be too 'Wagnerian'. But later audiences have echoed Nietzsche's praise of the opera. Halévy, one of Bizet's librettists, remarked on its thousandth performance that Bizet had discarded the conventions of the form and 'tried only to impart the greatest possible degree of truth and passion to his work'. He could even bring himself to say that Bizet in this piece 'scorned all cheap effect'. That avid opera-goer Tchaikovsky much admired the 'easy naturalism' of *Carmen*. It had, he remarked, characters 'whose feelings and experiences I shared and understood'. In this he thought it so unlike the melodramas of Verdi.

These are remarks which, however oddly they now sound, perfectly represent the common desire of the audience for an experience of opera which comes close to their own lives. Others have thought that the comic form of mixing speech with song deprives opera, however stirring the nearness of the action, of its proper importance. According to this opinion, if an opera is to render the significance of life in a manner employing the full potential of the art then everything should be conveyed within the music.

For some the *singspiel* and the *opéra-comique* have been so thoroughly devalued that for those works in these traditions which musicians and audiences recognize as having some distinction protective persons have composed settings for the spoken parts. I cannot recollect a performance at which anyone has been rash enough to attempt anything of the sort for Mozart's *Seraglio* or *The Magic Flute*, but it was only Karl Böhm's denunciation of the outrage that put a stop to the Metropolitan's custom of setting the spoken dialogue of *Fidelio* to music. Bizet is still badly served by those who have put his dialogues to tunes in their improvements of *Carmen*.

Gounod himself, seeking a single tone for *Faust*, decided that the speech of his first version had to be eliminated. After the first performances at the Théâtre Lyrique in 1859 he wrote accompaniments for recitative for the Strasbourg production of 1860. He certainly strengthened the formal structure of his work, but, paradoxically, his was a theme which might well have benefited by being presented in the disturbing juxtaposition of song and speech. Weber had, in *Der Freischütz*, shown how a devil might, by his speaking among the singers, show that he did not belong to the human world. Gounod was not intelligent or innovative enough to exploit the possibility of speech as an indicator of all not being uniformly well with Faust in a world of song. Later composers have made something virtuous out of the very sense of untidiness that speech produces in the opera house. Of these Schönberg is certainly the most inventive in exploiting the tension created by the gap between speech and song. In his unfinished opera *Moses und Aron* he presented the opposing sensitivity and temperaments of the two brothers by having one speak and the other sing. The interruption of a speaker in the midst of an opera is both grating and stimulating to the listener, making him shift his mode of attention and thus internalizing the division between two views of the world. This is a creative abuse of an admitted tradition. Schönberg assumes the audience's expectations of opera and deliberately encourages and disappoints them. Moses' speech is a designed shock. It works only because audiences are used to characters whose importance reaches to the mythic being set with a wholly singing context. There is here a disturbance carefully engineered by the composer and eminently recognizable by the audience.

In Iain Hamilton's *The Royal Hunt of the Sun* a parallel disturbance is obtained by a composer's use of silence. The Indian interpreter mimes his translation of Pizarro and the Inca as they sing. While he is their voice he is himself silent. When, most unexpectedly, the interpreter breaks into song we realize that he is, while still pretending to interpret, expressing his own desires. He has hopes of manipulating the great men for his private purposes. His mime was another's. His song is his own. Song is personal. At such moments opera makes perfect sense.

A COMMON SENSE

Opera audiences had come by the early nineteenth century to find nothing at all outlandish in Pepoli's bitter charge to the writer who wished to become a successful librettist that he should take a 'weird subject', give up all thought of 'whys and wherefores', and set off like a steamship, 'all spume and smoke and noise'. And things have not seemed all that more reasonable to those enthusiastic for opera even after Wagner had worked his revolution and centred attention upon something within the character rather than upon the machinery of the narrative. At any rate even the most enthusiastic persons are likely to make odd remarks about the events of his most serious operas. Madame Kirsten Flagstad, at a Viennese dinner, remarked cheerfully that she 'went along with Isolde in Act I until she drinks that potion, after that she's just soppy'. An audience's serious attention to the significance of Schönberg's work, cannot, therefore, be taken as a paradigm of the relation of composer and audience even now. There are many in the house who have come precisely to escape 'the real world' of aunts and mortgages and galoshes. They want a night 'out' of such a world. They expect the curtain to open upon a wholly fictitious and irrelevant amusement. People are so contrarily demanding that the charge of absurdity is often made still. But it is not so damaging as the charge of boredom. Sometimes an audience may be unkind enough to make both on the same evening. At the first night of Hans Werner Henze's *We come to the river* at Covent Garden my companion said on opening his programme and glancing through the synopsis of the plot, 'O, I see it is going to be one of those absurd things.' At the very end of the evening an elderly gentleman behind me remarked with great conviction to a small American boy: 'I'll tell you why they're clapping; they're clapping because they are glad it is over. They didn't enjoy it. None of them enjoyed it.' Perhaps Henze's combination of an obvious disregard of many conventions with a covert use of many others made it unlikely that he would delight and interest everyone. But he did have a serious intention, and he did make an effort to announce to his audience that opera might be a celebration of some seriousness.

In the late nineteenth century Busoni suggested that most members of the opera audience wanted 'to see powerful emotions on the stage because, as average individuals, they experience none in real life'. All this may, of course, be fair comment on earlier audiences, though I doubt it. But the good number of persons who now go to performances of opera, pay quite large sums for their tickets, and approve their governments' subsidies for the theatre, are unlikely to be all looking for a poisoning scene, a trilling soprano and a bear. In 1891, Mark Twain at Bayreuth thought that 'seven hours at five dollars a ticket is almost too much for the money'. In days when the private spending of most of us has to be inspected for some economies and the grounds for a subsidy must be looked at narrowly by some Treasury official, it is all the more likely that reasons other than sensationalism persuade so many people to buy tickets.

There has ever been a widespread suspicion that quite a number of opera-goers are simply ensuring that they are seen in the intervals between the acts, rather as people are said to become teachers because of the long school holidays. The slowly pacing procession, always anti-clockwise, I think, through the marbled halls of modern German opera houses may bear a hint of this. I can remember as my first acquaintance with the ugliness of the world's governors the parade of elderly men and splendid young women, all diamonds and gold lamé, at the intervals of the Bayreuth *Tristan und Isolde* in 1952. And sometimes at Covent Garden voices can be heard announcing loudly what Boris hinted to Evelyn at the embassy reception. But such things are not the rule. Commonly in the stalls, as in the gallery, the talk is of opera. This is to be expected because most of those who have bought seats in the stalls began their opera-going in the gallery. A liking for opera is commonly begun in late adolescence when few boys or girls have the money to indulge in luxury. An old man's memories of youthful enthusiasm may suggest that those in the gallery are there for the opera and that the tired persons sitting round him in the stalls are not. But in fact all, or almost all, are.

And all, or almost all – the old man in the stalls, the young girl in the gallery – are there with some sense of each other's presence. Opera is evidently not simply the result of the cooperation between those behind the scenes, on the stage, and in the pit. The audience is needed. And each member of the audience as much as those giving the performance needs the others in the house. And most of those who are present realize this, and realize it in the most inauspicious surroundings with no help at all from red plush and chandeliers. In the Hynes Auditorium at Boston, where a sadly depleted Metropolitan cast and orchestra gave a poor performance of *Fidelio* to an audience which had paid a great deal of money to sit on uncomfortable folding chairs, the peculiar operatic community was established. Beethoven's confidence in the communion of all human beings was justified as an unknown dowagerly lady turned to me at the interval saying 'Well, aren't you glad to be here?' We settled at once into talk of the great cry '*O Freiheit, kehrst du zurück?*'

At such a moment of the breaking of social restraints the revolutionary action of *Fidelio* is manifest, and the performance has become paradigmatic of what each opera performance makes its aim. The audience has realized its community in the music.

For the success of the evening there must occur a communication of appreciation between the members of the audience. Not simply in the talk of strangers to each other at the interval but in the shared realization during the performance that something of value is happening. And there must occur also a realization that what is happening has not simply been generated in the house that night but arises from all past performances of opera.

In going to an opera a man becomes not simply a member of an audience at a particular performance but also a member of a general tradition of performance. The repertory of a great opera house is certainly likely to include new works from season to season, but it will ordinarily be composed of revivals of older operas. Mozart, Wagner and Verdi are long dead, Puccini and Strauss not quite so long; between them these composers substantially fill the programmes of houses in every country. Anyone who goes at all regularly to performances of opera in a major city for more than a year or so is going to see several pieces again and again. That he expects. It is an attraction of opera that it represents the vitality of the past to those who would have a share in the Western cultural tradition. And for those who have come in for such a share it is almost impossible to be disappointed enough by a performance of one of the staple works, however inadequate or misconceived, to give up the practice of opera. The vitality of the tradition sustains the sharer. He has come with the conviction that it is in the opera itself, not in the performance of the singer, the producer, or the conductor, assisting though they be, that what is important persists. And singer, producer, and conductor, distracting though they be, cannot prevent his sharing what the composer is offering. Stendhal, attending a Vicenza performance of Rossini's *The Italian Girl in Algiers* in 1817, noted how the opera could 'fire a blaze of joy in a third-rate theatre where the highest attainment was unqualified mediocrity'. It is characteristic of opera audiences, therefore, to expect a good deal from a performance and to recognize the demand made for their careful attention. Critics have not always admitted that others in the house have come with such serious purpose as they.

Beaumarchais, having commanded the singers to 'Enunciate clearly' and the orchestra to 'Play more softly', went on to demand with some irony that the audience 'concentrate for three hours on a work created in as many years'. Most of those who buy tickets for an opera would wish to pay the composer such deliberate attention. They are all well aware of his having made an effort to communicate his meaning and even those like the gentleman reading a newspaper between the acts at La Scala, or the lady with green-painted face at Cincinnati, are there to hear what the composer says in his three hours. Busoni's remark that the member of the audience 'neither knows nor wants to know that he who would enjoy a work of art must actively contribute to the pleasure' is not, at any rate now, of general application. But the difficulty of concentrating for so long upon an operatic action remains. Our energies are not limitless. And the composer in expecting such an attention is accepting a responsibility to present his meaning as precisely as he can manage. It is for an appreciation of the particular cast of his mind that the audience has assembled.

The singer, producer, conductor, or the critic in the morning paper may each have some persuasive power, but the audience assembles in order to witness Gluck's *Iphigénie en Tauride* or Weber's *Der Freischütz* or Berg's *Lulu*. It is the composer who is recognizably in charge. The audience has bought tickets on his account. They are spending their time at the opera because thus they will be able to see for themselves what kind of order the composer has been making for himself. They think it a fair chance that what the composer presents will be not merely amusing, though they will not despise an offer of entertainment, but illuminating. They have some faint hope that it may even prove provoking enough to stimulate their own appraisal of experience.

Not everyone in the audience, nor any one all the time, of course, will have these notions of what he is doing in the theatre, but most, some of the times they attend opera performances, have entertained something of such a hope. And generally the expectation of an illumination of their lives through the music is at least partially fulfilled by what the audience receives from the opera composer. It is the rule not the exception for a composer to recognize the audience's right to hear something of themselves in an opera. At the very start of opera, Monteverdi had objected to making an opera out of a tale of the marriage of wave and wind: 'How can I, through these winds, affect an audience?' The history of opera is the history of that effort to affect audiences' awareness of themselves through the musical action of the drama. The greater intensity of expression achievable through the operation of music upon areas of human sensitivity largely untouched by the spoken word has customarily encouraged the composer to hope that from the telling of his drama's story audiences would become vitally aware of those areas within.

Though it is precisely through the musical telling of the drama that opera has its effect the peculiar stir of the operatic experience is not confined to the musicians in the audience, nor are musicians the only ones to make a proper judgement on what is offered them. Addison remarked, 'Music is not designed to please only chromatic ears, but all that are capable of distinguishing harsh from disagreeable notes; a man of ordinary ear is a judge of whether a passion is expressed in proper sounds, and whether the melody of those sounds be more or less pleasing.' This is a meagre account of what each member of the audience can expect from an opera composer. If Mozart's father was merely echoing Addison's thought when he advised his son 'when composing consider not only the musical but the unmusical public', Mozart's work shows that he intended much more than a pleasing of the ordinary ear. He meant the members of the audience, whether they were counted musical or unmusical, to experience, through his opera, an enlargement of sympathy. This is the intention of all opera composers of any interest.

No one can go humbly and questioningly to anything approaching a decent performance of *Figaro* or *Aida* or *The Mines of Sulphur* and not come away with a sense of wonder at the nobility of human endeavour, and the worth of human intellect, and the power of human will. And of his own sharing in a community of such qualities.

If there is any value at all, beyond a pointing to the common emphasis upon the will of the protagonist, in the traditional linkage of modern opera and classical drama, it is not to be located in the mirage of a musical renaissance of the Camerata, nor in grandiloquent theories of purgation, but in the sense an audience has of being active assistants in the experience. The Dionysian and Lenaean festivals of Athens were sacred events, and each one taking part, the author, the choregus, the actor, and the play-goer, had a share in the holiness of the event. For the duration of the festival each was regarded as a sacred person. In 363 B.C. Eponymus was condemned to death for thrusting out a spectator who had sat in the wrong seat. The spectator shared the dignity of the occasion. He was part of it. And a member of an opera audience knows himself to be part of a similarly sacred occasion. This sharing and its sacred character are accidentally acknowledged in Addison's remarking of the opera audience that 'the inclination to sing along with the actors so prevails with them that I have sometimes known the performer on the stage do no more in a celebrated song than the clerk of a parish church, who serves only to raise the psalm, and is afterwards drowned in the music of the congregation'. And if the peculiar vocabulary of the sacred has been dropped in Blanche Roosevelt's account of the La Scala gallery-goers, that of participation has not. They come 'to lend their presence to the event of what is to them the entire world: the annual opening of a new opera, or a first-night at their renowned opera-house; in short they are part of it'.

It is the awareness of being part of it which brings members of the audience to consider the language in which opera is sung. In the song-cycle the composer and singer conspire to frame a small world to which the outside audience pays attention, and it is natural that in such a distinct and alien world an alien tongue should be employed. The man in the opera audience shares the opera world, and, precisely because he is within the action himself, expects to know what language is being used around him. Since few in an audience are ready to follow the good example of the heroine of D. H. Lawrence's novel, *The Trespasser*, and undertake to learn German because they want 'to understand Wagner in his own language', and since, even if they were all willing to acquire the use of that language, it could not be expected that they should also learn French, Italian, and all those other languages, including English, in which operas have been composed, there is a demand everywhere expressed for performances in the vernacular of the audience. And everywhere, too, there is a counter-demand for performances to retain the original language.

IN WHAT LANGUAGE?

Some members of the audience in London or Vienna are aghast to discover on their first going to a performance in one of the great opera houses that they are in for an entertainment 'writ in choice Italian'. There seems no attempt to communicate with them, no invitation to a conversation, no suggestion that they are to be offered a meaning for things which the composer hopes that they may share. And they may well begin to complain that they are not being taken into proper account.

Those who, as they take their places in the opera house, are inclined to think that their part in the evening's proceedings is to remain awake in a wise passiveness, do, certainly, act as the true inheritors of some earlier and influential audiences. The old court performances must have been presented with such assumptions of the court musician's duty being, like that of other servants, to arouse the patron to approval. Mozart found that the Archbishop of Salzburg took such a circumstance for granted even when he was dealing with the greatest composer of his, or, perhaps, of all time. Such princelings, however, would never have been put to the inconvenience of attending operas in languages other than those they would accept. The modern listener and spectator, confronted with an unknown and an unwanted foreign tongue, is likely to complain to his neighbour about the thoughtless management. His neighbour may, however, suggest that he consider whether what the composer offers, what he is attempting to say, might not be rather altered, might be given a different tone, if the management were so hardy as to authorize a translation of the libretto for the performance. No communication would occur.

It is curious that some members of the audience should have to be reminded by their neighbours of the possible consequences of a translation of the text. It is evidence of how much people expect an opera's performance to be continuous with that ordinary life in which everyone talks their language. For we all know that there is a peculiar tone associated with each individual language. At school, another sixth-former and I used to present concerts for our fellows of gibberish which, we thought, had a most authentic sound: French *chansons*, German *lieder*, an Italian aria or two, and an encore in Japanese. Everything depended on getting right each nation's distinct and imitable tone. The composer, with far more precise an ear than we could ever boast, will hear the particular tone of the libretto. The sound of the language will be a part of what he offers the audience. It must be a part. It cannot be the whole.

Precisely because he is aware of the audience's demand for a lucid presentation of his view of things the composer is concerned with each characteristic of the language of the librettist. Through such a concern he may hope to speak to the audience. He has to begin from the character of the spoken language and to come, as he listens intently to its speech, to an appreciation of the relation this particular language might be capable of having with music. Not a few composers have made claims that the song they have made for their characters has been precisely fitted to the moods of the language of the libretto. Jacopo Peri, discussing the problems of language and music in his preface to the published version of *Euridice* in 1600, declared himself convinced of the intimate relation of ordinary speech and song. Though he wanted to gain a reputation as the renewer of a classical art, he was careful to state that in putting his opera together he had concerned himself more with the patterns of Italian than Greek speech. 'Even though I do not claim that this was the song used in the Greek and Roman tragedies, I believed that it was the only one which would lend itself to our speech.' Monteverdi, supposing that opera should be as 'natural' as possible, asked a librettist who had wanted to bring Tritons on to their stage, 'how, my dear Sir, can I imitate the language of winds which do not speak?' He was expressing the common opinion of the early opera composers, and of most later composers, that the song of opera was to be an imitation of speech. He could imitate winds well enough. It was their speech he could not imitate. And therefore he could not invent their song. The care with which successive composers attended to this matter encouraged Addison to state it as a rule in opera composing that 'a composer should fit his music to the genius of the people'.

Later composers have certainly observed such a rule. They have sought to express the peculiarities of the language of the libretto in their music. Mozart advised Aloysia Weber, who had complained about the difficulty she had in singing a piece he had given her: 'Study the words over and over, and their rhythm and feeling, and you won't find the aria difficult any more.' Mozart was offering rather more complex advice than he appeared to be. To attend to both the rhythm and the feeling at one time is exceedingly hard. The rhythm does not always help in communicating the meaning of a word. Madame Weber was to hear the word feelingly. This was a problem for her. But it is clear for us that Mozart was not advising her to study the music note by note, but the libretto word by word. The language would determine the singing because the language had determined the music. The key to the music was in the language. Mozart articulates in his music what is already within the spoken language. He hopes that the audience will first recognize his perfect articulation of the language that they speak in the street, and then consider whether he is not articulating what they ordinarily feel. The common conversation of men is unclear and fraught with misunderstandings; Mozart aims at making ordinary conversation lucid. And he can only do this if the music comes across to the audience as adapted to their ordinary expression. In quite the same way Verdi complained to Ghislanzoni, when he got a batch of particularly poetic text from the ambitious librettist, 'The characters do not speak as they ought to do.' He rewrote much of the last scene of

Aida with just this common speech in mind. He simplified every expression according to the paradigm of ordinary usage. And Wagner at a Bayreuth rehearsal remarked sternly to the singers that the dialogues they were attempting would only make sense to them and their audiences, 'if the tempo at which they are performed is just that of the words when they are spoken'. Mussorgsky's remark in 1868 that the composer in creating musical dialogue is presenting the audience with what is 'just ordinary conversation', and that he would be a rash man indeed who did not reverently attempt a 'reproduction of simple human speech', is a modest expression of a sentiment that most of the recognized masters of opera have entertained.

The characteristic tone of the particular vernacular has confronted the composer in the libretto, line by line, word by word, and syllable by syllable. It is his task to present something of the linguistic tone of line and word and syllable. The difficulty for him in this matter is that line and word and syllable offer different kinds of prompting. The statement of meaning which the librettist has made in the line is not the more general sequence of resonances that occur when the words are considered one by one, and the associations of the words are not discernible in the sounds of varying quantity and quality which the syllables present. Or not normally, at any rate. Few sentences and not all that many words are onomatopoeic. The composer must set himself to discerning which of the promptings he is going to observe at each instant of his score, and how the others may be brought into accommodation with that one at that time. His decision may be so often made in one way that it will be a recognizable characteristic of his style, Monteverdi's delight in words, for example, or Wagner's in syllables, but it can never be made automatically.

It might seem to follow that a composer would do well to keep to the language he himself has spoken since childhood. In the ordinary course of things this is what has happened. But there have been distinguished composers, Gluck in Paris, Mozart in Vienna, Handel in London, who have written operas to texts in a language not natively their own. And this oddity has been repeated recently. The language of *Oedipus Rex* was alien to Stravinsky, three of Henze's operas have been composed to librettos in English, and the Japanese composer Mayuzumi has recently attempted to do something with a German version of a Japanese story. Stravinsky, however, worked in the assurance that the Latin of Daniélou was a dead language to all his listeners of whatever country. The problems of the vernacular could not arise once the composer had made such a decision about the fit language of his piece. And *Oedipus Rex*, though a fine piece, is not quite an opera even when conducted with all the vitality of Mr Colin Davis. It was certainly not an opera when Stravinsky conducted it. Henze's latest effort often prevents, by the device of several lines being sung at once, anyone's being sure that he has mastered the qualities of English. And his previous English language works were translated into German for their first performances. Mayuzumi's first night fiasco in Berlin was in large part attributable to his total indifference to the peculiarities of German in particular and language in general. So these modern enterprises do not offer a deal of encouragement for composers to stray from their childhood language. The examples of Mozart and Handel might in themselves be enough to suggest that a composer who is ready to observe the characteristics of a language may set a text in any language, but it must be remembered that Mozart and Handel were dealing with Italian texts in cities where Italian was not the native language but simply the fashionable vehicle of such entertainments. No one cared what was being said. It remains, therefore, likely that a composer will be better able to manage proper music for a text written in his own rather than in a foreign language.

It is also likely that when an opera is performed to an audience which speaks the language of the libretto there will be a greater chance of the composer communicating what he wants to say than if he has to address those who generally speak another language. The words will be more likely to survive the distortion of being sung. It is a common experience to catch the drift of another's remarks if they are made in one's own language, however indistinctly one has heard them, from their recognizable tone. Gluck's success in Paris was due to his acting on the sensible dictum that 'the Italian manner of singing cannot suit the French'. It could not suit the language, the songs, or the audience.

It is more than likely, too, that an opera sung in the original language which confronted the composer and excited him into making his music will sound better than one sung in translation. Addison remembered that when he was young the imported opera stars sang in Italian surrounded by a chorus singing in English. Audiences became restive. Managements therefore changed the systems. They had, by the time Addison was middle-aged, 'so ordered it that the whole opera is performed in an unknown tongue'. They had not found it either possible or profitable to demand that the leading singers should join the chorus in singing English words. The consonance of sound seemed, evidently, more important than any gain in intelligibility that a translation offered. At least it must have seemed so to a great number of seventeenth-century opera-goers. But surely not to all. It is at this point that the debate about translation becomes rather more strenuous.

It is to be noted that the general literary argument that everything suffers in translation, except, of course, bishops, cannot be so forcefully alleged in this discussion. To suggest that meaning will be lost in translation is the common literary practice, but, though it is an argument for audiences learning other languages, it would in an opera context be an admission that the meaning of the line mattered a great deal, and this is not what the defenders of opera in original languages generally profess. There are certainly famous examples of bad translations giving an audience the wrong impression of what is going on, but even these cannot be employed in talk of opera in quite the way that they might in talk of poems, novels or plays. The music makes a difference here as in every aspect of opera librettos.

W. H. Auden, an experienced and talented librettist, who worked with Stravinsky and Henze, suggested that it was not the meaning of the librettist's sentences, intelligent or foolish, but the sound of the words which was important to a composer. 'The poetic value of the words may provoke a composer's imagination, but it is their syllabic values which determine the kind of vocal line he writes. In song, poetry is expendable, syllables are not.' The composers' attention is, on this view, to the rhythmic and syllabic structure of the language in which the libretto is written rather than to the verses of the writer.

If Auden has indeed got things straight then it begins to seem quite unreasonable to suggest that a composer's opera should be sung in any but the original language whose syllabic structure he had so carefully and exclusively observed. If the composer gave his best attention to the meaning of the libretto then he and his audience might well require a translation to be made so that he might communicate the sense of his opera at a foreign performance, but if he has rather given attention to the peculiar rhythms of a particular language and to the syllabic lengths of vowels in the libretto, then there must be some great loss of consonance and harmony, and a distortion of his design, in any performance at which the text is rendered in other rhythms and syllables. 'Wagner in Italian,' wrote Auden, 'or Verdi in English sounds intolerable and would still sound so if the poetic merits of the translation were greater than those of the original, because the new syllables have no apt relation to the pitch and tempo of the notes with which they are associated.' Auden's argument, which is concerned not with the original stirring of an idea in the composer's mind but with the final effect of what he makes, is, it appears, accepted by those influential persons who organize Covent Garden and the Metropolitan Opera, where the operas are customarily performed in the original language. And others who have less influence may come to accept such an argument or some form of it. A sense of what may be lost by an opera being sung in translation comes sometimes to the opera-goer who, on holiday perhaps, attends a performance of a work he knows already and discovers that it is not being sung either in the composer's language or his own, but in some foreigner's translation. An Englishman among the huge crowd at the Arena in Verona, say, could well have the sense that the audience around him is huzzahing a most un-French sound at the performance of *Carmen*. It will become clear to him during the event that Bizet must have heard something quite different in his head. Such a change of language, if it is so noticeable at a performance of *Carmen* in Italy, may convince him that he has been unaware of all sorts of oddities in English language performances of *Lohengrin* or *Rigoletto*.

Some brilliant translators, with a sense of the true difficulties of their profession, have the gift of working hard and long at the search for words which do not simply mean but sound the same as those of the original libretto. But such persons are rare. And some translations, especially those tolerated in the past, are appalling. There was a stupendous example of a translator's irresponsible deception of an audience in the loudly applauded eighteenth-century English version of the popular Bononcini's *Il Trionfo di Camilla*, where the great aria '*Barbara si t'intendo*' in which the furious lover declares that he at last sees the perfidious character of his beloved, became a sad lament: 'Frail are a lover's hopes'. But if a translator should attempt such a betrayal of the original a composer of any competence will certainly not have left the attentive members of his audience without any hint of what is really going on. The music will betray the betrayer. As Addison remarked about the Bononcini translation, 'it was pleasant enough to see the most refined persons of the British nation dying away and languishing to notes that were filled with a spirit of rage and indignation'. He himself knew from the music just what was going on in the composer's opera. Audiences cannot be expected always to be on the alert for such betrayals. They may just think that the translator has revealed again how foolish the words may be that a great composer is willing to accept from a librettist. The great duet between Tamina and Papageno in *The Magic Flute* with its lovely refrain of the married happiness of '*Mann und Weib*' became the Ivor Novello-ish nonsense of 'day by day, and year by year' in a recent English version. My expostulation to the translator resulted simply in the reply, 'You couldn't just have "man and wife", now, could you?'

And yet, despite every example of such enormities, the idea of opera in translation has its attractions. Auden's theory is not wholly convincing. It must be that those who appreciate the meaning of that third or so of the words which the singers can be expected to get across to the audience, have a richer understanding of the opera than those who do not. The experience of hearing an English opera sung in English must convince a native English-speaker that he is losing something when he attends performances sung in a language he does not comprehend. It may be that 'Verdi in English' sounded 'intolerable' to Auden but at any rate Verdi himself was not averse to being heard in French: when Verdi learnt of the Opéra's intention to produce *Otello* in the original language version, he wrote at once to express his surprise: 'There is something out of tune, shocking, about this mixture – the Opéra, and a work in Italian!' It is remarkable that this composer, famous for his care of the words of his opera texts, should have been so insistent that what he was attempting would not be communicated if the original language were not abandoned. It is interesting that he saw this in musical terms. The original would be 'out of tune'. There was some musical reason in Verdi's mind for the desirability of a translation. A musical reason evidently more intimately connected with the elements of line and word than with syllables. The word and the line may be recovered for an audience to some extent by a translation.

IN TWO LANGUAGES?

Most opera-goers attend a performance with a sense of two languages, the one in which it was written and is to be performed, and the one in which they have read a translation, or at any rate a synopsis, beforehand.

Armed with some rudimentary knowledge of the plot and characters a man may expect that the music will give him sufficient intelligence of what is going on. Certainly much of a composer's meaning, if he is at all competent, should be communicated to his audience through the sound. He is a composer precisely because he has discovered that he can communicate to other people through his music. And every opera-goer understands something of this. He appreciates what is happening on the elementary level of the sweep of violins and the blast of trumpets, and what is happening on the more sophisticated levels of the music. The famous modulation in the last act of *The Marriage of Figaro* is generally understood as well as felt by an audience. The notes themselves are communicative. Mozart is skilled enough for that. And once he has realized the relation of some snatch of Wagner's music to some incident in the story a man may get along quite well in the most complex passages, finding himself more and more at home as the performance of the *Ring* proceeds. And such an intelligent listener should have no difficulty at all in feeling the simple emotional tugs of the music in the operas Verdi wrote when a young man, and this despite the composer's being concerned with most complicated story-lines. And this is generally the case. There is sometimes a difficulty in realizing what is going on in the music of a modern opera because the composer is working further forward in the musical tradition than the listener. The composer is aware of what Mozart, Wagner, Verdi and others have done in the form, and the man in the audience, perhaps, is not. But, if that man listens carefully, a competent composer, who knows that he has to communicate with such a man, will by his music mediate the effects of the tradition to him. The early twentieth-century *verismo* of d'Albert's *Tiefland* depends as entirely as Verdi's nineteenth-century *verismo* on his capacity to make us attend to his musical invention. D'Albert has to use just such instruments as Verdi had to hand. The mistakes and distrust which dominate most of the action are simply presented. The audience can as easily recognize where the music is pointing in this opera as they can in those of Verdi's maturity. The audience have simply to hear the evident separation of the vocal line from the orchestral sound. They have simply to recognize what is equally evident, that the voices and the orchestra sound together in one splendid tune only at the moment when the boy and girl realize that they are loved by each other. From then on the music tells the audience that they will see the lovers escape from the lowlands of the title and reach the delights of the mountain country. The music tells the audience exactly what is happening.

So the man in the audience is right to expect a great deal from the music. The intelligence of the composer is exhibited there. But he is also right to suppose that the composer means him to get some information from the words. He is right, before he goes to a performance, to take up his translation for half an hour or so. He will have more confidence in his identification of *leitmotiv* and *parola scenica* and a turn of the plot if he has some literacy in the matter of librettos. An opera-goer may, therefore, however much the music has informed him of what is going on, and however helped he has been by his prior perusal of the translation, wonder whether it would not be better, as well as simpler for him, if the singers were to perform the opera in his own rather than the librettist's language. He will surmise that he would be much more at his ease, particularly in the long narrative monologues of Wagner's great cycle, or the complexities of the opening scenes of *Ballo in Maschera* or *The Force of Destiny*, or the instant when, in *Tiefland*, Pedro comes out of Marta's room most unexpectedly, if he did not have to rely on his recognizing a phrase once in a while. He would like to have a better and more continuous alertness to the text than his translation affords him during the performance. For not a few people an opera's being sung in translation removes a source of unnecessary nervousness, and allows them to attend more closely to the music.

And yet, on attending to the music they are brought back to wondering whether the vocal as well as the orchestral music ought not to be given in its original form.

There is in all this a progression from the way in which an opera-goer may consider how his private appreciation of the composer's intention may be furthered, to the way in which a public performance should be managed. Opera house managements, too, may come to the conclusion that the claims of both original and translation languages ought to be recognized.

If hearing an opera in translation does enable a linguistically deprived audience to come closer to some important aspect of the composer's work, if even the reading of a translation is really helpful in preparing for a performance in the original language, and if, also, the rhythm and the syllabic value of the original words are really integral to the character of the opera, then things seem complex enough to justify an opera house performing works in both the languages of the composers and the language of the audience, or at least in those cities where there is more than one opera house, to justify some coherent policy which affords the citizens chances to hear a good number of operas in the original languages and the vernacular. This policy, generally adopted in Germany, seems lately to have been attempted by Covent Garden and the English National Opera both by their independent recent productions of the *Ring*, and in their planned cooperation for a production of *Ariadne auf Naxos* to be given in original and translation at their houses. At Houston an opera is given a group of performances in the original language and then another group in English. This is managed by rehearsing two casts, one international, one native, and those who opt for the translated version may congratulate themselves on paying half the international evening's price for their seats. At Seattle, the *Ring* is performed in two cycles, one German and the other English. And similar things, not altogether by design, are occurring in New York where I once, in a weekend's shuttling across Lincoln Center from the Metropolitan to the New York City Opera and back, saw two productions of *Bohème* and two of *Figaro*.

The adoption of such a policy by these managements, which seems to many opera-goers to be a sane and practical way of dealing with a troublesome problem, seems to others of a more theoretical turn of mind to be a mean device to avoid making a judgement on evidence which the history of the form amply supplies. There is a difficulty, however, in interpreting the evidence. This any opera-goer must acknowledge if he examines his own experience. Certainly the Covent Garden production of the 'Ring' is for me more satisfying than the Coliseum version. But does not the experience of the English version enable me to realize so much more of what is going on in the German? And is not the experience of the English National Opera production infinitely more satisfying than the hotch-potch Bayreuth offers? And in New York, while the Metropolitan's *Figaro* was so much finer than the English language version, the City Opera offered a much more lively account of *Bohème*. The measurement, even for oneself, of appropriate effectiveness in such things is not easy to encompass. For, whatever the chosen instrument, it has to take into account not only the response a performance achieved from an audience, or some quite impertinently chosen members of the audience, but the loyalty of the performance to the composer's design, and who is so rash as to do more than guess at that? And who would wish to make from any one such judgement a generalization to govern the performance of all those other operas he had hopes of attending?

Things would not even be made altogether simple if each language group could rely on a steady supply of new operas by composers working in their language. Such a state of affairs would be highly desirable, but, though it might mollify the grumbles heard now, it would not prevent opera-goers wanting foreign operas of distinction to be performed alongside these vernacular works. The same language disputes would then arise.

Indeed the audience should not expect any theoretically satisfying resolution of this debate about translation. For the dispute occurs precisely because of the essential character of opera.

If opera were merely music then as few would be anxious for the words to be translated as now ask for those of the choral movement of Beethoven's Ninth Symphony or the *lieder* of Schubert to be put into English. If opera were merely drama then as few would ask for performances in the original language as now complain at Beaumarchais's *Le Mariage de Figaro* being given in English at the National Theatre. Opera is neither concert nor play. Its sharing of some characteristics of each leads some members of an opera audience to wish it would approximate to one and some to the other. Most, however, are uncertain of their opinion in this matter. They waver between wanting the composer to speak as he writes, and wanting to understand him themselves more precisely.

And a decision on whether opera be sung in his language or their own is not so easily to be had from them as a statement of their determination not to sacrifice anything of the particular excitement that opera affords.

The dispute about vernacular opera, like those fierce engagements between Rameau and the Encyclopédistes in the 1752 *guerre des bouffons*, or between the journalistic supporters of Piccinni and Gluck some years later, or the newspaper war between those Bohemians who thought 'Dvořák has defected to the West', and those who were sure that 'Smetana merely copies down folk tunes', and all those other lively quarrels between the adorers of rival singers, is a sign of how closely the audience may be touched by opera, how immediate may be the reactions opera provokes.

It is, however, more nearly related than those other disputes to the central concerns of opera-goers. The accommodation of both original language and vernacular performances in so many cities presents a paradigm of the two kinds of satisfaction that opera-goers are demanding. The performance in the original language offers an invitation for the member of the audience to leave aside the particularities of his own way of life and enter upon another. The performance in his own vernacular allows him to bring the opera into immediate contact with the pursuits of his everyday life. The dispute about language reflects, therefore, the tugs of opera as revelatory of mythic worlds and of opera as the celebration of individual value. The resolution of the dispute reflects the refusal of audiences to yield to either tug.

INDIVIDUAL AND COMMUNITY

The repertory that audiences impose on opera houses is largely made up of operas which celebrate the individual, operas which allow the member of the audience to thrill in sympathy with both the individual personage of the action and the individual singer on the stage. But anyone who thinks of the art as being more than a pleasant evening's entertainment will require the management of the opera house to proffer, and not infrequently, opera which prompts a member of the audience to consider what the composer, the singer, their neighbours along the row of seats, the hero, the heroine, and the villainess, share with themselves.

One does not have to attend all that carefully to what is going on in an opera in order to appreciate that it is a celebration of feeling, of passion, and of will. These are dangerous powers but, at least in the operas of those composers who are aware of the character of their occupation, celebration may be performed with sensitivity and intelligence and be, therefore, in its performance, educative. The attention an individual gives to the action of an opera may be for him not simply a revelation but an experience of the difference in his own life between the exercise of will and mere wilfulness.

A moralist might hope that opera would assist in the purging of the destructive elements of our characters so that we may the better engage in life. But opera's effect, whatever may be true of tragedy, Greek or modern, is not cathartic in quite that way. Opera purges men of those hesitations and worries which make it difficult for them to acknowledge their own importance to themselves. It is common that at a performance of opera a man may become unembarrassedly aware of the importance of his own emotions and entertain a belief in the effectiveness of his own will. A good performance of an opera quite unashamedly suggests that we should take ourselves seriously, and encourages us to make the demand that others take us seriously. Opera, that is, provides a language for us to speak of ourselves as we have always known we should speak. And, generally, the composers of operas suggest that, given such a language, we should learn to speak of the good that may come of human hopes.

Verdi may not seem to offer much hope to his characters but at least he is careful for the preservation of their personal integrity in a collapsing universe. Mozart and Wagner have both higher expectations of salvation. The divine salvation of Idamante and Ilea in *Idomeneo* is given precisely because they love one another enough to die, in *Figaro* the Count is redeemed by the pure love of the Countess, in *The Magic Flute* the steadfast love of Tamino and Pamina is the one safeguard they have in a world in which no one else seems trustworthy or reliable or kind. And the search of Papageno for Papagena is, for all its homely character, or perhaps precisely because of its homely character, a striking pointer to the need each human being feels for being made whole by another. It is highly significant in Mozart's design that the first love duet is not of two lovers but of Pamina and Papageno setting out to find their loves. It is evident that Wagner, too, was much concerned with the possibility of salvation and integration through love of another. The theme of *The Flying Dutchman* is of a man who can only be saved from eternal punishment by a woman's love. *Tannhäuser* is about a man who can only be saved from falling again into a pagan hell by a woman's loving sacrifice. *Parsifal* presents a woman who can only be saved from servitude to the powers of evil by a man's pure love. In *Tristan und Isolde* the lovers call themselves by the other's name, so total is their union and their sense of being made whole by each other. And in the *Ring* it is the love of Brünnhilde for Siegfried, who had once declared 'I am Brünnhilde', that prompts her to re-establish true order in the world by returning her marriage ring to the Rhine. It may be that all this represents some psychological quirk of Wagner's personality, but as he presents his mind in the music the listener is likely to agree that the love of another will set the world in order.

The persuasions in these operas of Mozart, Wagner and Verdi, like that of Beethoven in the greatest redemption opera of all, are made in contexts of political importance. The setting is almost always in the halls of kings and wizards and pontiffs. This is the preliminary convention which brings the audience to a willingness to enter upon the process of self-awareness. If this convention is ignored, as it is so often in the work of Puccini and *verismo* composers, the composer must find it more difficult to bring any but the most charitable members of the audience to an easy acceptance of the importance of the characters' emotions, for only the most charitable can think the world dependent upon Mimi's love or

Rudolf's jealousy, and thus must find it nigh impossible to bring the rest of the audience to the final realization of their own emotions' importance.

It is difficult for any of us actually to say that our emotions and will are important, but for the nicest as well as for the nastiest of us something like that is the case. To most of us, therefore, the oddity in *Tristan und Isolde*, if we can be brought by a good performance to recognize it, is not the hugeness of the passions shown to us, or the collapse of a kingdom in a clash of love and loyalty, or the final deaths all over the stage, the oddity is simply that it needs a magic potion to bring all this about. We know from everything that Wagner has shown us of Tristan and Isolde, and from everything he has shown us of ourselves, that such love brings about its own tragedy. And what he has also shown us is that we are people who think all the tragedy worth it. We do not go home purged of our feelings of fear and pity, because we have not been shown anything to fear or pity; rather we have been shown some usually hidden aspect of ourselves, and shown that it is not shaming but uplifting. This is a power common to operas quite unlike *Tristan und Isolde*. Nietzsche was professedly aiming at reducing the influence of such elemental music when he wrote *The Case of Wagner*, but his account of Bizet, whom he opposes to Wagner, suggests a similarity of effect. He begins that essay by stating that he had just been for the twentieth time to hear *Carmen*. 'How such a work makes one perfect! One becomes a "masterpiece" oneself.' *Carmen* enlarges his experience. He is, as he sits in his box, given a sense of life in the dry heat of Africa. 'I envy Bizet for having had the courage to express this sensibility which had hitherto had no language in the cultivated music of Europe.' Through a discovery of his capacity for new sensations a member of the audience may come to think better of himself. 'You see how much this music improves me?'

It was this assertion of peculiar will and its effect upon members of the audience which offended Schopenhauer. This great philosopher thought that music expressed the universal will, the force before things. He thought too that the purest musical form of will was that of melody in which are signalled the various efforts of will and their satisfaction in 'the final return to an harmonious interval and, still more, to a key note'. Music, and particularly melody, expresses universal will. And in opposition, poetry expresses individuality. Schopenhauer, therefore, disapproved of most operas because they allowed the play of individualism upon the field of will.

If that element which Schopenhauer defined in terms of universal will – which I have suggested is related to the general forms of myth, and which is at least a hint of some human sympathy within our culture – is to be manifest then some other operas must be played in the repertory together with those of individual import.

At the beginning of opera's history, Italian aristocrats celebrating the Christian nuptials of their peers were confronted by Peri's *Euridice*, a Greek tale about Pluto breaking up the marriage of an artist and his wife. Nothing of individual circumstance connected characters with audience. Yet the composer intended that his patrons should recognize the reference of the action to their own lives. Though Peri's opera is rarely performed, later composers have presented similar works for later generations to contemplate. They have roused images from our dim and unconverted past. Opera finds the pagan in us all. Those who expect a composer to present them with an expression of their cultural community may cite many such invitations for us to participate in the present act of myth.

Composers have not found it at all an easy matter to shape other acceptable expressions of our culture. Audiences have been prepared to receive all sorts of things as individual tales about someone else, but they have properly demanded that the composer who claims to be expressing a matter common to themselves must really speak a common language. Would-be universalist tales told in special or closed languages, however delightful, have not proved acceptable. Audiences have not given sustained approval to versions of primitive human apprehensions which have their origins in christendom or nation, sect or gang. Such settings, perfectly adapted to express individual will, have not yet been convincingly employed for the expression of the culture. 'Charles V not Charlemagne.'

Those operas which have been shaped as if everyone in the audience subscribed to a Judaeo-Christian view of the cosmos may be instanced as essays at universalist relevance which have rarely lasted long in the opera house. Handel, of course, is famous for such things, but Judaeo-Christian stories have been employed even in nineteenth- and twentieth-century opera. Verdi's *Giovanna d'Arco*, Meyerbeer's *Les Huguenots*, Saint-Saens's *Samson et Dalila*, Strauss's *Salome*, and Nielsen's *Saul and David*, for example. None of these biblical or hagiological pieces has held the stage except Strauss's opera, and that is a piece remarkable for its divergence of tone from the gospel narrative of John the Baptist's death.

It is not that these operas have been less musically mature than others. Each has some stunning musical moment. The joyous aria 'Let the bright Seraphim' in *Samson et Dalila* offered Joan Sutherland the opportunity to reveal her wondrous voice. Verdi's striking orchestration of accordions for angels and harmoniums for devils makes *Giovanna d'Arco* interesting from its opening moments. The first performance Bernard Shaw ever applauded was his mother's singing of the page's song in *Les Huguenots*. And everyone knows the tune of 'Softly awakes my heart'. These works have dropped from the repertory simply because audiences are unable to find in themselves the necessary sympathy with the action. Now and again, of course, they may be revived at the behest of a singer who fancies a part, or a producer who thinks to make them say something modern, but they are not for us. When my companion found no one with whom to identify, I began to doubt if even Mr Dexter could make *Dialogues des Carmélites* last long in New York.

Nor is it true that any myth which is not Jewish or Christian will work for us. Tales of Siva, of the Buddha, or of the Poro men, would have no greater call upon our common response. The most impressive composers of opera have known this. However they may have wanted to treat matters of serious religious import they have resisted the temptation to express their sense of these things in a traditional religious frame. Wagner considered writing *Jesus von Nasareth*, he got as far as sketching a scenario for *Der Buddha*, but he actually composed the *Ring*. Mozart does not demand any great sensitivity to the gods in *Thamos* or *The Magic Flute*, but when Elizabeth Lutyens determines to take us through a version of their relations in *Isis and Osiris*, even though it is that put about by Plutarch, she makes her opera task impossibly difficult. She might have done better with Ishtar. A Cambridge don of this century, after all, died murmuring 'Tammuz, Tammuz'. Few, certainly, of her audience were likely to feel that the religion of ancient Egypt expresses their own sense of the anxieties of life. If we are to have an Egyptian opera it had better be about the passions of men and women, not those of strange and peculiar deities. It had better be *Aida*.

Again, operas in which composers have made their appeal to racial or nationalist sentiments have generally been neglected even by those who share them. *I Lombardi* worked well enough for a while but is now a rarity in the opera house. Britten's coronation celebration in *Gloriana* is as little performed. Scott Joplin's *Treemonisha*, whose heroine starts life as an abandoned baby and becomes the leader of her people in their escape from the terrors of superstition, failed in a Harlem run-through in 1915. There is less surprise, perhaps, in the failure of Robert Sessions's bicentennial *Montezuma*. Boston audiences should not have been expected to thrill to anything but songs of Concord and Lexington. But Sessions's pupil had no greater luck in San Francisco with a more promising theme. Andrew Imbries's *Angle of Repose*, when produced among the descendants of those who made California great, found no enthusiasm for its presentation of a modern man in search of his pioneer ancestors. Despite the libretto being derived from Wallace Stegner's 'epic-realist' novel, and the score having elements of folk-song, waltz tune and protest march, despite even the whole being bound together by psychological references in text, music and production, this opera also failed to convince its audience that it was saying something for everyone.

Nor has any individual, in the public exploration of the images which tenant his own mind, had success in making an opera that satisfactorily expresses the collective sense of things. No man can invent a myth for his society. While audiences have accepted the myth of love at first sight as it is exampled in Sophie and Octavian, and have even been ready to respect the symbolic value of the glass of water in *Arabella*, they have remained unmoved by the esoteric nonsenses that litter the life of the Dyer's Wife in *Die Frau ohne Schatten*. Hofmannsthal's imagery for this opera was so personally straitened that even Strauss could not move freely within it. It is the most muddled of his compositions. A similar structural individualism makes it difficult to remain interested long in Alberto Ginastera's *Bomarzo*. The composer claimed that his opera was structured according to a classical Greek pattern of 'exposition, crisis, and conclusion'. He claimed, too, that he had made an opera about 'a man of our time'. The work, whose action takes place in the mind of the hero, flash-backing to images of lust and violence, remains a self-indulgent parade of one man's fantasies, however common such day-dreams may be. It is a psychopathic, not a sympathetic work. The opera is neither of the classical nor of our own time. It seems to me that it is precisely because it is not the one that it is not the other. We cannot all be patient of such a funnelling down of our experience. Equally insistent in its reference to 'men of our time', and more urgent in its mythological message, Josef Tal's *Ashmedai* also remains locked in the imaginations of librettist and composer. It is not enough to tell us that a demon from the *Book of Tobit* is wreaking Nazi horrors among us, for an audience to recognize in this opera a present share in the myth of 'The Destroyer'. Mr Tal may believe in the viability of such images of external demons from another clime, but if the rest of us are to talk of devilries then our culture has brought us to think of rather more human desires that some other may take our place in present hell. Gaspar in *Der Freischütz*, the Duke in *Rigoletto*, Nick Shadow in *The Rake's Progress*, have to find a substitute victim if they are to escape torment themselves. Our demonology is of more complex a kind than Mr Tal's parable can express.

Only by working from our shared language may librettist, composer and producer express the inner truths of our shared experience. The expectations that men have of opera as communicative of their culture's tone is not to be satisfied by the inventions of an individual, any more than it is by the constructions of churches and nations. Such an expectation derives from the sense that opera may reach more deeply into our experience. That it may reach into the source of our common sense.

The peculiar cultural reference of opera, European in origin, and but little adapted in response to the differences of New York or Sydney or Cape Town, effectively demands that anyone who would discriminate among its resonances should himself be native to the culture. The success of *Il Seraglio* in the palace court of Istanbul, or of *Madama Butterfly* in Tokyo, is, like that of other less nicely localized operas in the repertory of Tehran Opera and the Colon in Buenos Aires, most easily supposed to be related to the Westernization of the educated members of those societies. It is a delightful oddity, an oddity that, if it were to be expected at all, would be connected with the wonder of Mozart, yet an oddity still, that a huge bodyguard, recruited by a black President from the wilds of his country for the duration of the Geneva Conference on Southern African affairs, excited at his first hearing of such a sound, should take back to his village a recording of *Idomeneo*.

He and the Professor of Law, on whose door he had knocked at midnight to ask what 'that wonderful music' might be, had, as they listened, shared in the wonder proposed by the composer. An exceptional man, the bodyguard had leapt the barriers between our cultures to claim a part in whatever Mozart offered. We, more ordinary, but by our cultural condition most happily excused such a demanding effort, entertain, as we assemble for a performance in the opera house, like hopes of participating in the wonder that black bodyguard heard sounding in the music.

AT CURTAIN FALL

It is within this context of participation that we ought to speak of the final burst of applause that provokes six-monthly annoyance among gentlemen who write to *The Times*. Opera audiences are notoriously demonstrative, and not only those in Naples or Hamburg, where rowdy booing seems to be common. Opera audiences realize, if the performance in any way releases the composer's will upon the house, that they are sharing in an occasion and they refuse to allow the pit and the proscenium to cut them off from the rest of the sharers. They clap, almost always, before the last note sounds, not because they are wilfully disregarding the composer's final wishes but because, as any opera composer knows well enough, they want to have a share in the company of harmony before the door in the hill closes. Mozart took it for granted that he should encourage such a sharing with a rousing final sound. 'Noise,' he thought to be 'always appropriate at the end of an act.' That way an audience would recognize the signal for their entry. 'The more noise the better and the shorter the better, so that the audience may not have time to cool down with their applause.' A composer may take the precise timing of an audience's applause as a test of his management of the opera. For an audience the clap is an expression not only of thankfulness that the event is accomplished but of determination not to let the glory fade.

It is, therefore, explicable that opera singers, and in my experience Italian tenors particularly, should reserve their intensest emotional response for these plaudits, rather than for the love, danger and death of the action. It would be splendid if they could manage to fulfil the demands of both stage action and auditorium occasion but they are at their bow at least attempting to make their own lives and those of the audience continuous with the opera. And they are doing so at the moment of crisis when the music has ceased and the lights have come up and whatever there is of illusion in the performance has come to an end. The singer and the audience would keep hold together on the reality created among them. And each is acknowledging what the composer has done. There can be few among the audience who are not in their applauding wishing to express their appreciation of the composer, and there can be few among the singers who do not accept this, at least in their more realist moments. The audience's applause and the singers' hands on hearts, then, are directly and indirectly expressions of excitement at being sharers of such a wonder, and gratitude to the composer for making them realize that such things are possible not only in the opera house but in their customary occupations. At the end they applaud in the recognition that entertainment has become the paradigm of experience.

It is evident to audiences that human beings of real distinction, of fine feeling and intelligence, have seen in opera the ready medium for their communication with their fellow men. It is the utter seriousness of their endeavour which impresses above all other characteristics. It is that seriousness which distinguishes opera from operetta. It is not that *Die Fledermaus* or *La Belle Hélène* are funny, or full of swinging tunes, or give the soubrette a chance to shine or the patter man a hope of an encore, which distinguishes them from operas. *Die Meistersinger* is as funny and in just as vulgar a way, *Figaro* is as full of tunes, *The Force of Destiny* gives the soubrette just as good a chance, *Don Pasquale* does as much for the patter man, *The Magic Flute* encompasses all four of these delights and more. It is simply that while Strauss and Offenbach and their ilk hope but to distract an audience for a while, Wagner and Mozart and Verdi, and even Donizetti, have thought by opera to make themselves known, and to persuade others to attend to their most serious declaration of mind.

At their communication of mind there is no other appropriate response but wonder. The music discloses their impressive power. And this is the relish of opera-going.

Through an experience of the variety of such powers a member of the audience may discover in himself a complementary largeness of mind. He may come to enjoy that catholic appreciation exhibited in an anecdote da Ponte tells in his memoirs. The great librettist delighted in the recollection of that day when the three most distinguished composers in Vienna, Martini, Mozart, and Salieri, 'came all three at the same time to ask me for texts'. Da Ponte took up the challenge and set to work on all three librettos at once. He told the Emperor Josef II that he wrote for Mozart in the evening, because he was like Dante, for Martini in the morning, because he was like Petrarch, and for Salieri in the afternoon, because he was like Tasso. The Emperor 'found my parallels very apt'. *Don Giovanni*, *Arbore di Diana* and *Axur, Re d'Ormus*, were well on their way by the time the composers called next day. Da Ponte's quickness, he admitted modestly, astonished the composers. The interest of the story, however, is not so much in the speed of the librettist's invention, but in his discernment of the differing personal distinctions of his composers. Da Ponte and the Emperor and less exalted members of the audience may be brought by opera to appreciate the composer as having such a particular vision, and as impressive, as that of the great poet, and as exciting his hearers with such a discovery of inward wonder as the reader experiences at the prompting of a poet. Opera is to be heard with that attention civilized men and women have acknowledged is appropriate to epic.

The recognition of the composer as the discoverer and proclaimer of meaning does not, of itself, enable a man to enjoy such a life as he has been shown in the theatre. He may, considering how the composer has presented the structures of experience, ask himself Wallace Stevens's question:

> How mad would he have to be to say 'He beheld
> An order and thereafter he belonged to it?'

To belong to such an order as Mozart or Beethoven suggests is, at curtain fall, the hope of those who come from the opera. That they belong to such an order as Verdi or Wagner suggests is their fear. Things have become rather more complex since that once upon a time when Jacopo Peri, at the conclusion of his preface to *Euridice*, confidently bade his audience, 'Live joyously.'

Reading List

I have set down here a list, in some elements eccentric, of divers books which, by their lively accounts of the excitements of opera, helped me to recognize the substantial worth of the form and provided me with the language for my enthusiasm. I hope that, if I have not been properly persuasive here, a reading of some of these books may yet prompt a like enthusiasm.

PREFACE

There are three works of general usefulness which offer diverse ways of understanding what composers have supposed themselves to be attempting.

Ulrich Weisstein's *Essence of Opera* (Norton Library, New York, 1964), contains a grand selection from the discussions of opera by librettists and composers from 1600 to the present day.

The Earl of Harewood's revision of Kobbé's *Complete Opera Book* (ninth edition, Putnam, 1976), contains details of over three hundred operas, their plots, their musical character and their performances.

Joseph Kerman's *Opera as Drama* (Vintage Books, New York, 1956), is an idiosyncratic and argumentative and stimulating defence of the thesis that 'in opera the dramatist is the composer'.

ONE WHAT DOES IT MEAN?

William Mann, music critic of *The Times*, has in 1977 produced what must become the authoritative English study of *The Operas of Mozart* (Cassell).

Charles Osborne's *The Complete Operas of Verdi* (Pan, 1973), provides always reliable and often exciting individual accounts of each opera.

Though Ernest Newman's *Wagner Nights* (Putnam, fifth impression, 1974) and Robert Donington's *Wagner's Ring and its Symbols* (Faber, third edition, 1974), each provide an interesting interpretation of the operas, I would think that the selections from Wagner's own writings in Robert Jacobs and Geoffrey Skelton, *Wagner writes from Paris* (Allen & Unwin, 1973), and Albert Goldman and Evert Sprinchorn, *Wagner on Music and Drama* (Gollancz, 1970), offer more satisfactory starting places for a study of his work. And there is a deal of instructive fun in Jacques Barzun's *Darwin, Marx, Wagner* (Doubleday, New York, 1958).

TWO IS IT FOR REAL?

A more sympathetic treatment of Puccini's enterprise than I have offered may be engendered by a reading of William Ashbrook's *The Operas of Puccini* (Cassell, 1969), or, better still, by a sampling of *Letters of Giacomo Puccini* (Vienna House, New York, 1931).

THREE DO THE WORDS MATTER?

Patrick J. Smith's *The Tenth Muse*, (Gollancz, 1970), is an easily written and highly allusive account of the history of the opera libretto and the relations between librettists and composers.

Charles Osborne has selected, translated and edited a representative group of *Letters of Giuseppe Verdi* (Gollancz, 1971), and these show the composer's particular understanding of his relationship with those many others concerned with him in the making of an opera.

A relationship of quite another sort is presented in *A Working Friendship: The Correspondence between Richard Strauss and Hugo van Hofmannsthal*, translated by H. Hammelmann and Ewald Osers (Vienna House, New York, 1974).

FOUR HOW DID IT BEGIN?

Michael F. Robinson's *Opera Before Mozart* (Morrow, New York, 1967), is an efficient short guide to what was happening in opera entertainments from the Camerata to the eighteenth-century *opera seria*.

There are older and more particular studies of Gluck by Alfred Einstein (Dent, 1936), and Ernest Newman (Dobell, 1895).

FIVE HOW IS IT DONE?

Sir Rudolf Bing's racey account of his memories of *5,000 Nights at the Opera* (Doubleday, New York), is quite useful as an introduction to opera as a business. Sir Victor Gollancz's careful inquiry about Wieland Wagner and *The Ring at Bayreuth* (1966), leads him into some rewarding thoughts on operatic production generally, and Geoffrey Skelton's *Wieland Wagner* (Gollancz, 1971), is most helpful in forwarding an appreciation of the kind of thing the composer's grandson achieved.

Though Anthony Pollard's *Recordmaster* series includes some informative short essays on the work of individual artists, it is difficult to discover any lasting usefulness in the many enthusiastic books about singers. Those who would make themselves aware of contemporary discussion of singers should, like those who wish to know more of conductors, producers and composers, subscribe to *Opera*, the monthly review edited by Harold Rosenthal (Seymour Press Ltd).

The programmes produced by opera-houses in our time are generally so enticingly informative about the plot, the history and the meaning of what is about to happen that I do not risk much in suggesting that wise members of the audience will claim their seats some quarter of an hour before curtain rise and, by attending to these programmes, equip themselves for the enjoyment of the performance.

Those who have the misfortune to arrive just in time for the conductor's entrance must content themselves with some profitable but retrospective reading in the train on their way home.

Hamish F. G. Swanston

Acknowledgements

The quotations on pp. 37–8 and 262, from Mr Colin Davis's conversation were originally printed in Alan Blyth, *Colin Davis*, Recordmasters 2 (Ian Allan, 1972); those on pp. 53 and 182 from Wagner's prose works are given in the translation by Albert Goldman and Evert Spinchorn in *Wagner on Music and Drama* (Gollancz, 1970); those on pp. 138, 140, 149 are from Hanns Hammelmann and Ewald Osers, *A Working Friendship* (William Collins, 1961); that on p. 213 is from Francis Hueffer, *Correspondence of Wagner and Liszt* (Vienna House, New York, 1973); those from Nietzsche are given in Walter Kaufmann's translation, *The Case of Wagner* (Random House, New York, 1967); those on p. 203 from Thomas Mann's *Death in Venice* in H. T. Lowe-Porter's translation (Penguin Books, 1955); those on pp, 81, 119f., 212 and 255 are from Charles Osborne's translation of *Letters of Giuseppe Verdi*, (Gollancz, 1971); and those on pp. 105.f. 1119f., 130, 169, 173f., 177, 179 and 240f., from the writings of Corneille, Beaumarchais, Stendhal, Grétry, Weber, Saint-Évremond, Marcello, Voltaire, Algarotti, and Peri, are given in the translations collected in Ulrich Weinstein, *The Essence of Opera* (Free Press of Glencoe and W. W. Norton and Company, New York, 1969).

Index

Abduction from the Seraglio, The, see *Die Entführung aus dem Serail*
Addison, Joseph, 277; and Italian opera, 284, 286; and librettists, 105
Aegyptische Helena, Die (Strauss), 148, 152f
Aida (Verdi), 7ff, 10f, 14, 88, 100, 119, 123, 134, 259
Alceste (Gluck), 180, 185
Alceste (Lully), 170
Arabella (Strauss), 147, 149
Ariadne auf Naxos (Strauss), 133, 142ff, 152, 154, 195, 251
Arianna (Monteverdi), 146, 165
Arthurian legend in opera, *see Lohengrin, Parsifal, Tristan und Isolde* (Wagner)
Auden, W.H.: and ensemble, 76; as librettist, 149, 198, 284f, 287; and singers, 101
audiences, 71f, 209, 217f, 243f, 261, 267, 272–9, 301ff (*see also indvidual operas*)

Bassarids, The (Henze), 100, 149, 197ff
Beaumarchais, Pierre Augustin Caron de, 25, 28f, 41f, 106, 139, 275f, 291
Beethoven, Ludwig van: and revolution, 21, 25, 90f;
Fidelio, 19–25, 28, 68, 76, 91, 142, 274
Bejart, Maurice, 220f
Bellini, Vincenzo: and librettists, 109–14; and madness, 92; and revolution, 42; and singers, 246f, 252f, 265
Norma, 111f, 247f
Benda, Jiři, 155
Bennett, Richard Rodney, 104
Berg, Alban, 69, 94
Berlioz, Hector, 167, 260f
Bizet, Georges, 82
Carmen, 80f, 88, 268ff, 286, 295
Les Pêcheurs de Perles, 82
Bohème, La (Puccini), 67, 84, 86, 88, 221
Boito, Arrigo, 104, 122–5
Bonynge, Richard, 265
Bouilly (author of *Leonore*), 20f
Britten, Benjamin, 199ff; and heroes, 200, 202ff; and madness, 207f; and singers, 207f
Death in Venice, 199, 200–208
Owen Wingrave, 201, 218
Peter Grimes, 68, 93, 95f, 200
Busenello, Giovanni, 90, 166–8

Cadmus et Hermione (Lully), 169, 171
Calzabigi (librettist), 179f, 185
Capriccio (Strauss), 147, 150f, 153f
Carmen (Bizet), 80f, 88, 268ff, 286, 295
Casti (librettist), 108
Cavalleria Rusticana (Mascagni), 82, 86
Cavalli, Pietro Francesco, 166f
Chéreau, Patrice, 288
Clemenza di Tito, La (Mozart), 36f, 41

Corneille, Pierre: and ensemble, 75; and librettist, 105
Corregidor, Der (Wolf), 18, 56, 104, 133
Così fan Tutte (Mozart), 35f, 37, 39, 76, 107f, 216f, 238, 244f

Dafne (Peri), 156f
Daphne (Strauss), 152f
da Ponte, Lorenzo, 28f, 32, 107ff, 303
Davis, Colin, 37f, 231, 253, 256, 260f
Death in Venice (Britten), 199, 200–208
Debussy, Claude:
Pelléas et Mélisande, 19, 62–5, 134f, 232
Dexter, John: and *Aida*, 233; and *Dialogues des Carmélites*, 235f; and *Le Prophète*, 234f
Dialogues des Carmélites, Les (Poulenc) 235f, 297
Diderot, Denis: and Gluck, 120; and *opera buffa*, 267; and singers, 241f
Don Carlos (Verdi), 13, 44f, 77
Don Giovanni (Mozart), 32ff, 35, 37, 39, 46, 68, 107
Donizetti, Gaetano, 80f, 93, 111, 220, 246
Dryden, John: and librettists, 70f, 105; and origins of opera, 156, 167; and opera plots, 172

Elektra (Strauss), 137ff, 148
Entführung aus dem Serail, Die, (*The Abduction from the Seraglio*) (Mozart), 106f, 244
Ernani (Verdi), 45, 47, 69, 121
Eugene Onegin (Tchaikovsky), 59–62, 250
Euridice (Peri), 156, 158, 240, 280, 296, 303

Falstaff (Verdi), 47f, 87, 124
Fanciulla del West, La, (*The Girl of the Golden West*) (*Puccini*), 84f
Fidelio (Beethoven), 19–25, 28, 68, 76, 91, 142, 274
Fliegende Holländer, Der (*The Flying Dutchman*) (*Wagner*), 53, 55, 220, 270, 294
Forza del Destino, La (*The Force of Destiny*) (Verdi), 45f, 50, 120, 122, 289
Friedrich, Götz, 147, 228f

Gabrieli, Andrea, 156
Galsworthy, John: and *verismo*, 83
Ghislanzoni (librettist), 9, 119, 122f, 281
Girl of the Golden West, The, see *La Fanciulla del West*
Giulio Cesare (Cavalli), 166ff
Giulio Cesare (Handel), 75, 193f
Gluck, Christoph Willibald, 242, 252, 292
Alceste, 180, 185
Écho et Narcisse, 179, 252
Iphigénie en Aulide, 180, 185f
Iphigénie en Tauride, 74–5, 179f, 186–8
Orfeo ed Euridice, 180ff, 183f, 188f
Gounod, Charles, 249, 271
grand opéra, 114f, 137
Greek myth in opera, *see Alceste* (Gluck); *Alceste* (Lully); *Ariadne auf Naxos* (Strauss); *Arianna* (Monteverdi); *Bassarids, The* (Henze); *Cadmus et Hermione* (Lully); *Dafne* (Peri); *Daphne* (Strauss); *Death in Venice* (Britten); *Elektra* (Strauss); *Euridice* (Peri); *Idomeneo* (Mozart); *Iphigénie en Aulide* (Gluck); *Iphigénie en Tauride* (Gluck); *King Priam* (Tippett); *Orfeo* (Monteverdi);

Orfeo ed Euridice (Gluck); *Pelléas et Mélisande* (Debussy); *Phaëton* (Lully); *Ritorno d'Ulisse in Patria, Il* (Monteverdi); *Semele* (Handel); *Troyens, Les* (Berlioz)
Grétry, André: and Italian companies, 120; and *opéra comique*, 266, 268

Hall, Peter, 216, 260f
Handel, George Frederick, 75, 192, 282f
Giulio Cesare, 75, 193f
Semele, 67, 193–5
Henze, Hans Werner: and madness, 98; as producer, 253
The Bassarids, 100, 149, 197ff
Elegy for Young Lovers, 97
The Prince of Hamburg, 97
We come to the river, 98ff, 253, 273
Hofmannsthal, Hugo von, 9, 136–51, 299
Huguenots, Les (Meyerbeer), 116, 126f, 297
Humperdinck, Engelbert, 133

Idomeneo (*Mozart*), 31f, 35ff, 44f, 75f, 141, 189, 293, 300
Incoronazione di Poppea L' (Monteverdi), 142, 166
Iphigénie en Aulide (Gluck), 185f, 180
Iphigénie en Tauride (Gluck), 74f, 179ff, 186–8
Italiana in Algeri, L' (*The Italian Girl in Algiers*) (Rossini), 41, 275

Kierkegaard, Sören Aabye: and *Don Giovanni*, 32, 35
King Priam (Tippett), 100f, 153
Knot Garden, The (Tippett), 96, 101, 218

leitmotiv, 55f, 132f, 225
Leoncavallo, Ruggiere, 19, 82ff
Lohengrin (Wagner), 218, 226, 233
Lombardi, I (Verdi), 12f, 43, 77
Lucia di Lammermoor (Donizetti), 59, 80f, 93, 220
Lully, Jean-Baptiste, 168–71, 185f
Alceste, 170
Cadmus et Hermione, 169, 171
Phaëton, 25, 67, 169, 217

Madama Butterfly (Puccini), 80, 84f, 86ff
Magic Flute, The, see *Die Zauberflöte*
Mann, Thomas, 203–6
Marcello, Benedetto: and audiences, 240f; and the bear, 210; and librettists, 173ff
Marriage of Figaro, The, see *Le Nozze di Figaro*
Mascagni, Pietro, 82
Meistersinger von Nürnberg, Die (Wagner), 54, 76f, 133, 142, 159
Metastasio, 75, 90, 107, 115, 127, 175–8
Meyerbeer, Giacomo, 99, 115f, 231f, 297
Les Huguenots, 116, 126f, 297
Le Prophète, 116, 127, 233ff
Robert le Diable, 115f, 126
Midsummer Marriage, The (Tippett), 100f
Milhaud, Darius, 155
Mines of Sulphur, The (Bennett), 104
Moniuszko, Stanislaw, 82
Monteverdi, Claudio, 59, 159; and librettists, 277, 280f
Arianna, 146, 165;
L'Incoronazione di Poppea, 142, 166
Orfeo, 67f, 159–65, 167f, 170, 180, 188, 199
Il Ritorno d'Ulisse in Patria, 130f

Moses und Aron (Schönberg), 271
Mozart, Wolfgang Amadeus, 19, 26, 27ff, 44f; and audiences, 301; and force of will, 92; and heroes, 90ff; illogicality of experience, 33f; and librettists, 106–9, 126; and money, 211; and revolution, 25, 33, 41, 44, 49, 90; and singers, 75f, 244ff, 281; and *verismo*, 89f
  La Clemenza di Tito, 36f, 41
  Così fan Tutte, 35f, 37, 39, 76, 107f, 216f, 238, 244f
  Don Giovanni, 32ff, 35, 37, 39, 46, 68, 107
  Idomeneo, 31f, 35ff, 44f, 75f, 141, 189, 293, 300
  Die Zauberflöte, 25, 37ff, 67f, 73, 108, 190, 286, 294
  Le Nozze di Figaro, 28ff, 31, 33ff, 35, 37, 107f, 126, 141, 216, 288, 293f
Muti, Ricardo, 259, 264

Nabucco (Verdi), 13, 43
Nietzsche, Friedrich Wilhelm: and *Carmen*, 269f, 295; and Wagner, 52, 226
Norma (Bellini), 111f, 246ff
Nozze di Figaro, Le (*The Marriage of Figaro*) (Mozart), 27ff, 31, 33ff, 35, 107, 126, 141, 216, 288, 293f

Offenbach, Jacques, 189f
opera buffa, 91, 106f, 146, 267ff
opéra-comique, 268ff
opera seria, 37, 174, 176
operetta, 189f, 302
Orfeo (Monteverdi), 67f, 159–65, 167f, 170, 180, 188, 199
Orfeo ed Euridice (Gluck), 180ff, 188f
Otello (Verdi), 47f, 104, 124, 287
Owen Wingrave (Britten), 201, 218

Pagliacci, I (Leoncavallo), 19, 82f, 86
Parsifal (Wagner), 52, 55, 68, 100, 130, 133, 218, 227
Pêcheurs de Perles, Les (Bizet), 82
Pelléas et Mélisande (Debussy), 19, 62–5, 134f, 220, 232
Peri, Jacopo: and librettists, 280; and singers, 252
  Dafne, 156f
  Euridice, 156, 158, 240, 280, 296, 303
Peter Grimes (Britten), 68, 93, 95f, 200
Phaëton (Lully), 25, 67, 169, 217
Piave (librettist), 120–22
Piper, Myfanwy, 204f
Ponnelle, Jean-Pierre, 220
Prophète, Le (Meyerbeer), 116, 127, 233ff
Puccini, Giacomo, 84ff; and singers, 252; and *verismo*, 84ff, 88, 164, 221, 294
  La Bohème, 67, 84, 86, 88, 221
  Madama Butterfly, 84f, 86f
  Tosca, 84ff, 87, 221
  Turandot, 67, 84f, 88, 135, 221

Quinault, Philippe, 25, 114, 169, 186

Rake's Progress, The (Stravinsky), 94, 299
Rigoletto (Verdi), 46f, 68, 77ff, 80f, 120f, 248, 262, 299
Ring der Nibelungen, Der (*Ring of the Nibelungs, The*) (Wagner), 51, 55, 72, 93, 129, 131f, 141, 147, 202, 216, 219, 222f, 226f, 228ff, 258, 290f, 294
  Götterdämmerung, 51, 56, 72, 130, 135, 224
  Das Rheingold, 55, 67, 257, 261
  Die Walküre, 55, 131, 133, 255

Rinuccini, Ottavio, 156–9, 165f, 209f
Ritorno d'Ulisse in Patria, Il (Monteverdi), 130f
Robert le Diable (Meyerbeer), 115f, 126
Romani, Felice, 109–14, 115
Roman myth in opera, *see Giulio Cesare* (Cavalli); *Giulio Cesare* (Handel); *L'Incoronazione di Poppea* (Monteverdi); Metastasio
Rosenkavalier, Der (Strauss), 140ff, 150, 154, 236
Rossini, Gioacchino Antonio, 41, 237, 275
Rousseau, Jean-Jacques and *opera buffa*, 267

Salome (Strauss), 137, 146f
Sanjust, Filippo: and *Aida*, 12f; and *Rigoletto*, 236
Schikaneder, E. J., 19f, 108, 211
Schönberg, Arnold, 271
Schopenhauer, Arthur, 295f
Schumann, Robert, 17f, 26
Scribe, Eugene, 52, 114–18, 126f, 129
Semele (Handel), 67, 193–5
Shaw, George Bernard: and Meyerbeer, 297; and Sardou, 63; and Richard Wagner, 231; and Siegfried Wagner, 261
singers, 15, 74ff, 207, 214, 236–52, 263f, 265, 272, 301ff; *castrati*, 178f, 240ff; *prima donna* and *prima uomo*, 239, 241
singspiel, 143, 268, 270f
Stendhal: and librettists, 119; and Rossini, 243, 275
Stephanie (librettist), 106f
Stevens, Wallace, 73, 303
Strauss, Richard, 9, 136ff; and librettists, 136–51; and singers, 74
Die Aegyptische Helena, 148f, 152f
Arabella, 147, 149
Ariadne auf Naxos, 133, 142ff, 152, 154, 195, 251
Capriccio, 147, 150f, 153f
Daphne, 152ff
Elektra, 137f, 148
Der Rosenkavalier, 140ff, 150, 154, 236
Salome, 137, 297
Stravinsky, Igor, 283
Striggio, Alessandro, 159–65
Szymanowski, Karol, 103f, 196f

Tal, Josef, 299
Tannhäuser (Wagner), 53, 159, 226, 257
Tchaikovsky, Piotr Ilyitch, 17, 58ff; and realism, 78f; and singers, 250
Eugene Onegin, 59–62, 250
Tippett, Sir Michael, 100ff; as librettist, 102ff
The Ice Break, 102
King Priam, 100f, 153
The Knot Garden, 96, 101f, 218
The Midsummer Marriage, 100f
Tosca (Puccini), 84ff, 87, 221
Traviata, La (Verdi), 46, 59, 73, 78f, 86, 88, 121, 241
Tristan und Isolde (Wagner), 56f, 62, 92, 130, 135, 225f, 258, 272ff, 294ff
Trovatore, Il (Verdi), 46f, 72f, 78f, 81
Turandot (Puccini), 67, 84f, 88, 135, 221
Troyens, Les (Berlioz), 167, 260

Verdi, Giuseppe, 1–14, 78, 87f; and the absurd, 47ff; and aria, 88, 95; and conductors, 255f, 259; and ensemble, 73, 77; and honour, 45ff, 69f; and madness, 81, 93;

Verdi, Giuseppe, (*cont.*)
parola scenica, 119f, 132; pessimism, 44–6, 48f; and producers, 221ff; and revolution, 42f, 49f, 79, 120, 122f; and Scribe, 116ff; and singers, 248f; and *verismo*, 77ff, 89, 288
Aida, 7ff, 10f, 14, 88, 100, 119, 123, 234, 259
Don Carlos, 13, 44f, 77
Ernani, 45, 47, 69, 121
La Forza del Destino, 45f, 50, 120, 122, 289
Otello, 47f, 104, 124, 287
Rigoletto, 46f, 68, 77ff, 80f, 120f, 248, 262, 299
La Traviata, 46, 59, 73, 78f, 86, 88, 121, 241
Il Trovatore, 46f, 72f, 78f, 81
verismo, 77, 81–6, 88f, 221, 288, 294
Voltaire, 128, 266; and librettists, 74; as librettist, 25; and Metastasio, 177f; and Mozart, 41
von Karajan, Herbert, 255, 258, 263f

Wagner, Richard, 11, 17, 62f; and conductors, 256f, 261f; and force of will, 92; and *leitmotiv*, 55f, 132f, 225; as librettist, 52–3, 128–32, 136; and madness, 92f, 130; and money, 212f; and Nietzsche, 269f; and realism, 72; and revolution, 50f; and singers, 236, 239
Der Fliegende Höllander, 53, 55, 220, 270, 294
Lohengrin, 218, 226, 233
Die Meistersinger von Nürnberg, 54, 76f, 133, 142, 159
Parsifal, 52, 55, 68, 100, 130, 133, 218, 227
Tannhäuser, 53, 159, 226, 257; (*see also Der Ring der Nibelungen*; *Tristan und Isolde*)
Wagner, Siegfried, 99, 261f
Wagner, Wieland: and *Aida*, 10–12; and *Orfeo* (Gluck), 184; and *Parsifal*, 260; and *The Ring*, 233ff; and *Salome*, 264
Wagner, Wolfgang, and *Parsifal*, 227
Walton, Sir William, 95f
We come to the river (Henze), 98ff, 253, 273
Weill, Kurt, 91
Wolf, Hugo, 18, 26, 58, 104, 133

Zauberflöte, Die (*The Magic Flute*) (Mozart), 15, 25, 37ff, 67f, 73, 108, 190, 286, 294
Zeno, Apostolo, 75, 174–5

More About Penguins and Pelicans

Penguinews, which appears every month, contains details of all the new books issued by Penguins as they are published. From time to time it is supplemented by *Penguins in Print*, which is our complete list of almost 5,000 titles.

A specimen copy of *Penguinews* will be sent to you free on request. Please write to Dept EP, Penguin Books Ltd, Harmondsworth, Middlesex, for your copy.

In the U.S.A.: For a complete list of books available from Penguins in the United States write to Dept CS, Penguin Books, 625 Madison Avenue, New York, New York 10022.

In Canada: For a complete list of books available from Penguins in Canada write to Penguin Books Canada Ltd, 2801 John Street, Markham, Ontario L3R 1B4.

The New Penguin Dictionary of Music

4th Edition

Arthur Jacobs

The New Penguin Dictionary of Music, compiled by Arthur Jacobs, a well-known music critic and Professor at the Royal Academy of Music, is a basic and comprehensive reference book. It covers orchestral, solo, choral and chamber music as well as opera and the ballet. Full and detailed entries deal with composers and their works, instruments of all sorts, orchestras, performers and conductors. Entries dealing with well-known authors whose work inspired musical composition are a new feature of this up-to-date dictionary which includes both information about the music of modern composers and the results of the considerable research that is going on into the music of the past.

This fourth edition will completely supersede its predecessors. It is longer by several hundred entries; many of the old entries have been considerably enlarged in the light of new research. Both new and old material combine into a work of reference that will be indispensable for anyone interested in music.

Arthur Jacobs is also the author of *A Short History of Western Music*, which is published by Penguins.

Introducing Music

Ottó Károlyi

Some acquaintance with the grammar and vocabulary of music – enough to understand the language without speaking it – greatly broadens the pleasure of hearing it.

Introducing Music makes the attempt to convey the elements of the art to music-lovers with no technical knowledge. Setting out from the relatively open ground of tones, pitches, timbres, sharps, flats, bars and keys, Ottó Károlyi is able to conduct the reader out into the more exciting territory of dominant sevenths and symphonic structure. His text is clearly signposted by musical examples and illustrations of instruments described, and no intelligent reader should have any difficulty in following the path. On arrival at the end, in place of being confused by the technicalities of a programme note, he should be within reach of following the music in a score.

'Here is one of those rare things – an instruction book that seems to succeed completely in what it sets out to do . . . The author develops the reader's knowledge of the language and sense of music to the stage where he can both follow, though not necessarily read from scratch, a full score, and even make sense of some of the exceedingly complex programme-notes' – *Recorder*

'He has presented the grammar of music with great clarity' – *The Times Educational Supplement*

'A great deal of information is packed into the 174 pages' – *Music in Education*

'The book is well organized in the way one subject leads progressively to the next, terms are crisply defined and explanations are lucid' – *The Times Literary Supplement*

The Pelican History of Music

(*In three volumes*)

Edited by Alec Robertson and Denis Stevens

The concert-goer and music-lover anxious to discover some of the hidden wealth of musical history will find in this series of three volumes an account of many kinds of music: primitive and non-Western, liturgical, medieval, renaissance, baroque, classical, romantic, and modern. Although there is some technical analysis, the authors and editors have concentrated on fitting music into its proper frame, whether ecclesiastical, courtly, or popular.

Each musical epoch is discussed by an expert who considers the music at its face value, instead of thinking of it merely as a link in a chain of development ending in the music of Beethoven or Boulez. The reader can therefore come to understand musical trends and styles both within and without the normal orbit of concerts and opera, and will be able to enjoy unfamiliar music as well as the accepted classics.

A special feature of the first two volumes is the group of illustrations that have been chosen to set the scene rather than to illustrate any specific points in the text.

The Symphony

(*In two volumes*)

Edited by Robert Simpson

The two volumes of *The Symphony* provide, composer by composer, a comprehensive introduction to the whole symphonic scene from Haydn to the present day.

Robert Simpson – himself a well-known symphonist – has done more than compile programme notes of the great symphonies: he has, in his two introductions, analysed the essence of symphonic form. By identifying the elements of rhythm, melody, harmony, and – vitally important – tonality as *all* being present in full measure in any successful symphony, he has provided a frame of reference which binds together symphonists from Haydn to Holmboe, from Mozart to Martinů.

His team of distinguished contributors, which includes Deryck Cooke, Hans Keller and Hugh Ottaway, has thus been able to provide a connected, unified study of all major composers who have 'attempted to achieve in an orchestral work the highest state of organization of which music is capable'.